MYSTERY
OF
REINCARNATION

About the Author

A native of Minnesota but a resident of Colorado since 1969, Jeff's life has been a journey that has taken him down many different paths. Besides writing, his hobbies include reading, art, politics and political history, world and military history, religion and spirituality, numismatics (coin collecting), paleontology, astronomy (and science in general), and Fortean subjects such as Bigfoot, UFOs, and things that go bump in the night. His personal philosophy is that life is about learning and growing, both intellectually and spiritually, and that is the perspective from which he approaches each project he undertakes. Currently Jeff resides in Lakewood, CO, with his wife, Carol, and their two sons. Visit his website at www.ourcuriousworld.com.

To Write to the Author

If you wish to contact the author or would like more information about this book, please write to the author in care of Llewellyn Worldwide and we will forward your request. Both the author and publisher appreciate hearing from you and learning of your enjoyment of this book and how it has helped you. Llewellyn Worldwide cannot guarantee that every letter written to the author can be answered, but all will be forwarded. Please write to:

J. Allan Danelek
℅ Llewellyn Worldwide
P.O. Box 64383, Dept. 0-7387-0704-X
St. Paul, MN 55164-0383, U.S.A.

Please enclose a self-addressed stamped envelope for reply,
or $1.00 to cover costs. If outside U.S.A., enclose
international postal reply coupon.

Many of Llewellyn's authors have websites with additional information and resources. For more information, please visit our website at http://www.llewellyn.com.

MYSTERY
OF
REINCARNATION

THE EVIDENCE
&
ANALYSIS OF REBIRTH

J. ALLAN DANELEK

Llewellyn Publications
St. Paul, Minnesota

First Edition
First Printing, 2005

Book design and layout by Joanna Willis
Cover art © 2004 by PhotoDisc, Inc.
Cover design by Ellen Dahl

Library of Congress Cataloging-in-Publication Data
Danelek, J. Allan, 1958–
   Mystery of reincarnation: the evidence & analysis of rebirth / J. Allan Danelek.—1st. ed.
      p.   cm.
   Includes bibliographical references (p.) and index.
   ISBN 0-7387-0704-X
      1. Reincarnation. I. Title.

   BL515.D26 2005
   133.9'01'35—dc22   2004065774

Llewellyn Publications
A Division of Llewellyn Worldwide, Ltd.
P.O. Box 64383, Dept. 0-7387-0704-X
St. Paul, MN 55164-0383, U.S.A.
www.llewellyn.com

Printed in the United States of America

CONTENTS

Part II: The Mechanics of Reincarnation

Appendices

Acknowledgments

It is said that nothing of importance is ever accomplished without the help of friends, and that is as true of writing a book as it is of shoveling a sidewalk. As such, I would be remiss not to acknowledge those who have been "in the loop" while I was putting this manuscript together, both for their willingness to read through the earliest drafts—when a work is still encased within its primordial goo—and for their willingness to make helpful suggestions. I'd especially like to thank Carmen Barber for her time and patience in this process, as well as Marcus Danneil and David Brunacci for providing me with their opinions of this work. I would also like to thank Mr. Jim Schwartz for his invaluable assistance in explaining the process of hypnotism and past-life regression to me, as well as for sharing his personal opinions and anecdotes about some of the theories articulated in this book in regards to how they play out in his own work as a hypnotherapist. A special note of appreciation goes to my sister, Cheri, for permitting me the rare opportunity of witnessing a past-life regression firsthand, and allowing me to be a part of both her past and her present. And, finally, my wife Carol deserves a special thanks for holding down the fort while I spent many an hour laboring away at the library. She is a young soul who travels well, and fills my life with love and laughter. Thanks to all.

Introduction

What happens to us when we die?

It is a question that cuts across racial, social, political, economic, and gender lines to remain the only element of our existence common to all human beings. Yet ever since Homo sapiens first began pondering the question a hundred thousand years ago, the answer has eluded us. What *does* happen when we die? What becomes of our soul, our mind, our personality—our very essence? For that matter, do we even have such a thing as a soul, or is it all an illusion we have created to give ourselves a sense of permanence and the hope of immortality?

For the atheist, the answer is simple. Since our brains are nothing more than tissue encased within a mantle of bone, nothing *can* happen to us when we die. The essence, personality, mind—soul—or whatever we wish to call our consciousness, ceases to exist. Like the brain cells that provide us animation, once they die the mind they animate dies with them, endowing our time on this planet with no more meaning than that which we choose to give it during our brief sojourn here.

To most people, however, that answer is unsatisfactory. It suggests that we are little more than some great cosmic accident and that, consequently, our lives have no ultimate purpose. No matter how powerful or famous or wealthy we may become, in a few generations our name will be, at best, but a footnote in history. Even the greatest among us will be, in a matter of a few hundred centuries at most, forgotten as completely as if we'd never been born. Such a premise leaves us to contemplate an existence without meaning and a universe that, despite all its beauty and splendor, has no more permanence than a flower that briefly blooms in the spring only to wither and die after a few short days of life.

Yet something deep within the human heart knows better. We instinctively understand that we are more than the sum of our parts. That is why most people believe that their personalities will survive physical death in some form or another, and continue to go on long after their bodies have turned to dust.

Some people imagine that we become ghosts and remain little more than disembodied spirits aimlessly wandering the earth, capable of perceiving the physical realm but unable to interact with it in any meaningful way. However, in my opinion, this would constitute an excellent description of hell and render the whole point of survival moot.

Others, however—in fact, most people—believe that we don't simply exist forever as ghosts, but that we actually move on to some other plane of existence. Heaven is the favored destination for most; a place where our conscious personality, no longer shackled to the limitations and burdens of physical existence, survives within a perpetual state of bliss and joy throughout eternity. Some add to this by also embracing a belief in hell; a perpetual state of agony for those who turn to evil and are doomed to exist forever within a conscious state of torment, regret, and fear.

All of these positions, however, have the unavoidable consequence of making our time on this planet but a blink of the eye of eternity, with the decisions we make—or fail to make—while "in the body" having profound and eternal ramifications. Unfortunately, this reduces the physical world to little more than a cosmic "hatchery" that exists only to birth new souls, each of which spend a tiny millisecond of time here before winging (or, potentially, plunging) to their ultimate estate. While, admittedly, this idea does manage to make this single life of paramount importance, it also forces one to wonder why a physical realm is even necessary. If the universe exists merely as a vehicle for our creation, why couldn't the process be circumvented entirely, so that we are birthed directly into the spiritual realm? Why all the unnecessary pain and hardship of a physical existence—especially one in which there exists the very real danger that we might earn hell through our misdeeds—if the spirit realm is the only destination that awaits us? In such a context, physical existence seems not only pointless, but, potentially, even hazardous.

There is, however, yet another position to consider. It is one that until recently has been largely ignored in the West but has been embraced by literally billions of people around the world for thousands of years; a belief that maintains this physical existence to be neither insignificant nor transient, but instead to be perpetually ongoing. It is the idea that our soul lives on not in some ethereal Eden—or Hades—somewhere, but realizes perpetual existence through a process of continual rebirths into the physical realm, making our time on this planet not one single, brief experience, but a repetitive process realized through literally hundreds of lifetimes. It is a timeless belief—one that predates both Christianity and Islam by many centuries—that is known by many names in many cultures, but is perhaps best known to us today as *reincarnation*.

Reincarnation has traditionally proven to be neither popular nor a widespread belief in the Judeo-Christian and Muslim world. Commonly, it has been perceived as a "fringe" concept embraced by purveyors of the New Age movement and Eastern-based cults, or, worse, a "tabloid" faith with no more substance than astrology, tarot cards, and healing crystals. As such, until comparatively recently reincarnation has not been considered a viable option within modern theological debate, and so has been traditionally relegated to the back room of Western religion like some crazed but generally harmless relative.

But that perception, especially as we move further into the twenty-first century, seems to be changing. People are more willing to challenge and, when necessary, abandon long-held religious beliefs when the dogmas fail to answer their questions, and as Westerners are becoming increasingly curious and tolerant of other belief systems, reincarnation is experiencing something of a renaissance in the West. In fact, a 1998 Harris poll[1] found that a quarter of all Americans believe in some form of reincarnation (fully a third among non-Christians), and even many scientifically literate people, intrigued by a multitude of increasingly well-documented past-life memory cases, are willing to consider the idea. No longer as easily dismissed as an exotic oddity as it once was, reincarnation is becoming mainstream and shows signs of growing increasingly popular as humanity moves further into the new millennia.

This burgeoning renaissance toward a belief in reincarnation is the reason for this book. It is my contention that there are many people out there who are curious about the idea but lack the kind of objective and straightforward information—preferably presented in a decidedly easy-to-read, nonacademic format—on the subject from which to decide for themselves whether the concept has anything to say to them. New Age prophets or religious and secular debunkers are often intent on attacking reincarnation as a dangerous heresy or as unscientific, unenlightened pseudo-science. As such, seldom does one have the opportunity to examine the pros and cons of the idea without being influenced by propagandists of all ilks intent on telling only their side of the story.

It is this oversight that this work hopes to correct. Think of this as a reincarnation "primer" if you will; designed not to provide a complete and comprehensive understanding of the subject (which would make this a far more expansive work), but instead provide a basis for intelligent discussion. It is the sort of book I would have benefited from had I come across it twenty years ago, and one I hope others intrigued by the possibilities of rebirth will find helpful.

---

1 Harris Poll, no. 41, August 12, 1998, by Humphrey Taylor.

Of course, I would be dishonest if I tried to pretend I have no opinion on the matter. I believe in reincarnation, though the idea was never a part of my original belief system. I come from an evangelical Christian tradition, and for twenty years maintained the assumption that reincarnation was an alien, unbiblical, and possibly even demonic teaching designed to lead millions astray. It was something I personally fought against, not from a position of knowledge but from the more comfortable perspective of ignorance. I believed then that I understood what reincarnation was and how it worked, but the years have shown me how little I really knew about a belief system I was so quick to denigrate.

Yet how can I present a book on the subject that portends to be unbiased and balanced while holding to the concept of reincarnation as a fact? One would assume I should have no greater capacity for objectivity than either the determined debunker or the enthusiastic proponent.

While I don't deny that this is a valid concern and that my personal beliefs cannot help but shade my own understanding of the subject, perhaps it is the fact that I have looked at the issue from both sides with equal sincerity that makes me uniquely qualified to revisit it. I understand the reincarnationist's position as well as that of the anti-reincarnationist with equal clarity, and so can perceive reincarnation's strengths and weaknesses better than those who have traditionally held to one position exclusively. Whether this will translate into anything approaching genuine objectivity I leave for the reader to decide; it is, however, my intention to give both sides as fair a hearing as possible.

For the sake of clarity, I've divided this material into two sections. The first part of the book—chapters 1 through 9—will provide a brief history of the concept and deal with the evidence for and against reincarnation from a scientific and rationalist perspective. It is designed to bring the novice up to speed on where the concept stands today as well as provide a comprehensive outline of the main points within the debate. The second—or theoretical—section of the book will deal purely with the mechanics of reincarnation: how it supposedly works, what it's trying to do, and what it all means. It is designed to examine the various hypotheses being bandied about and show how they stack up against each other, as well as consider the logic behind each theory to see how they fare in the face of both rational thought and scientific evidence. Obviously, this is the more speculative element of the book, but one that should satisfy the curiosity of most people who are seeking as complete a picture of the concept as possible.

Finally, it should be noted that unlike many books of this genre, none of the material presented here is channeled information acquired from disembodied spirit guides, nor anecdotal accounts gleaned from past-life regressions. That's not to say information acquired through such means may not be valid or have something of value to say on the subject, but I have chosen instead to approach the subject from a more analytical perspective. While I may occasionally refer to such information, this is, as best as I am able to ensure, a work based on confirmed case studies by men and women of considerable scientific expertise and credentials, as well as arguments for and against each position based on pure logic. Whether my sense of "logic" happens to coincide with anyone else's remains to be seen, but that, at least, is the spirit from which I approach this material. As such, there is only a single past-life case recounted here—used as an example of how the logical processes operate in attempting to explain or "debunk" a good reincarnationist case—and a few personal anecdotes designed to illustrate how a past life could possibly affect a current life. The rest of it is based on documented evidence and some "sleuthing" on my own part that hopefully doesn't wander too far from reason.

It is my profound hope that this work will bring the reader a little closer to understanding how sincere, rational, and intelligent men and women can come to maintain a belief system as unique as reincarnation while, at the same time, possibly helping—in some small way—the reader define his or her own spiritual path. This book is about possibilities, not only of the human spirit, but of the human heart; it is about the hope of eternity that comprises all human philosophies in their efforts to explain the inexplicable and touch upon the face of the Divine. Hopefully, this work will help some find at least a piece of the answer, which is all any book that attempts to speak to the question of immortality can aspire to do.

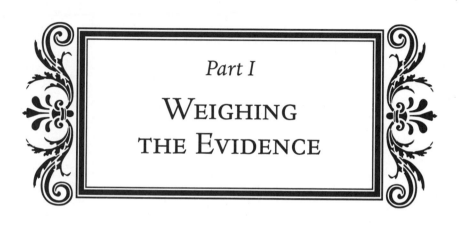

Part I

WEIGHING
THE EVIDENCE

As one would expect of any idea that deals with the question of life after death, the issue of reincarnation has always been, and will likely always remain, a subject of considerable controversy. Whereas we once lived in an age where such issues were left to the church to decide, today we live in an empirical, rationalist age—or so we like to believe—that defines reality in very different terms than those used by our ancestors. To them, the words of the prophets and the writings in the holy texts were sufficient to explain the world around them, but that age is long past. We may still revere the words of the prophets and even attempt to apply their teachings to our daily lives, but when it comes to matters of what happens to us when we die, more often than not they leave us with more questions than answers.

What is needed is the opportunity to weigh evidence that is of a verifiable, historical nature from an objective and dispassionate perspective, and for this we must turn to religions' ancient nemesis—science—to find some answers. Not that science has all of the answers, mind you; it cannot proclaim truth where the evidence does not conform to rigid scientific standards, yet it still has a few things to say on the subject. It can tell us, for instance, about how the human brain operates in all its intricate complexity, and, working through the objective and precise standards of mathematics, can demonstrate when an event lies outside the realm of mere coincidence or is the product of statistical probability. Further, historians (who are often overlooked) can tell us with often unwavering confidence if a prior life claim is historically and culturally accurate—or at least plausible—or whether it is nothing more than the enthusiastic musings of a deluded mind. It is hoped that in taking more of an analytical approach to the question, we might be better able to examine the evidence free from the religious or cultural biases that tend to cloud our vision, and this will allow us to make a more informed decision as to whether reincarnation has anything to say to us personally.

As such, this part of the book will concentrate exclusively on those evidences that are suggestive of reincarnation and examine each of the main objections to the idea commonly presented by the scientific and religious communities. It will also examine a pair of actual cases—one that details how a possible past-life experience might have impacted a present life, and one of a documented and highly verifiable past-life memory from the annals of regression therapy—in an effort to gauge how one of the better cases on record stands up to the scrutiny of science, psychology, history, and logic. Far from comprehensive, I present this material purely as a primer for those who are not entirely decided about the issue but are curious enough to want to know more. It is my hope that the reader will come away from this with a foundation upon which to understand the pros and cons of the debate more clearly, and so be able to make a more informed decision.

chapter one

THE SEARCH FOR BRIDEY MURPHY

T he date was Saturday, November 29, 1952. In the home of Colorado businessman and self-taught hypnotist Morey Bernstein, a
twenty-nine-year-old woman by the name of Virginia Tighe was being
put into a hypnotic trance in the presence of her husband and a few
close friends. While such casual demonstrations of the remarkable powers of hypnotism were becoming increasingly popular within the world
of middle-class suburbia as a form of amusement, Bernstein's reason for
hypnotizing the young woman was far more than merely the desire to
provide his audience with some light entertainment. He was attempting
to find answers to some of the deeper questions he had been pondering
for some time—answers he hoped his willing but uncertain subject
might be able to provide. Bernstein was on nothing less than a quest to
discover the truth about reincarnation.

Bernstein had been studying the ancient concept for several months
and was curious as to whether hypnosis could access memories of a previous life lost to the conscious mind but accessible to subconscious recall.

Virginia Tighe, a woman he had hypnotized on two previous occasions (in an apparently successful effort to end a life-long smoking habit) and who had proven to be an especially good subject, had kindly agreed to let him use her for his "experiment," despite having no interest in the subject of reincarnation herself. Turning on his tape recorder and surrounded by witnesses, Bernstein quickly put Tighe into a deep, hypnotically-induced trance and at last was ready to see for himself if reincarnation was mere fantasy, or whether it had some basis in fact.

At first the session went as many previous regression therapy sessions had gone: Bernstein easily regressed Tighe through a litany of early childhood memories all the way back through elementary school, effectively demonstrating the remarkable abilities hypnotism has in accessing lost or hidden memories. Normally this was where the session would conclude due to the natural assumption that infancy was as far back as it was possible to go, but curious as to what would happen if he continued to regress her further, he instructed the young woman to continue going back in her mind until she found herself in "some other scene, some other place, or some other time" and describe what she saw. Even he was surprised at what happened next.

Quietly speaking in a mild brogue, Virginia identified herself as an Irish woman named Bridey Murphy who claimed to have been born in the town of Cork, Ireland, in the year 1798. Supposedly recounting a life lived in nineteenth-century Ireland, "Bridey" went on to describe in considerable detail a number of facts about her previous existence, all of it told in a lilting and progressively growing Irish accent that proved at times difficult to understand. It was as if the woman sitting on his couch and talking into his tape recorder was no longer a twentieth-century Colorado housewife but a genuine nineteenth-century Irish woman.

While much of what she recounted was little more than anecdotes and disjointed stories from her alleged past life, some of it was detailed enough to be verifiable. Claiming to have been born to a Cork barrister named Duncan and his wife Kathleen Murphy, she recounted her marriage to a man named Sean Brian McCarthy, and living a life in Belfast until her death in 1864 at the age of sixty-six. Further, she named a number of places and acquaintances from her previous life and remembered other unique details that appeared too detailed to be simply "made up" or some sort of errant fantasy. For example, she used archaic terms that only someone who studied the local dialects of Ireland would recognize, and she correctly identified several household items by their nineteenth-century terms. She correctly identified the currency of the era and was able to give the names of geographic locations that had long since been renamed but were in use in the nineteenth century. She even correctly named two Belfast grocers "Bridey" had dealt with in the 1850s, both of whom were eventually proven to have actually existed.

Intrigued by the unexpected results and uncertain of what to make of them, Bernstein conducted five more sessions with Virginia over the next year, each of them tape-recorded and witnessed by both Mrs. Bernstein and Mrs. Tighe's husband (as well as others). Finally, after some months of uncertainty as to what to do with the information, Bernstein and some journalist acquaintances hired investigators to check out Tighe's story.

Not all of it proved to be smooth sailing, of course. For starters, there was no written record of a Bridgett (of which Bridey was a common nickname at the time) Kathleen Murphy being born to a Cork barrister named Duncan Murphy in 1798, nor any mention of a Brian McCarthy from Belfast. However, these problems were quickly—and, some might say, conveniently—explained by the fact that accurate record keeping was practically unknown in Ireland during the time period in question. In the end, many details of her story proved to be true, and Bernstein was convinced that Tighe's story was genuine evidence of reincarnation. Fascinated by what it might mean to mankind's quest to understand what happens after death, he decided to write a book on the incident. Bernstein didn't know it at the time, but he was about to ignite the public imagination in a way it had not anticipated.

Though Bernstein was a first-time author, *The Search for Bridey Murphy* became an unexpected bestseller, selling over 170,000 copies within the first two months of its release in January of 1956. An overnight sensation, Bernstein's riveting account of past-life recall was serialized in thirty-nine newspapers, an abridged version appeared in the prestigious *True* magazine, thirty thousand LPs of his recorded sessions with the woman he identified by the pseudonym Ruth Simmons (agreed to in an effort to protect Tighe's and her husband's privacy) were sold, and a Hollywood movie dramatizing the story was made. There was even a popular song inspired by the event, and almost overnight the concept of reincarnation—a belief held by only a tiny minority of Westerners at the time—entered the public consciousness in a major way.

Unfortunately for Bernstein, things did not last long. A reporter from the *Chicago American* sent to Ireland to investigate Bridey's claims and dig further into the background of Tighe soon uncovered some disturbing facts. Aside from there being no written records to confirm Bridey's existence (as Bernstein had admitted himself), more significant problems soon emerged. For instance, no record of the Belfast church she named, St. Theresa's, or the priest, a Father Gorman, who had supposedly officiated at her wedding, could be found. Additionally, other seemingly minor but important details from her story—such as recalling as a child "scratching the paint off a metal bedframe" when iron beds had not yet been introduced to Ireland, and living in a "wood" house in forest-poor Ireland—also challenged the veracity of her "memories." Most damaging of all, however, proved to be the discovery that when Tighe lived in Chicago as a child, she had a neighbor named Bridie Cottrell who happened to have the maiden name of Murphy. Other damaging facts soon emerged: Tighe had an aunt of Irish extraction who supposedly regaled the young and impressionable girl with stories of Ireland, as well as allegations that she enjoyed speaking with an Irish brogue as a teenager and learned to dance Irish jigs as a high school girl (something she had demonstrated during one of her sessions). When the newspapers had finished their hatchet job, it seemed the highly suggestive "Ruth Simmons" was simply recalling hidden memories of long-forgotten stories she had heard as a child but was able to recall only under hypnosis.

As suddenly as it began, the mystery of Bridey Murphy was, as far as science and the general public were concerned, solved, and overnight the intriguing story of the middle-class American housewife who could recall having lived a previous life in nineteenth-century Ireland was relegated to the scrap heap of pseudo-science, the incident serving ever since as a glowing example of the power of persuasion and the effect "hidden" or "lost" memories can have on the subconscious mind.[1]

LETTING THE GENIE OUT

Whether the Bridey Murphy case was a genuine case of past-life recall, a cleverly perpetrated hoax, or an example of the power of the mind to recall even the most minor events of childhood, there was no denying that *The Search for Bridey Murphy* was instrumental in bringing reincarnation into the mainstream of Western consciousness. Until then the belief was held by only a tiny fragment of the population, but once Tighe's story hit the bookstores—and despite its later debunking—interest in the subject grew. By the late 1960s it was becoming increasingly popular, especially among the young, who, turned off by traditional Western religion and enticed by the swan song of Eastern gurus and New Age masters, had become much more open to foreign ideas and concepts. Further, the seventies and eighties saw a burgeoning of books on paranormal and occult subjects, while books by channelers (people who supposedly act as conduits for disembodied personalities) and works by such well-known celebrities as Shirley MacLaine began to make reincarnation increasingly acceptable and an openly viable option for many. The reincarnation genie, so to speak, had been let out, and there seemed to be no way of getting it back in the bottle.

---

1 Later investigation brought some of the skeptics' "facts" into question as well, and Bernstein continued to maintain the authenticity of the Murphy case right up to the time of his death. For a more complete treatment of this case, see appendix A.

It was not just New Age gurus and Hollywood starlets beating the reincarnation drums either; a few careful scientists and researchers also began looking into the idea from a decidedly secular standpoint. The past-lives research studies of psychologist Helen Wambach, an eminently qualified therapist and professional hypnotist who charted the past-life memories of over a thousand regressed subjects over a ten year period, brought a degree of demographic validation to the concept, while the meticulous and careful work of Dr. Ian Stevenson, a clinical psychologist and one-time head of the psychology department of the University of Virginia, documented thousands of past-life memories in children (more on this later). Though both of these pioneers and others who labored in the field often felt the sting of professional and personal ridicule for their efforts, they hit a scholastic nerve with the public, and, despite the best efforts of a growing cadre of professional secular and religious debunkers, interest in the subject continued to grow. No longer was reincarnation considered a bizarre belief held to by a few people who fancied themselves the reincarnation of Napoleon; it was fast becoming a serious field of study in its own right, and one that begged to be more fully explored.

The belief in reincarnation has proven to be more than just a harmless outlet for some people's curiosity—it has proven to possess some useful benefits within the field of psychology and mental health as well. Once it was discovered that patients suffering from severe but idiomatic phobias and fears could be hypnotized and "regressed" back to a past life to determine the source of their trauma, past-life regression therapy became another valuable tool in the open-minded mental health professional's tool box. As a result, today there are literally thousands of therapists across the country who are regressing people back to past lives in a quest to ease present life problems, often with extraordinary success. Even therapists who do not necessarily believe in reincarnation themselves find the curative powers of past-life regression therapy nothing short of astounding. It seems that the mere *belief* in reincarnation—regardless of whether or not it's true—appears to be helpful in dealing with trauma and restoring mental health when more traditional therapies have proven ineffective; a fact that is, in itself, remarkable.

As such, as the twenty-first century dawns, reincarnation is increasingly becoming an idea whose time has come. There is overwhelming evidence that something is going on that needs to be carefully and, as much as possible, objectively studied. There have been entirely too many well-documented and inexplicable past-life stories for all of them to be casually dismissed as New Age ramblings or "junk" science. Despite the dogged and determined attempts to explain away everything as hidden memories, fantasies, hoaxes, and coincidence—explanations that are proving increasingly unconvincing to all but the most ardent skeptics—now is the perfect time to reexamine reincarnation in a somber and serious manner.

Unfortunately, it is my experience that the vast majority of people who reject the concept out of hand have never looked into the subject at all, much less examined the evidence for and against it with anything approaching objectivity. It is simply "assumed" to be untrue, and therefore it is dismissed without a second thought. As a result, the average Westerner has only a superficial understanding of the concept, which is a pity, for reincarnation offers answers to many of the important questions we all have about life, God, and eternity in general.

Why are we in the West so generally skeptical of an idea that has been a part of the religious heritage of billions of people around the world since antiquity? It is a belief that has been and continues to be held by many cultures around the world, from the Lapps of Finland to the Igbo of Nigeria, and from the Aborigines of Australia to the Tlingit Indians of Alaska. It is, in fact, almost as universal as the belief in God and the immortality of the soul. One would imagine that a concept that predates Western religion (and, for that matter, Western civilization itself) by thousands of years should illicit more respect than what it has been traditionally shown.

Additionally, few people are aware of the fact that some form of reincarnationist beliefs have been a part of Western religion as well, having been a major element of the teachings of the Sufi branch of Islam, the Gnostic wing of Christianity, and the Kabbalist and Hasidic traditions of Judaism. It was a belief shared by the ancient Druids of England, the Egyptians of 2000 BC, and even the Greeks of Plato's day. To understand reincarnation, then, is to understand ourselves, for, like a subtle shadow, it has always been a part of our thinking. To dismiss it outright is to deny an important part of the human experience, as well as lose the opportunity to better understand the world we live in.

But where did this belief system originate, and how has it evolved into the various permutations it has taken on today? While I appreciate the fact that history doesn't interest everyone, a brief historical sketch might be helpful in understanding the very large footprint that reincarnation has left in the dusty tracks of history, and how its history has traditionally influenced our own society and continues to do so to this day.

chapter two

A VERY BRIEF HISTORY LESSON

It is not known when and where the earliest notions of reincarnation first emerged. Like the nearly universal belief in God, it seems to have arisen spontaneously in various societies around the world, and, while the concept is interpreted through each culture's own unique filter, every tradition has proven remarkably consistent in its basic understanding of the idea, demonstrating reincarnation's nearly universal appeal.

Though largely conjecture, it is likely that reincarnationist ideas first emerged when the earliest humans began noticing strong similarities between recently born offspring and their deceased ancestors. Perhaps the mannerisms or interests a child displayed reminded one of a deceased loved one, or a birthmark mimicked one that was prominent on a long-dead grandparent, leading village elders to imagine that the dead ancestor had returned a second time—a reasonable assumption in a culture in which the soul was naturally believed to survive death. Additionally, since cases of spontaneous past-life recall have been recorded in nearly every society on earth, it's reasonable to assume that such "memories" were recounted then just as they are today. Whatever the cause, however, it appears to have effected many cultures in similar ways, until reincarnation eventually became the dominant theme in many of the earliest religions of Asia (particularly on the Indian subcontinent). It was when these various traditions began to merge their different and unique—as well as common—beliefs into a single faith that Hinduism was born over six thousand years ago, making the doctrine of reincarnation a firmly-established element of the religious landscape over four thousand years before Christ was born.

Around 490 BC, Buddhism—an offshoot of Hinduism inspired by the teachings of a wealthy prince named Siddhartha Gautama (later revered as the Buddha)—further refined reincarnationist beliefs and added elements to them. Whereas Hinduism generally taught the cycle of rebirth to be never-ending, Buddha introduced a means by which the endless cycle might be broken through self-discipline and purging oneself of all desire. Not surprisingly, the Buddha's teachings were perceived as a threat to the social structure of Hindu society, resulting in considerable tension—and not infrequent bloodletting—between these two great branches of Eastern thought that continues in some quarters to this day. These days, however, both religions combine to account for the faith system of nearly two billion people throughout Asia, and they remain two of the largest faiths, next to Christianity and Islam, in operation today.

Reincarnation in the West

While the evidence is spotty and far from complete, it appears that reincarnation has always been an element of the earliest beliefs and teachings of the ancient Western world as well. In fact, it may have played a far more extensive role in Western thought than traditional histories have led us to believe.

Egyptologists, for instance, generally agree that some form of reincarnation seems to have been a part of the belief system of the ancient

Egyptians, whose purpose in practicing mummification was due to their belief that the soul remained with the body as long as the body existed, without which it would be forced to leave and find another body, thus restarting the process of attaining heaven from scratch. As such, mummification was a means to, among other things, circumvent rebirth—or at least delay it as long as possible.

Reincarnationist ideas also worked their way into the thoughts and writings of some of the earliest Greek philosophers and writers. Aristotle, Socrates, Plato, and Pythagoras all taught and believed in some form of rebirth, as did Ovid, Virgil, Cicero, and a host of other great thinkers of antiquity. Some of these ideas were so prevalent in the centuries immediately preceding the birth of Christ that reincarnationist concepts became an element of many of the "mystery" religions of the Mediterranean; religions that were to become the template for other later mystic-based faith systems of the region. Reincarnation, far from being an uncommon idea, was in fact widespread, and may have strongly influenced the shape and thrust of Greek and Roman philosophy.

THE SUPPRESSION OF REINCARNATIONIST TEACHINGS IN THE WEST

The reason reincarnationist teachings as a common element of ancient Western thought has not been more widely acknowledged in our history books is due in large part to the role the Catholic church had in not only the later development of Western society, but in reworking and, when necessary, rewriting the history of the ancient world to reflect its own anti-reincarnationist philosophy. What makes this especially curious is that the Christian church itself started out with a belief in reincarnation, only to see it later exorcised from all Christian doctrines and writings, a fact that remains largely unknown to most Christians today. While some within the church would argue with this premise, it is a fact that much of the history of the early church has been extensively edited in an effort to marginalize and, when possible, eradicate these teachings that were believed to have been a threat to orthodoxy. Its success in doing so came about only after the greatest threat was finally destroyed in the fourth century—a threat known as Gnosticism.

A somewhat exclusive and scholarly group of Christian mystics that flourished during the first four centuries of the common era, the Gnostics were known for teachings that challenged nearly every point of the more widely held and prevailing opinions about God and the nature of the Christ that were then in vogue within the Roman world. It is becoming increasingly evident to scholars that many of the earliest and most important Christian writings and teachings—though practically exterminated in the fourth century—were generated by this small but important sect, and that their influence on the development of early Christian theology was far more substantial than scholars previously imagined.

Among the beliefs the Gnostics included in their writings that put them at variance with the main church was a unique form of reincarnation. Gnostic beliefs differed somewhat from those taught within Eastern religion (which are closer to how we might understand the concept today), and, though they had much in common, the Gnostics' perspective on reincarnation remains unique even to this day.

The Gnostic "take" on reincarnation works from the premise that all humans are, in essence, emanations of God, and, as God is a spirit being (or, more correctly, spirit in general), our natural state is also that of pure spirit. As such, Gnostics consider being born into the flesh a condition that prevents one from realizing his or her original state of pure spirit, and dooming him or her to an endless series of rebirths into ignorance and pain. It is a cycle that can only be broken through acquiring gnosis (or knowledge, from which they derive their name), which provides one with the enlightenment necessary to permanently return a person to his or her true spiritual state. Salvation, then, wasn't about avoiding judgment and eternal damnation; it was about being saved from ignorance and confusion and, with it, rebirth into the flesh (which was the spiritual equivalent to flunking a school course and being forced to retake the entire class again).

Not surprisingly, these teachings proved to be at odds with the more dominant non-Gnostic wing of Christianity who maintained that salvation came through the saving power of God through the sacrificial death of his son, Jesus the Christ. Also, since the doctrine of reincarnation was at odds with a belief in a final judgment and bodily resurrection (two ideas the Gnostics found repugnant), it proved to be a threat to the control of the hierarchy within the established church as well. Judgment (or hell) and the promise of an eternal reward were the control mechanisms of traditional Christianity, without which there would be no means of maintaining the obedience of the masses. Clearly, reincarnation, despite being taught and held to by many of the earliest church leaders, had no place in the changing church and had to go.[1]

To be fair, it was not the doctrine of reincarnation alone that got the Gnostics in trouble. The Gnostics taught a number of ideas that could only be considered controversial, the most important among them being their view of Jesus, whom they considered a spirit being that only took on the "illusion" of matter in order to teach mankind how to break the grip of the physical realm and return to the divine source. This idea, not remarkably, led them to deny a number of the basic doctrines of orthodox Christianity, such as the virgin birth, the humanity of Jesus, and his bodily resurrection from the dead, so it wouldn't be correct to contend that reincarnation alone is what brought about the Gnostics' eventual demise. In any case, the Gnostics' days—and the church's teachings on reincarnation—were numbered, and once the Emperor Constantine embraced literalist Christianity as the national religion in AD 321, Gnosticism was doomed. Armed with the authority of the state, Gnostic teachings—including reincarnation—were soon declared anathema (the formal term for "heresy"), and the Gnostics were driven underground,

---

1 For a more complete account of Gnostic reincarnationist teachings, see appendix D.

their writings burned and their leaders driven into exile, imprisoned, or, in a few cases, even killed. By the end of the fourth century the sect had been largely eradicated from the Roman Empire, and with their demise reincarnationist precepts practically disappeared in the West for the next 1,500 years.[2]

It's interesting to consider the response of the modern church to these facts. When it acknowledges the existence of the Gnostics at all (and few Christians are even aware they existed), they are routinely portrayed as a dangerous fringe group who attempted to corrupt the clear and simple faith handed down by Jesus, Paul, and the disciples. How surprised many Christians would be to learn that for a time Gnosticism may have been the intellectual and spiritual soul of the early church, and that it was stilled only through the political maneuverings of a church hierarchy that was apparently more interested in political power than spiritual growth. It's intriguing to imagine what the modern Christian church—not to mention Western civilization in general—would look like today had the Gnostic branch of Christianity dominated.

The Resurgence of Reincarnationist Beliefs in the West

Though reincarnation continued to be held to by a few indigenous cultures in Africa and the new world, it remained largely unknown in Europe and the Americas for many centuries. While it did manage to find its way into some of the more mystical branches of Islam (the Sufis) and within Judaism among the Hasidic and Kabbalist traditions, for the most part, reincarnation remained a tiny, minority belief held to by only

---

2 Reincarnationist beliefs were still evident among a few Christian-based sects that later arose to challenge the power of Rome, such as the Cathars (known as the Albigenses in France), but with their eventual extermination by the end of the thirteenth century, reincarnation as an integral element of Christian thought was effectively dead.

a very few people—a condition that was to remain constant until fairly recently.[3]

Reincarnationist ideas did not find their way into America in any significant way until late in the nineteenth century when an eccentric (and, some said, unstable), English woman by the name of Helen Blavatsky established the Theosophical Society in 1875. A woman of considerable intellect and energy, the controversial and volatile Blavatsky and the highly mystical organization she founded echoed the beliefs of the earlier Gnostics and incorporated numerous elements of Eastern thought, of which reincarnation was a major element. Fortunately, the unusual Blavatsky and her small band of followers lived in an age when spiritism and the occult arts were in vogue, allowing her free reign to articulate and write extensively on her unorthodox beliefs without fear of persecution. However, even though she and her organization were successful in reintroducing many traditional reincarnationist beliefs to the Western consciousness, they never managed to attract more than a tiny following, so reincarnation remained largely foreign to the belief systems of Americans well into the twentieth century—a condition that was to remain until a unique and curious man by the name of Edgar Cayce entered the stage to awaken a whole new generation of Americans to the concept of rebirth. And, remarkably, he did it almost by accident.

ENTER THE SLEEPING PROPHET

Edgar Cayce was not a likely candidate for a man destined to reintroduce reincarnation into the mainstream of American thought. In fact, by most accounts his life started out about as undistinguished and unspectacular as one could imagine. Born on a small farm in Hopkinsville, Kentucky,

---

3 That "minority," however, included such notables as Dickens, Emerson, Thoreau, Shaw, Dostoyevski, Tolstoy, Melville, Benjamin Franklin, Shakespeare, Da Vinci, Kant, Dante, and Voltaire, among others—an impressive "who's who" of reincarnationists by anyone's standards.

in 1877, Cayce proved to be an average but reasonably intelligent boy who, due to the demands of working on a small family farm, was forced to quit school early and so never received more than a ninth grade education. While this was not unusual in the farmlands of the Midwest in the nineteenth century, it did mean that young Cayce would have to make his way in the world with few prospects and, by most estimates, little chance of escaping the poverty of his youth.

Forced to take what work he could find to support himself, it was while working as a store clerk that Cayce's life took an even sharper downward spiral. He developed a severe case of laryngitis—a condition that not only made it increasingly difficult to work, but one that refused to respond to traditional treatments of the day. Facing the twin prospects of financial destitution and possible long-term physical distress made Cayce understandably depressed and anxious about how he would make a living. Unknown to him at the time, however, the illness was to prove a godsend and profoundly change his life.

One night, a traveling hypnotist arrived in town and, hearing of young Cayce's predicament, offered to try and cure his laryngitis through hypnotism. Now hypnotism (or "mesmerism," as it was known as in those days) was a fairly new phenomenon, so Cayce was a little hesitant to take the man up on his offer. However, he was growing desperate enough to try anything, and so he relented and allowed himself to be hypnotized. Fortunately, Cayce proved to be an especially good subject, and while under hypnosis he found that he was able to speak in a normal voice for the first time in months. When he was brought out of the trance state, however, he discovered that he was once again unable to speak, a phenomenon that repeated itself each time the hypnotist put him under.

Apparently unable to affect a permanent cure for young Cayce's condition, the hypnotist finally gave up and moved on to his next engagement, leaving the young man in his original predicament. Fortunately, however, another man had witnessed the event and, being an amateur hypnotist himself, offered to help. He reasoned that if Cayce could speak while under hypnosis, perhaps he could describe what was wrong with him. Willing to give it a try, Cayce was once again put under and, as predicted, was able to not only diagnose the reason for his condition (a restriction in the blood supply to the vocal chords), but affect a treatment as well. Within days, so the story goes, Cayce was healed.

Convinced that if he could diagnose his own illness while in a trance he might be able to do the same for others, Cayce soon proved capable of giving remarkably accurate diagnoses to others while in a self-induced trance. Now armed with this new ability—which Cayce presumed to be a gift from God—he went on to become one of the most successful and prolific "diagnostic prophets" of modern times, successfully identifying and correctly prescribing treatment for literally thousands of patients right up to the time of his death in 1945. Eventually a research center was established in Virginia Beach, Virginia, to catalogue and study his remarkable abilities (a facility that exists to this day, over half a century after his death), making Edgar Cayce a household name within the psychic community and earning him the title the "Sleeping Prophet" because he always worked his "miracles" while in a deep trance.

Though most famous for his ability to diagnose and treat illnesses, Cayce was also known for something else. It seems that while in a trance, he would occasionally begin talking about his subjects' past lives and revealing other information of a decidedly paranormal nature as well. Being a devout Christian, however, made this problematic. Reincarnation was considered inconsistent with his faith, but what was he to make of the information his sessions were providing that insisted there was such a thing as previous lives? Confused and anxious, he at first dismissed the information but eventually came to accept it as a valuable tool in understanding an individual's condition more thoroughly. Apparently, Cayce decided, many ailments were karmic in nature—that is, they could find their root cause in actions committed in previous lives—information that proved invaluable in facilitating his sessions even more. Without ever abandoning his Christian faith, Cayce went on to become an expert on the subject of previous lives, as well as what supposedly occurs in those periods between lives, penning (or, at least, inspiring) a number of books and articles on the subject before he died. Reincarnation, while not yet firmly established in the Western psyche, was at least knocking on the door.

To be fair, however, Cayce was not without his detractors. While he did demonstrate a remarkable ability to successfully diagnose illnesses while in a trance state (some claim an astonishing 90 percent success rate), he was also occasionally wrong, a point frequently pointed out by his detractors. It has also been charged that many of his diagnoses were so general and vague that they were little better than guesses (a charge commonly leveled against modern psychics as well), which, while a valid objection that needs to be considered, does not explain how he managed to be uncannily correct in so many cases. Considering that Cayce had no formal medical training (though he was to eventually become well-read on the subject) makes the notion that he was simply good at guessing simplistic.

His teachings on reincarnation, on the other hand, suffered not in being wrong, but in being unsubstantiated. Cayce was not terribly concerned about proving his beliefs, so he rarely kept detailed records that might be useful in obtaining empirical evidence to support his past-life claims. Like so many things in Cayce's life, such ideas were simply to be taken on faith, and so, for the reincarnationist, Cayce does little more than provide some interesting ideas that must be taken with a grain of salt (as were his equally bizarre and unsubstantiated beliefs about the lost civilization of Atlantis—another interest of Cayce's). Yet it is difficult to imagine that reincarnationist ideas in the West would have been as conceptually developed as they were had it not been for the "Sleeping Prophet" and his apparently remarkable abilities. Whether one believes Cayce possessed any special powers or not, his contribution to bringing reincarnationist ideas into the Western consciousness cannot be understood, especially in the half century since his death.

Though Cayce's work was interesting, he did not have the following during his lifetime that he was to acquire after his death, so his reincarnationist views were not widely known outside of paranormal circles.

Yet Cayce set the stage for Bernstein's later work, and, as such, was instrumental in launching the modern reincarnationist movement in America. Today, Cayce's work is widely read and studied, making him one of the most important reincarnationist teachers of modern times as well as a driving force behind what was later to be the called the "New Age Movement"—a way of thinking about the world around us that has revolutionized the way we understand God and death and what happens to the human soul when we die.

Modern Reincarnationist Beliefs

While Cayce's and Bernstein's books made their marks in the national psyche, it wasn't until the 1960s that reincarnationist ideas began to become popular in Western culture. The introduction of Eastern philosophies onto college campuses and among the young during the Vietnam War era fueled debate on religion in general and often challenged the anti-reincarnationist teachings of the churches, while the popular writings of Shirley MacLaine, Jane Roberts (the Seth series), Neale Donald Walsh, Sylvia Browne, and others—much of which deal extensively with reincarnation—further popularized the notion. Today, reincarnation remains a mainstay not only in the New Age movement, but in the rapidly growing New Thought churches (Unity and Religious Science among others), and is even getting a hearing within the more liberal branches of Christianity. Clearly, as a belief system it is now firmly entrenched within the Western mindset, and is growing in popularity daily. Apparently, and in spite of the best efforts of both its religious and secular detractors, reincarnation is here to stay.

The point of this extremely brief and very sketchy history lesson is to emphasize the point that reincarnation is not some new or alien belief system that suddenly emerged in the 1960s when the first gurus arrived on our shores, but instead has been a part of this country's beliefs—at least in a small way—for over a century. Therefore, in considering the evidence for reincarnation, one is not treading on new and unexplored territory, but is harkening back to a rich past that begs to be more closely examined and better understood. History is an ally in our search that must not be ignored if we are to have any success in unraveling the mystery of reincarnation, for it is in the whispers of ages past that we might find our own future and, with it, a better understanding of the intricacies of the universe within which we live.

chapter three

EVIDENCE FOR REINCARNATION: THE PHYSICAL EVIDENCE

It is one thing to understand the extent of reincarnationist beliefs around the world and appreciate the profound role reincarnation has played in history, but what is the evidence for reincarnation and, in the same vein, how trustworthy is that evidence, considering the intricacies of the human mind and our ability as a species to delude ourselves into believing all sorts of nonsense? Is reincarnation, as the skeptics maintain, nothing more than a collection of anecdotal stories told by highly suggestible people and, in some cases, clearly unstable personalities, or is there something more to it?

It is not generally recognized by the average Westerner that reincarnation has a good deal of hard evidence to support it, and that the evidence is frequently more impressive than many people are aware. In this chapter, we'll take a look at some of the more compelling evidence that supports reincarnation, all the while remaining conscious of the fact that even the best evidence is not flawless, nor is any of it in itself capable of "proving" reincarnation to the satisfaction of its critics. If examined objectively, however, it can be intriguing.

Conscious Past-Life Memories in Children

Perhaps the strongest and best-documented evidence in support of reincarnation comes from the work of Dr. Ian Stevenson, a Virginia psychiatrist of impeccable credentials who began studying cases of conscious past-life memories in children in the late 1950s. Since then, Stevenson has collected almost three thousand cases of children—most of them between four and ten years of age—who were allegedly able to recall having lived past lives, complete with names, dates, and even details about the villages in which they believe they previously lived. Many were able to instantly identify members of their "former" family and were often able to recount pet names and intricate details of their previous lives with uncanny accuracy. Additionally, many of the children Stevenson studied could even recount how they had died in their previous lives, providing details of their deaths with a degree of certainty and knowledge inexplicable for children.

What's most impressive about these memories is that these children were not hypnotized or "regressed" into remembering previous lives, but had exhibited conscious memories of past lives spontaneously from a very early age. In fact, Stevenson specifically made it a point to ignore past-life memories acquired through hypnosis precisely because he considered them unreliable and fantasy prone. While children are, of course, capable of fantasizing as well, what impressed Stevenson was the wealth of personal and often intimate details the children were able to recount—details he thought would be unlikely for a child to imagine or learn from an adult. Children were simply not capable of retaining anything like the vast amount of information his subjects frequently provided—even after lengthy coaching—nor were their stories consistent with the type of fantasies children are famous for.

Even more impressive than the sheer quantity of detail the children could provide was the fact that much of it proved to be verifiable. Names often (though not always) proved to be accurate and, in most cases, turned out to be those of complete strangers who had died just prior to the child's birth. They correctly recalled former spouses, siblings, parents, and even children they had parented in their previous incarnation, and were able to describe the home they had lived in with remarkable accuracy though they had never been within fifty miles of the spot during their present life. In a few cases, the children identified so strongly with their past life that they insisted on being called by their former name and even felt alienated from their present family, preferring (and, in some instances, becoming clearly upset when not permitted) to spend more time with their previous family. While these memories and inclinations tended to fade after a few years and disappear completely by adolescence, they remain among the best evidence for reincarnation to date. If reincarnation could be proven in a scientifically satisfactory manner, these children are the best evidence science could expect.

Though Stevenson was occasionally attacked for his methodology and sometimes accused by skeptics of "coaxing" children into creating their fantastic stories (charges that have never been substantiated), for the most part those who have bothered to study his data objectively are usually impressed with his thoroughness and the care he took in ensuring that neither he nor anyone else consciously or unconsciously influenced his subjects in any way. Even more impressive is the fact that he frequently discounted promising prospects if he believed there was even a hint of collusion or coaching involved, or found significant discrepancies in their "memories."

Another objection often leveled against him was that since his subjects came almost entirely from Asia—a continent where reincarnation was already a part of the culture—they were more likely to possess memories of past lives simply because they were culturally predisposed to the idea, thus implying that such memories were nothing more than a reflection of the local mythology. Such objections are countered, however, by the fact that Stevenson also recorded scores of cases of past-life memory in children from Western nations where reincarnation is not a significant element of the culture's beliefs. While there was an admittedly vast disparity in the number of Asian children versus those from Europe and the Western hemisphere, Stevenson maintains that this is a result of anti-reincarnationist bias in the West. In effect, since Westerners are generally less open to the idea of previous lives, they were far less likely to encourage or report such memories in their own children. As such, since Western children who recall past lives are frequently ignored and their memories rejected as childish fantasies, it is only natural that more stories would come from the children of Hindu or Buddhist parents than those with a Judeo-Christian or Muslim background.

What's important to remember is that Stevenson was not setting out to prove reincarnation (he only maintains that his data is *suggestive* of reincarnation—not proof of it), but was simply collecting data on a remarkable phenomenon he believed science needed to study, often frequently putting himself at great personal risk in his travels through sometimes hostile environments to do so. In committing his entire life to studying these past-life memories when he could have easily made a much more comfortable living for himself by simply ignoring the question entirely speaks volumes for the man's integrity and perseverance. If reincarnation is ever "proven" to be true, much of the reason will be due to the work of this extraordinary man.

CORRESPONDING BIRTHMARKS

One of the more interesting and potentially solid pieces of evidence suggestive of reincarnation also came from Stevenson's research. During the course of his travels he noticed that occasionally some of the children he investigated revealed marks on their bodies that precisely corresponded with the fatal wounds they claimed their previous personality had suffered at the time of their death. For instance, one of Stevenson's subjects, an eleven-year-old Turkish boy, recounted having been accidentally shot in the head with a shotgun by a neighbor in a previous incarnation. Curiously, the boy was born with a badly deformed right ear that closely mimicked the wounds the deceased man had received, a fact later confirmed by medical records and photographs Stevenson was able to obtain from local authorities during his investigation. And this was by no means an unusual case; Stevenson recounted scores of similar cases, some in which toes and fingers—and in a few cases, even entire limbs— that had been lost in a previous incarnation were missing in the current incarnation, as well as even more startling instances in which there were multiple birthmarks that closely resembled the precise wounds received by the past-life subject. In one case, he even found matching entrance and exit wounds in a subject that closely corresponded to those of the previous personality who had died from a gunshot wound to the head. Of course, the chances of such perfectly matching marks occurring naturally even once are astronomical, and Stevenson had a number of such cases on record.

Noting that such peculiar birthmarks were most common in subjects who recalled an especially violent death in their last incarnation, Stevenson theorized that traumatic deaths may imprint such a powerful impression on the psyche that the marks of that death may actually be imprinted upon the unborn fetus to follow the subject into the next incarnation. Precisely how this might be possible remains, of course, a mystery, but corresponding birthmarks remain some of the strongest evidence for reincarnation on record. While not conclusive in their own right, they defy natural or biological explanations, and, while they may be written off by skeptics as mere coincidence, the fact that Stevenson has recorded scores of such cases is highly significant.

DEMOGRAPHIC STUDIES

In the late 1960s another psychologist, Dr. Helen Wambach (1932–1985), began a series of experiments that dealt with the demographic consistency of past-life memories. Intrigued by several personal experiences she had encountered in dealing with patients who had described previous lives while under hypnosis and curious to know if there was more to it than simple imagination, she decided to compare their recollections with anthropological, sociological, and archeological studies made of the cultures they mentioned to see if there was any demographic consistency in their recounted memories. For instance, if gender and social-class ratios proved to be inconsistent with what anthropologists and sociologists had estimated them to have been,[1] that would demonstrate that her subjects were either making up stories or inadvertently fantasizing. If, on the other hand, there proved to be a correlation with the known demographic data, that would bring significant weight to the idea that human beings continue to live on through the mechanism of multiple rebirths, for the only other possibility—that literally thousands of subjects had innocently and spontaneously manufactured demographically accurate past-life memories from their imagination—was statistically and logically untenable.

Convinced that such a study was both feasible and potentially valuable, she began regressing volunteers—often several at a time—into remembering past lives and then having them carefully record details about their gender, race, economic status, and other often mundane specifics of their daily past lives. By the time she finished regressing just over one thousand subjects over a ten year period, she realized she had some interesting data on her hands.

What Wambach found was that the information she obtained proved to be remarkably consistent with what demographers know of the ancient past. For instance, as the majority of Wambach's subjects were women (by a 3 to 1 ratio), and working from the premise that most people would be unlikely to imagine themselves to have been a member of the opposite

---

1 Obviously, since record keeping is a fairly modern phenomenon, demographers, utilizing the best socio-economic models and anthropological studies, can only make educated guesses as to population sizes, economic status, and so on, of ancient cultures. While not precise, the numbers they produce are generally accepted as reasonable by demographers.

sex, there should have been a disproportionately higher number of individuals remembering themselves to have been females rather than males in a past life. Instead, she was surprised to find a large number of women remembering past lives as men (as well as a smaller number of men remembering past lives as women) that when tallied resulted in a biologically accurate 50/50 ratio of men to women throughout every time period recorded. If these "memories" were based upon pure imagination, such a consistent male/female ratio should be impossible to achieve, suggesting that a high number of authentic past-life memories existed within her sampling.

Additionally, social classes proved to be not only remarkably consistent, but also in line with demographic studies. Wambach had her subjects recount whether they were poor, middle class, or upper class in a previous life, presuming that a disproportionate number of subjects would opt for more interesting or affluent lives, which would strongly suggest that the memories were manufactured. To her surprise, however, most subjects recalled having lived rather ordinary and even drab lives, often in desperate poverty. In fact, fewer than 10 percent of her subjects recalled living an upper-class lifestyle, and about a quarter to a third recalled being artisans or merchants (middle class) in a previous incarnation, which corresponded very closely to sociological studies from the various periods in history she covered. Her data, then, on top of demonstrating an inexplicable consistency when compared to accepted scientific expectations, also destroyed the commonly held notion that most people recall living past lives as famous or wealthy people.

Other details proved to be accurate as well. Subjects frequently described architecture, clothing styles, and even the coinage in use at the time that was consistent with what archeologists know of the past. Even mundane details such as types of footwear used, common eating utensils, primary diet, and the methods used to cook their food—details a would-be hoaxer would be unlikely to consider—were also consistent with the known historical record. Additionally, racial distribution and ratios proved to be correct as well, demonstrating again that either one of the most wide-spread and carefully maintained hoaxes was afoot, or that maybe people really do live more than one life. No other explanation seemed plausible.

Wambach was as surprised by the results as her skeptical colleagues later proved to be, but her data seemed airtight. Though skeptics questioned her methodology (hypnotism) and scholars disputed some of her conclusions, no one could deny that she had produced some fascinating and remarkable results with her study. Unfortunately, her data has been largely ignored by the academic community to this day, despite it being one of the best and most objective pieces of evidence for the validity of reincarnation in existence, demonstrating not a weakness in her methodology, but a potentially fatal chink in science's armor.

VERIFIABLE PAST-LIFE MEMORIES

A fourth type of evidence for reincarnation, and the best known (and most controversial), is the memories of a past life that are acquired through hypnotism and produce verifiable details (of which the Bridey Murphy case was typical). Unlike Stevenson's subjects, these are not consciously recalled past lives, but memories that can only be obtained during a deep hypnotic trance. Also, unlike Wambach's subjects, who often failed to recall specific personal details of their past lives such as their name or place of residence, these memories are far more specific in the information they provide, with subjects often being able to provide full names, occupations, names of spouses and family members, and other pertinent details of an alleged past life (sometimes even to the precise street and address at which they previously resided).[2]

---

2 Why the degree of detail patients recall during traditional regression therapy and that recalled by Wambach's subjects varied so much is unknown. Perhaps in regressing her patients so far back, much of the personal information was lost, or perhaps some of her subjects were not as deeply hypnotized as others.

Though similar to the kind of information Stevenson obtained during his examinations of children who professed to remember a past life, these memories are different. Most of the children he studied could only recall details from their immediately preceding life, and these memories were of people who had died only a few years (and, in a few cases, months or even weeks) before the child's birth. Regressed memories, however, tend to go much further back in time—sometimes centuries, in fact—and to often distant locales that often provide a plethora of verifiable historical and personal detail; details that could only be explained through forgotten memories, fraud, or reincarnation.

Obviously, those who reject reincarnation presuppose the first two explanations to be the most likely, and while there are a number of cases that have proven to have been the result of lost or hidden memories, these account for only a small number of the many scores of well-documented cases on record. Genuine hoaxes are even rarer, though not unheard of (and are usually exposed as such fairly quickly). That some of these recollections may be actual evidence of reincarnation, then, must be taken seriously.

Unfortunately, while most of these cases prove to be imbued with enough detail to make them plausible as past-life memories, none has proven to be irrefutable proof of reincarnation. There are always a few erroneous details thrown in among the verifiable facts to cast doubt on their authenticity, and so while they remain good evidence for reincarnation, they must always remain just outside of the veil of provability. We will examine one of these cases in depth in a later chapter and demonstrate how difficult it is to reach a final verdict, but for now it is enough to realize that though the evidence acquired from past-life regression is far from airtight, it is also better than most people suspect.

XENOGLOSSIA
[INEXPLICABLE USE OF A FOREIGN LANGUAGE]

One of the more interesting, and uncommon, evidences for reincarnation remains those well-documented cases in which people reliving a past life suddenly begin speaking in a language that they have never learned. Sometimes it can be as simple as a few foreign words or phrases, or, in a some instances, as complex as an entire, fluent conversation being carried out in a language the subject is not even aware exists. In some of the most credible and compelling cases of xenoglossia recorded, the subject may not only speak in a foreign language, but may even use an archaic version of it that has not been in regular usage for centuries, making it extremely unlikely to be a fantasy, a hoax, or a case of cryptomnesia (forgotten memories).[3] As such, a good case of xenoglossia remains one of the more compelling evidences for reincarnation, but because they are so rare they have not generated enough hard data to allow researchers to come to any conclusions.

A similar but more common phenomenon sometimes seen in past-life regressions is when the subject does not speak in a foreign language, but in a foreign dialect or accent (the Bridey Murphy case—during which the subject spoke in a heavy Irish brogue when describing her previous life as a nineteenth-century Irish woman—was a classic example of this phenomenon). Even when the vocabulary the subjects use to describe their past life is contemporary, heavy (and, usually, convincing and appropriate) accents are still sometimes heard. For example, an English-speaking woman who recalls a past life lived in Germany may

---

3 One of the better known cases of xenoglossia was seen in a past-life regression episode experienced by the late, well known actor Glenn Ford, who was able to speak French while reliving a past life, despite it being a language he did not know. Linguists listening to a recording of the session afterward confirmed that Ford was speaking a seventeenth-century version of the dialect, with a long-extinct but accurate Parisian accent.

abruptly take on a German accent, though still recounting her memories in modern English. It is as if the current or "modern" personality is filtering the statements of the past personality through its own brain—essentially acting as its own translator—but even though it is successful in translating the language, enough of the former personality's native tongue survives to be heard as a distinct dialect or accent.

Of course, some people have a good ear for dialects and can even mimic a few of them, so this is probably not particularly significant. However, as someone who enjoys attempting to mimic foreign accents (with varying degrees of success), I can attest to the fact that it is not as easy as might be assumed. To produce a convincing accent takes hours of practice and often can't be replicated accurately at all unless one has the opportunity to spend some time in the country whose dialect one is attempting to mimic. Even professional actors are not usually capable of pulling off a believable foreign accent (although there are a few who get close), so it is difficult to imagine how a person with no particular interest in foreign accents or training as an actor could produce a convincing dialect on the spur of the moment. But, of course, such *is* possible, and so foreign accents are not particularly good evidence that one is genuinely speaking with a past-life personality.

SAVANTS AND PRODIGIES

Another phenomenon that might be pointed to as possible evidence of reincarnation is that of savants and child prodigies, those rare individuals who possess some remarkable gift or ability far beyond what is either natural or explainable.

Savants differ from prodigies in that they are individuals born with severe physical impediments (such as blindness) and/or extreme mental retardation, but who still possess some unique and often astonishing talent that utterly defies logic. For instance, a severely retarded man who, for all practical purposes, lives a life that approximates that of a seven-year-old child, may possess the ability to perfectly replicate any piece of piano music after hearing it played only once, an ability well beyond not only his—but most people's—capacity to learn.

Such cases are frequently explained away as prenatal brain damage being overcompensated by the undamaged parts of the brain, resulting in a sometimes greatly enhanced ability to perform some unique and astonishing skill. This may well be the case, too, since such skills that savants possess are rare—if not nonexistent—in the natural world, making it difficult to see how they might be evidence of a past-life talent resurfacing in a present incarnation. As such, savants do not appear to present a very strong case for reincarnation.

A prodigy, however, is a different story. Prodigies differ from savants in the respect that from all outward appearances they appear as very normal children who just happen to have a seemingly inherent ability to learn a particular skill at a greatly accelerated pace. Good examples of prodigies include the German composer Mozart, who was able to compose simple arrangements of music at the age of four and entire symphonies by adolescence, and the seventeenth-century mathematician Blaise Pascal, who managed to outline a new geometric system by the age of eleven.

Unlike the savant, however, the prodigy isn't born with the ability to write music or understand the complexities of geometry; he or she must learn it the same way everyone else does. The difference, however, is the *speed* at which prodigies learn, and their capacity to grasp the material so easily. As such, most are able to digest years of material in a matter of months, enabling them to master a particular discipline years ahead of their peers.

Modern science attributes these rare gifts to simple brain chemistry, which is fine as far as it goes. The question that needs to be explored, however, is "*Why* are their brains wired differently than other people's?" Or, precisely, "In which way are they wired differently?" Is it some genetic mutation, or a one-in-a-million mix of DNA (and if so, why does it not seem to similarly affect their normal siblings?). Or could it be that these special people possess their remarkable ability because they have done it all before? In effect, could the child who shows a special gift for geometry have been a mathematics professor in a previous life? Was Mozart able to accomplish his amazing feats of music because, precisely as he claimed, he had been a musician many times before?

Is it possible that a lifetime of learning can somehow survive death and manifest itself in the next incarnation? While far from conclusive, it is an intriguing idea. The problem, however, is that if previous knowledge can be brought into a fresh incarnation, why doesn't it happen more often? Surely there are many people who possessed great knowledge or skills in the past, so child prodigies should be reasonably common. Yet in reality such gifted children are rare, which seems to suggest other, more prosaic reasons for such early ability.

However, one possibility does present itself, at least from a reincarnationist perspective. It should be recognized that only recently have there been such large numbers of scientists, musicians, artists, and academicians upon the planet; in past centuries such people were comparatively rare. As such, there would have been a very small nucleus or "pool" of highly knowledgeable (or academic) souls out there looking to reincarnate, making prodigies exceedingly rare (although it could be argued that there should be more prodigies in the future as more trained professionals die and their souls are continually added to the "mix"). Additionally, some may be born into a Third-World culture in which such innate skills lie dormant and undiscovered, and it is even possible that only some souls are capable of transferring knowledge gained in one lifetime into the next, or that it may be done only in special cases for specific reasons.

For the most part, however, it appears more beneficial for a soul to drop all memories and acquired knowledge from a previous incarnation precisely so that it can start fresh with no "baggage" from a past life to contend with. Probably so much of the "old" knowledge is out-of-date and of little use to the present personality that to discard it in toto and start with a "clean slate" would be the best course of action. For example, medical knowledge has increased so profoundly over the last century that the training and experience held by an early nineteenth-century physician would be woefully out-of-date by today's standards and probably better left in the past. In fact, to retain that "old knowledge" might actually prove detrimental to learning the "new" knowledge, so the soul would be wise to make a point of shedding its past education and move on with a new and fresh perspective. There may be cases, however, where certain past knowledge might be useful in the present, so it is purposely retained by the soul and integrated into the next personality (possibly as a means of helping with the spiritual/social and scientific evolution of human society in general). Then again, the retention of past knowledge—like the memory of past lives in general—may be a fluke.

One final thought: while child prodigies are rare, gifted children are not. Everyone knows children who are especially quick learners and seem to operate on a higher academic level than their peers. Could it be that those children we consider "gifted" or especially bright were actually educated individuals in a past life who, while no longer retaining the specific knowledge they held in that earlier incarnation, still retain the habit of learning that they had acquired then? The knowledge itself may not survive, but perhaps simply the *desire* to learn is the residual echo of an educated past life. Could that explain the apparent disparity we see in much of the academic world, where some students seem to excel while others struggle or drop out entirely?[4]

---

4 Of course, parenting and environment are also factors in determining a child's
   scholastic capabilities, though academically astute children sometimes hail from
   dysfunctional homes in which education was marginalized or ignored. Perhaps
   it's not so much one's intelligence that emerges from an educated past life, but
   a love of learning that marks a prior academic tradition.

DÉJÀ VU

Have you ever had the strange feeling that you're repeating an experience you're certain you've never had before, or entered a building that seems strangely familiar to you, though you know for a fact you've never been there before? If so, you have experienced what is referred to as *déjà vu*—the phenomenon of repeating an event or having inexplicable knowledge of a place you've never previously visited.

To some people, such experiences are considered evidence of a past life—an "echo" or ill-defined memory that has somehow survived the rebirthing process, only to be inadvertently triggered by some event in the present. It can be as simple as a subtle sense that you've had a particular conversation or experience before—much like the feeling you get when reading a book you've read before but can't recall when—or as extraordinary as knowing the precise layout of a building or even an entire town that you have never visited before.

Science insists that such experiences are simply a coincidental similarity between a present and a similar but forgotten past experience. For example, people may feel a special familiarity with a house they have never visited before not because they lived there in a previous life, but because they have at one time or another visited a similar home that unconsciously reminds them of this one. And how many of us have had a long-forgotten conversation suddenly repeat itself in the present? Memory is a tricky affair that is capable of playing all kinds of pranks on the mind.

However, this possible solution does little to explain the sheer amount of detail that is sometimes recalled in the best cases of déjà vu. Even a similarity of places or events cannot explain, for instance, how a person can correctly name and describe the maze of streets that lie just ahead in a small village that he or she is visiting for the first time, nor does it seem to comfortably account for how a person can recall with unerring exactitude the precise layout of a home that he or she has never visited before. A similarity with places or things experienced in the past can go only so far; at some point the odds against correctly guessing the street layout of a city or the location of various rooms within a sprawling mansion become astronomical. Reincarnation, in such cases, must be considered at least a possibility.

DREAMS AND NIGHTMARES

All of us from time to time have had extraordinarily vivid dreams and terrifying nightmares from which we've awakened either perplexed or frightened. Occasionally dreams will even repeat themselves, almost demanding that we pay attention to their message.

Such dreams, however, are almost always triggered by events in our present life and seem to be the subconscious's way of processing important information we might not be aware of in our conscious world. We really don't know why our brains do this exactly, though some have postulated that dreams are the subconscious's way of identifying some repressed trauma that needs to be dealt with, or a bit of make-believe constructed by our imagination designed to fill a need we unconsciously possess. In any case, dreams seem to be an important part of the human experience and a valuable resource to understanding the hidden parts of our sometimes troubled psyches.

Once in a while, however, individuals may have dreams that seem unique and strangely different or out of place. They may dream they are living in the distant past, interacting with people they do not know and generally dealing with some obscure situations that they are thoroughly unfamiliar with. Such dreams may repeat throughout a person's life (sometimes with monotonous regularity) or they may occur only once; in either case, however, these dreams seem completely detached from the subject's present or "normal" world and remain largely inexplicable. It is these dreams that reincarnationists have sometimes pointed to as echoes or memories of a past life manifesting themselves in the present.

While an intriguing idea and one not at all inconsistent with what one might expect if reincarnation were true, dreams probably constitute some of the weakest evidence in support of reincarnation. They are usually too vague and lack verifiable specifics to be of any empirical value. Occasionally, however, a few dreams are sufficiently specific and detailed enough that the images in them can be verified, though such cases are exceedingly rare and problematic.

Conclusion

Though the quality of the evidence may vary greatly, the casual belief held by many that the physical evidence for reincarnation is simply not there is entirely erroneous. While reincarnationists have yet to produce incontrovertible "proof" that we have lived before, it is not a belief that exists without significant and, some might say, impressive evidence to support it. That some may choose to ignore this evidence is not an indictment against reincarnation, but a testimony to the human propensity to reject anything that does not fit into our carefully wrought—and often culturally and religiously maintained—world view. Reincarnation may not be true, but if it's not, then the mystery of what is going on with past-life regression, conscious past-life memories in children, and coordinating birthmarks must be explained in other ways. To simply dismiss the entire issue as coincidence or mere New Age nonsense not only is dishonest and intellectually lazy, but ignores the larger issues involved. Something is going on that needs an explanation, and the search to find that explanation may prove to be as fascinating a quest as the possibility of reincarnation itself may be.

chapter four

EVIDENCE FOR REINCARNATION: THE SOCIO-PSYCHOLOGICAL EVIDENCE

If reincarnation were true, it might be imagined that it should effect us in ways both obvious and subtle in many areas of our lives. While demographic studies and verifiable past-life memories constitute the empirical evidences for reincarnation, such evidences are uncommon and exceedingly rare in most people's lives. To most, the evidence will not be so obvious, but will instead be more likely perceived in subtle, less definable ways, such as through the outward nature of our personalities and personal likes and dislikes. It is difficult for most people to comprehend the many ways a past life might shape our current understandings, beliefs, tastes, and tendencies, but it is through these outward manifestations of the soul that the past is most commonly revealed. In effect, the reason we perceive things the way we do and the things that shape the sort of person we are may have more to do with our past lives than we might appreciate.

Of course, some (if not most) of our personal characteristics can be explained away by our environment and upbringing, but too often we find ourselves sharing an environment with a sibling or acquaintance and still emerging a very different person from him or her. The fact that two siblings can grow up in nearly identical circumstances within the same household only to take two very different paths upon reaching adulthood is a mystery of human behavior; that one is extroverted and has a good head for business while the other remains shy and has a remarkable aptitude for music cannot be easily explained away with either genetics or upbringing. Some third element must be at work, forging very different personalities from what is essentially the same raw material.

In this chapter we will explore this mysterious mechanism of human nature, and look for the evidences of reincarnation within ourselves. This is, of course, a far more introspective and subjective search for such evidence, but one each of us can do for ourselves if we only take the time to search our lives for the telltale clues that our distant past continues to touch our lives still.

PERSONALITY

Most people are aware of the often vast differences in personality evident among even the closest siblings. I have two sons whose personal histories couldn't be more similar: born in the same hospital (in the same delivery room, no less) twenty-eight months apart, they lived in the same room together throughout most of their lives, watched many of the same television programs, had many of the same friends, attended the same schools (often with the same teachers), and yet they still demonstrate significant differences in their personalities. Whereas one is more naturally academic, the other is mechanically gifted; one has a hair-trigger temper that erupts with sudden force while the other possesses far greater levels of restraint; one child possesses a penchant for increasingly unpopular practical jokes while the other has an entirely different sense of humor. It makes one wonder how they could both have come from the same set of genes, considering how very different they are in so many ways.

So what is it that determines our personalities exactly? Why are some of us naturally more patient than others, and why do some of us enjoy reading while others would never consider cracking a book? Further, why are some of us drawn to museums and art galleries while others are drawn with equal passion to shopping malls and sporting events?

Behaviorists tell us that this is all due in part to genetics, in part to the environment each child grows up in, and in part to the result of the personal experiences each child has had. While siblings may have similar experiences, each child's experience is still uniquely his or her own. In other words, even though siblings may live in very similar environments, they have different experiences that shape their individual personalities in distinct, one-of-a-kind ways. Then, as they mature into adulthood, these individual traits become set, and a fully formed but unique adult personality is the result.

And yet, why does it appear that children often emerge from the womb with very different and distinct characteristics—characteristics that emerge long before the child is old enough to experience anything that could conceivably shape his or her personality? Additionally, many child psychologists claim that a child's basic personality is often set by the age of four, but, if so, how exactly are later experiences molding the future personality? If a child is naturally impatient, for instance, being put into a situation in which patience is called for will more likely be perceived as tortuous rather than a growth experience. The child may learn to deal with his or her impatience in more constructive ways as he or she grows older, but the underlying impatience will still be there—it's simply under better control. If experiences shape our personality, however, then being forced to wait should eventually result in a more patient persona, yet this is seldom the case. Life experiences may shape our coping mechanisms or even reveal to us things we need to work on, but they rarely alter a person's basic nature. Shy people may push themselves to be more personable at parties, for example, yet even if they attend a hundred social gatherings it will not likely turn them into flamboyant extroverts. How we choose to experience particular situations merely defines who we already are—the experiences themselves do not determine who we will become.

So how do we explain personality, then? Do we explain it in terms of chemical reactions in the brain, environmental factors, or even genetic proclivities? Or, as some reincarnationists believe, could our basic personality be set even before we are born? Are we, in fact, simply a reflection of our soul's own basic personality, reflecting its attributes and characteristics through each new incarnation?

This, of course, brings up the question as to whether there are different "types" of souls, just as there are different personality types. For instance, is there such a thing as a "party" soul that routinely manifests itself as a gregarious, fun-loving extrovert, and a "meditative" soul who repeatedly manifests as a quiet, shy introvert? Further, if the human personality does survive death relatively intact, it has to go somewhere; could that "somewhere" be the next fetus it chooses to inhabit? It's not clear how much of our personality survives death, but it could be far more than we imagine.

Hobbies, Interests, and Obsessions

In the same vein, then, could our hobbies and interests also be an "echo" from a previous incarnation? For example, if one was an artist in a past life, wouldn't we expect that person to be drawn toward expressing himself or herself through drawing and painting in this life as well? By the same token, is a Civil War buff simply pursuing a new interest, or is that person in some ways still clinging to a past incarnation in which he or she was a participant in that war? Even if we have no conscious memory of that past persona, might not our present personality and hobbies be a modern reflection of our past-life experiences and interests?

I have often wondered where we get our interests from. Certainly, some of them we acquire in this lifetime from various sources, yet it is also equally true that if you subject two people to the same hobby, one will frequently be fascinated with it while the other will consider it one great exercise in boredom. So what determines what makes one sibling an avid fisherman while the other couldn't care less about the entire issue? Is it really all just a matter of environment?

Reincarnation, while not the only possible answer, must at least be considered, especially in those cases where one develops a hobby or interest that seems quite out of the ordinary. Is a boy growing up in land-locked Iowa, for example, who develops a fascination for eighteenth-century schooners despite having no nautical background, responding to some unknown stimulus, or could it be a response to a past life lived as a crewman on an eighteenth-century schooner? In the next chapter we will explore an authentic case in which a hobby that came to border on an obsession may have had its basis in a possible past life, but for now it is enough to be aware of how much of our past we may retain in our present, albeit in the most subtle and subconscious ways. Our past, then, may be far more tied to our present (and, by extension, our future) than we can begin to imagine.

PHOBIAS

Phobias—those unusual and often overwhelming fears of things that do not constitute a genuine danger to us—are a common phenomenon almost everyone has experienced at one time or another. How one acquires a phobia is a well-understood process; phobias are the result of some trauma or event from one's past (often childhood) that manifests itself in later life as a panic-inducing fear. For example, a boy who nearly drowns may develop an unnatural fear of water, or a girl who was lost in a store as a toddler may have an irrational fear of abandonment as an adult. As such, phobias of one kind or another affect most people, though usually they are mild enough (or unusual enough) that they do not seriously impact a person's life.

That these irrational fears are the unfortunate consequences of prior traumas, however, is not the problem. It is those phobias that seem to develop *without* an accompanying trauma that remain inexplicable. For example, a therapist may find that a man with an irrational fear of water has never experienced a near drowning (and may, in fact, never have been near water in his life) but has been terrified of drowning for as long as he can remember. With nothing in the patient's past to explain how he developed such a fear, these phobias can be the most difficult to treat, as there is no apparent way to identify and deal with the underlying trauma. Past-life regression therapists, however, frequently discover that while a person may not recall nearly drowning in a present life, he or she frequently *does* recall drowning in a previous one—an event that terrified the individual to such a degree that he or she managed to bring that trauma into his or her current incarnation. Once so identified, in many cases recovery can be surprisingly quick and complete, allowing the patient to recover far faster than might have been the case with more conventional therapies. Even the medical community agrees that such therapies are an effective means of dealing with severe, unexplained phobias, though they generally dismiss reincarnation as a viable explanation. To most clinical psychologists, such past-life "memories" are mere fantasies specifically manifested by the human psyche for the purpose of identifying the hidden phobia by placing it in a safe context outside the patient's own past. At last safe from any perceived danger, it is conjectured, the mind is finally able to deal with the underlying trauma and effect a speedy recovery—a type of self-induced placebo effect. We will deal with this objection a little later, but for now it is enough to recognize that whether reincarnation exists or not, the very *belief* that it does seems to have curative powers, which is a remarkable admission in any event.

What this phenomenon does force us to do is ask ourselves whether many of the things we fear—especially those fears and phobias that seem out of place and far more severe than might seem reasonable—are but mere echoes from a distant past. It's no secret that phobias frequently play into past-life memories and are often the doorway that reveals that past; could it be that modern hypnotherapy techniques developed over the last half century were inadvertently crafted specifically to cure the emotional traumas of past lives? It's an interesting possibility.

Homosexuality and Transgender Tendencies

Until fairly recently it was assumed that homosexual behavior was a freely chosen lifestyle choice that could be resisted with sufficient will power, but evidence has subsequently shown just the opposite to be true. According to recent studies, approximately 2–3 percent of the population develop or realize an almost exclusively homosexual orientation from adolescence, while other studies further suggest that the proclivity toward same sex attraction may also have a genetic link. Yet what would cause such a proclivity, especially considering the negative consequences such a lifestyle "choice" has traditionally incurred in some societies? Is it a question of environment and upbringing, or is it entirely a matter of biology?

Or could there be another factor involved? What if the underlying cause of homosexuality is neither environmental nor genetic, but is instead the result of a previous opposite-sex incarnation? Since regression therapists frequently encounter cases of men remembering that they were women in their immediate past life—and of women remembering they were men—could cross-gender reincarnation have a more profound impact than might seem immediately evident? In essence, are homosexuals (and bisexuals and transgender individuals, in general) "trapped" in the wrong body, as some have actually complained?

Perhaps in so closely identifying with their previous gender, some find it difficult to adjust to their new gender and so retain many of the characteristics they possessed in their last incarnation. As such, a man may be attracted to other men because on some level he still retains feminine proclivities from his past life (despite the degree of masculinity he may possess in other areas of his present life). While far from irrefutable evidence for reincarnation, does it not answer a few questions rather nicely?

But what of the possible genetic factor? If it can be conclusively proven that some people are genetically inclined toward homosexuality, doesn't that preclude transgender reincarnation as a possible cause?

Not necessarily. As is suggested in the cases of prior-life wounds emerging on the bodies of present incarnates in the form of unusual birthmarks, it could be argued that the physical realm may well respond to the desires of the spiritual realm and manifest those aspects of a past life the soul desires to carry with it into a present incarnation. In other words, the soul creates the genetic template its next body will adhere to before that person is even born, whether it be the manifestation of past-life wounds or a proclivity toward homosexuality. In essence, our physical manifestation—even our genetic coding—could be determined by the spiritual realm; our personality then is not shaped by biology, but the other way around.[1]

But what then of bisexuality and those who change sexual orientation? If a man reincarnates as a woman but as a result of retaining a strong identification with that previous gender remains attracted to other women, what are we to make of those who seem to be attracted to both sexes equally? Doesn't this also seem to challenge the idea of cross-gender reincarnation?

Possibly, but then the entire issue of human sexuality is a complex one. Is it possible that some bisexual tendencies are the result of a *partially* successful gender shift, but not a *completely* successful one? In other words, when souls move from one gender to the other, is it possible that the new personality the soul has generated may take some time to reacquaint itself to its new sexuality, and that the process of gender confusion is a part of that reorientation process? If one had lived several incarnations as a man and was suddenly reincarnated as a woman, one might be forgiven for imagining the process to be something less than simple. While some souls might make the transition easily, others may have to struggle to fit

---

1 This also, incidentally, could hold true for genetic proclivities toward alcoholism and drug abuse. In effect, could an alcoholic be simply "echoing" a past life as an alcoholic through the mechanism of his or her own DNA?

in to their new gender, producing a period of uncertainty in terms of sexual identity (an uncertainty that may be even more pronounced in pure homosexuals). In fact, it may take more than one incarnation into the same gender for a soul to accept its new sexual orientation (which is why a homosexual man may still recall a past life as a man, even though he still demonstrates transgender proclivities in his present life).

This is not to suggest that homosexuals or bisexuals are "flawed" in some way, or that experiencing life from the perspective of a homosexual/bisexual person may not possess certain benefits in terms of spiritual growth; it is simply to suggest that reincarnating may not be an easy or effortless process. Along the same lines, could our past sexual experiences be reflected in this incarnation in other ways as well? In effect, could a person who was sexually brutalized in a past life enter this life in the form of a serial rapist, or could promiscuity in one lifetime be passed on to the next (or result in an irrational fear of or even disgust for sexual activity in general)? For that matter, could those who choose a celibate lifestyle be doing so in an effort to counter a promiscuous past, or could a promiscuous present be the result of repressed sexuality in a previous incarnation? Our past sexual experiences—as is true of all life experiences—may have more to say about our present practices, preferences, and attitudes than we imagine. But then if it is true that we take "bits" of ourselves from one incarnation to the next, should we expect anything less?

SCHIZOPHRENIA AND MULTIPLE PERSONALITY DISORDERS

Some reincarnationists maintain that certain mental disorders in which a person exhibits two or more distinct personalities could be construed as evidence of reincarnation. It is thought that perhaps the various personalities are not simply bits and pieces of a single, splintered personality, but are in fact past-life personas manifesting themselves alongside the present personality. In effect, the theory goes that if the soul is a repository of all our past lives, might the soul not occasionally lose the ability to keep these past-life personas "in their place," resulting in a rather chaotic emergence of many of them all at once?

While, on the one hand, this might explain the distinct and often dramatically different personalities MPD and schizophrenic victims frequently exhibit, it fails to account for several variables. First, it doesn't address the issue of why the different personalities that exhibit themselves within MPD sufferers do not recount personal histories of past lives. In other words, they don't seem to be "out of synch" with the present, but appear fully cognizant of their environment and surroundings, which is difficult to explain if they were truly past life personas. I would imagine that if a seventeenth-century personality suddenly emerged into our current time and culture, it would find its surroundings strange and unfamiliar; as such, we might imagine that since it had no frame of reference within which to understand the concept of manned flight, for example, we should expect it to be terrified of flying on a modern aircraft. This does not seem to be the case, however, and we are forced to wonder how ancient personalities could function so well in a modern world (and without even mentioning the disparities it was experiencing).

A second problem with the theory is that the treatment for MPD is to successfully reintegrate the various personalities into a single, whole personality. However, it seems that if we are dealing with multiple past-life personas, it should be impossible to find them willing to subjugate themselves to a single dominant personality. In essence, they should resist being merged with the other personalities, just as we would resist all efforts to merge our own current personality with someone else's. They might simply choose to stop manifesting themselves (perhaps for their own protection), but that decision should have no effect upon the "core" or "base" personality; it should remain unaffected by the decision of the past persona to leave in the same way that an unwanted relative choosing to leave my home should have no impact on my personality (other than, perhaps, that of providing a sense of relief). As such, it appears that the various personalities exhibited in an MPD patient don't seem to be separate people so much as contending facets of a single personality, each fighting for dominance and control.

Finally, within regression therapy, it has been repeatedly demonstrated that the various past-life personalities are not aware of each other, whereas the various personalities demonstrated by MPD sufferers frequently are. In fact, each personality often has very strong opinions about the "others," which is something rarely if ever seen within past-life regression. This begs the obvious question, then: if MPD personas know about each other, why don't the various past-life personas exhibited during regression therapy do the same? In other words, why isn't my eighteenth-century persona aware of my thirteenth-century persona? Or is it?

As such, MPD and schizophrenic episodes do not appear to be particularly compelling evidence for reincarnation, though I do believe such experiences are not without some spiritual ramifications. For example, they could be evidence of more than one soul residing within a single body (an idea we will examine more extensively in chapter 15), or even of the presence—in some cases—of a malicious or parasitic disembodied personality attaching itself to the host personality, but that's an issue we will examine later.

CONCLUSION

Though far from irrefutable evidence of reincarnation, these elements are all important indicators that something might be happening that we do not entirely understand. Individually, none of these "evidences" may be compelling in and of themselves, but when combined they are a powerful clue that this single life we are living now may be neither the first nor the last, but merely the most recent.

If true, it seems that we may not be so different from our "old" selves as we imagine. We may be different manifestations of the same soul, separated only by the limitless expanses of time and space, but deep down inside we may remain essentially the same person. It is a question we will look at in later chapters dealing with the mechanisms of reincarnation, but for now it is enough to say that if we *have* lived before, why should we imagine we are not that same basic person now as we were then?

chapter five

ECHOES

In an effort to demonstrate how past-life experiences may unknowingly influence our present life, I present this account of a man whose life may have been heavily affected by just such a past experience—an "echo," if you will, of another life lived in another time that somehow managed to influence and indeed dramatically steer the course of his adolescence. I do not relate it here because it is a remarkable story, for it is not. It is a story that is common to perhaps millions of people, so it is not even unique to the human experience. It is, however, *typical* of the human experience, and so I present it here not as evidence that the human soul lives on through numerous incarnations, but to demonstrate as best I can how, if reincarnation is true, it might manifest itself in an ordinary life in ways that the person so affected may be entirely unaware.

I know the person behind this story well, and I can assure you he is not particularly anxious to share it with the reading public, yet he feels it is necessary that he do so for the sake of clarification. The subject recounts these experiences and observations only after great internal debate and no small amount of trepidation, but believes it so important in illustrating how reincarnation might work in the daily lives of ordinary people that he is willing to put himself under the high glare of scrutiny and, quite likely, subject himself to some degree of ridicule. Yet sometimes personal privacy must be sacrificed upon the altar of knowledge so that learning can take place.

The man I speak of here is, of course, me. The events I'm about to describe are true insofar as I remember them, and I will endeavor to present them as objectively and dispassionately as I am capable of doing. I realize many will simply dismiss them as adolescent fantasies or, at best, unusual coincidences, and I make no claims to the contrary. I only present what happened to me in a straightforward manner and let the readers decide for themselves whether my story has anything to say to them.

An Adolescence for the Ages

My story begins around the time of my twelfth birthday. Until then I had been a rather ordinary boy growing up in a large, Catholic family on a farm near St. Cloud, Minnesota. I was not an unusual child in any way. I was perhaps a bit more precocious than most and certainly imaginative, but from all outward appearances I was a very typical product of the American Midwest. Like most boys at that time, my hobbies tended toward stereotypical male interests such as dinosaurs, racing cars, and toy trucks, and while my parents had a difficult marriage, for the most part I remember my childhood as being a relatively carefree and happy one.

My parents divorced when I was ten, and my siblings and I had just moved with my mother and stepfather to Colorado when things began to change. Whereas previously my interests had been rather conventional, as I approached adolescence I began developing an unusual fascination with things having to do with the military. Where this newfound interest came from was inexplicable. My family was not connected with the military in any way, nor did my family possess a significant military history. As such, there seemed no obvious external influences that might explain my unusual interests, and yet as I moved into my teen years, my fascination for all things military—from toy soldiers and plastic tanks to war movies on television—grew exponentially. Most of my reading material dealt with military history (specifically the Second World War), and, not surprisingly, once I became a competent model builder, my bedroom became a virtual museum of aircraft, tanks, and ship models. Further, once I had acquired the financial means, I also began accumulating a considerable collection of bayonets, helmets, insignia, and even a few World War II–era rifles and pistol duplicates. One could say I was a "military nut" bordering on the obsessed, and while it's not that I didn't have other interests as well, they paled in comparison to the time and energy (and financial resources) I put into my hobby/obsession. The military in general and World War Two in particular *were* my life, or, at least, a big part of it.

More than that, as I moved further into adolescence I found myself increasingly sliding into a largely imaginary world in which I fantasized about being a soldier in combat. Always something of a loner (partially as a result of growing up in a remote area of the mountains west of Denver), I would spend hours in the nearby forests fighting fantasy battles with nothing more than a steel rod as a rifle. Growing increasingly elaborate and complex in detail the more times I played out each "game," my obsession soon became so focused and grim that I could almost visualize the gruesome carnage in my mind's eye. Additionally, my imaginary battles were remarkably similar in both scope and depth: I invariably imagined myself an infantryman battling an influx of enemy tanks in a forest. The script never varied, and I seemingly never tired of my unchanging role in the drama. It was as though it were a play I had performed a hundred times before, and seemed content to play out another hundred times.

My fascination for the military manifested itself in other ways as well. At thirteen I joined a local chapter of the Civil Air Patrol, a paramilitary Air Force auxiliary, which gave me the opportunity to wear

oversized Air Force uniforms and march about like a soldier for hours at
a time. I genuinely enjoyed the military atmosphere the CAP exposed
me to, from drilling to moving up through the ranks, as well as the
occasional "orientation flights" I was able to take courtesy of the Air
Force reserve group at a nearby base. I even had the opportunity to
spend a week at the Air Force Academy near Colorado Springs one
summer, an experience that gave me my first real taste of military life,
and one that seemed to set my immediate path for me. It was inevitable,
then, that I would eventually find my way into the armed forces upon
graduation from high school, enlisting in the U.S. Navy in November of
1975. I seemed "born" to be a military man, and as such was able to
endure the discipline and drilling of basic training much easier than
many of my shipmates.

This obsession for all things military stayed with me for the next few
years, and didn't wane even after I left the military and married. Pursuing a career in art, I noticed that even in art school many of my projects
had a decidedly military theme to them. This preoccupation stayed with
me well into my thirties, by which time it at last began to fade significantly as I made a concerted effort to expand my areas of interest.

Today I no longer retain my fixation with the military. My models
are long gone and my military collection was sold years ago. I still possess a few books on the subject, but they sit on a shelf collecting dust,
rarely opened, and while I still occasionally find myself watching a history channel feature on the Second World War, it no longer holds me
captive as it and programs like it once did. I have outgrown my earlier
obsession, and try now to be the peacemaker rather than the warmon-
ger I once was. In fact, I look back upon my childhood fascination with
a mixture of curiosity and embarrassment, and wonder to this day what
it all meant, and what might have triggered such a unique adolescence.

A Question of Environment

Where did this fascination with the military come from? In particular, why the obsession with World War II?

Again, I did not come from a military family. My birth father was a factory worker; my stepfather, the manager of the local Elks Club. Although I had the usual mix of male relatives who were World War II veterans, their experiences were never recounted (at least not around me), nor were they important to our family's dynamics. In my home, the war rarely came up as a topic of conversation, and if it did it was in hushed tones, as though it were something to be fervently forgotten. As such, it was clear I couldn't blame my obsession on a steady diet of war stories told to an impressionable boy by a phalanx of veteran uncles.

Television? Certainly that was an influence. The late fifties and early sixties were the golden age of war-theme television programs, and movies like *The Longest Day* and *Twelve O'Clock High* were popular fare at the time. Did these programs trigger within me an unusual interest in military history, or did I naturally gravitate toward such programs because of an already inherent interest in the military and then reflect what I saw back into my fantasy world? In other words, did the shows I watch instill within me a military obsession, or did I watch such programs because they fed into the military obsession I already possessed? Undoubtedly, these programs enhanced—and, perhaps, even helped define—my growing preoccupation, but what was it about war-theme entertainment that so attracted me in the first place, especially considering my non-military upbringing?

Further, why only the Second World War? I showed no similar interest in the First World War, the Civil War, Vietnam, or other American or foreign conflicts. Why this particular era only? My collection of airplane models contained close to fifty aircraft, but while I counted a few modern jet fighters and a smattering of ancient bi-planes among them, the bulk of it was made up of aircraft from World War II. I just wasn't as interested in aircraft from other eras, and preferred to keep with the "theme" to which I had gravitated.

As I look back over my life, I recall other idiosyncrasies I developed during that time as well. Perhaps the most curious of these was a penchant for only one type of footwear—black Wellington boots. I never cared for athletic footwear or hiking boots (though either would have made more sense considering the amount of walking I did). Why Wellingtons, which are far from the most comfortable shoes available? And why only black? I didn't care for any other kind of boot, even though cowboy boots were popular when I was growing up.

Students of military history, however, might find my footwear fetish interesting. Boots very similar to what we now refer to as "Wellingtons" were standard issue for German soldiers during the Second World War (and had, in fact, become something of their "trademark"). Had I developed a preference for such impractical footwear in a vacuum, or were they already unconsciously familiar to me by virtue of having worn them in some long-forgotten past?

There were other signals as well: the only foreign language I had ever taken an interest in while in high school was German, and though I never became particularly proficient at it, I enjoyed the classes. I especially liked listening to the instructors from Austria and Germany who taught these courses, finding their musings about their homes as interesting as learning the language itself. I had an almost insatiable interest in their countries and felt I would be comfortable living there, though I could not begin to imagine why.

Some readers may wonder if these stories related by my instructors might have been more influential on my militarism than I imagined, but I doubt it. These young student teachers—most of them in America on teacher exchange programs and not much more than five to ten years older than me—were far from militarists. In fact, like most young teachers during that era, they would be more accurately portrayed as pacifists, and they certainly did not easily discuss the war (which often proved to be a sensitive and uncomfortable topic in any case). While their observations were useful in painting a general impression of their homelands, they were far from detailed and did not contain much that was relevant to my military preoccupation.

Finally, another curious interest of mine at the time was dirigibles, those massive lighter-than-air vessels that floated majestically through the skies between the world wars. By the time I was sixteen I had already become something of an expert on them, and spent many hours drawing pictures of the great airships. I even produced a few simplistic designs of my own. Interestingly, my fascination with such vessels did not extend to their modern equivalent, the blimp, but seemed fixated upon the great rigid ships of the late twenties and thirties. Was it a mere coincidence that most of these vessels were of German manufacture? And, again, where did this particular interest derive from? There certainly was nothing in my immediate environment (or, for that matter, on television) to have triggered such a fascination.[1]

PUTTING THE CLUES TOGETHER

What are we to make of all this? Why the fascination with a war that ended over a decade before I was even born? Why the preoccupation with all things military in a boy who had no contact with the real world of the military, and why the preference for black Wellington boots, the affinity for German, and the intense interest in airships?

Any one of these elements alone would not be particularly significant, but together they seemed to be pointing me toward something. There was a unifying theme to them, and most of it had to do with Germany and the Second World War (or, in the case of the airships, the immediate prewar years). But what did it all mean?

---

1 A full-length feature film about the last flight of the German airship Hindenburg was made in the late 1970s, but my interest in dirigibles had begun to wane by that time, and so could not have been an influencing factor in my earlier preoccupation with the great ships.

Environment does little to account for these obsessions. My five siblings showed no similar interests despite comparable family backgrounds. Only I had these proclivities. Something was drawing me to these things—something outside the realm of my normal daily experiences and cultural inclinations. I assumed they meant I was simply odd, but I wonder: could they have been more than inexplicable eccentricities? Could they have been snippets of a past life resonating within my modern incarnation?

I have no conscious memories of having been in a World War II infantry/armored battle of the kind I described earlier, yet it appears I retained "impressions" of having had just such an experience imbedded in the deepest recesses of my subconscious. Such battles—which I assumed at the time to have been "imaginary" or "make believe"—were actually quite common in Russia throughout much of World War II. Was it merely a coincidence that Hitler's drive into Russia in the summer of 1941 was a favorite historical theme for me, and the one element of the entire war that seemed most poignant?

Imagination or Memory?

What am I to make of this unusual aspect of my adolescence? Are these elements merely—as the rationalist would maintain—the product of an overactive imagination, perhaps enhanced by a sense of isolation and lack of maturity? No doubt psychiatrists could offer a purely natural rationale to explain my unusual past: these things occurred because of the way my brain is "wired," or perhaps I was a far more suggestible child than most, and television had impacted me more profoundly than I realized.

There are many possible explanations for my experiences, yet none of them seem to add up. They were too specific, too consistent, too theme-oriented to be mere boyhood fantasies. Background, environmental influences, television—none of them answers the question of why there was an extremely limited and frequently Germanic theme to my interests. If it were all a product of television, shouldn't my interests have been all over the board, so to speak, with little correlation or consistency to them? Shouldn't they have likewise extended to other conflicts as well, such as the American Civil War or even some of the great wars of the Roman and Greek eras (all of which were common movie themes of the sixties and seventies)?

The possibility that I was unconsciously recounting a past memory—diluted and incomplete as it was—never occurred to me until many years later. It wasn't until I began examining the concept of reincarnation that the possibility that I had actually lived another lifetime—perhaps as a German soldier in World War II—became a distinct possibility. Were the "imaginary" tank battles, an affinity for black Wellington boots and the German language, and my fascination with World War II but "shadows" of a brief and violent past that haunted me into this new incarnation?

For the sake of argument, let us suppose for a moment that I had been a young German soldier in the Second World War. Further, imagine that I had fought a desperate battle in the forests of Russia—a battle that ultimately cost me my life—and then, after a brief sojourn in limbo (or wherever it is disembodied souls may loiter), I entered the body of a fetus in a St. Cloud hospital in 1958.

What would be the potential consequences of such a transfer? Could the young soldier's death have been so traumatic that even the process of rebirth could not entirely obliterate the deep scars it left on his soul, and so he carried them into this newest incarnation—not as a consciously recalled memory, but as an impression that influenced him in subtle and inexplicable ways? Could it have ultimately manifested itself in this preoccupation with the circumstances surrounding this young man's death—the greatest and most horrific war known to mankind—and could it have left vague "memories" of a language he had spoken long ago but had since forgotten, and even a preference for a type of footwear he wore every day in his forgotten march across Russia? And wouldn't his interest in dirigibles perfectly mirror those of a German boy growing up in the

1930s who had personally seen the great airships of his day glide gracefully across the sky (and who would have been of the approximate same age he was when he first developed such an interest)?

I call these "echoes" from the past, not memories. Memories are specific and data driven; echoes, or, more technically, "resonance effects," are more akin to impressions or inexplicable affections, interests, likes, and dislikes we develop almost spontaneously that shape our nature in subtle ways that we are not aware of. One needn't even believe in reincarnation for echoes to shape our persona; the process goes on regardless of and, in fact, often in spite of, our beliefs. It is the nature of the soul, and it is relentless.

But why would such residual interests and fascinations remain? What purpose, if any, might they serve?

Who knows? Perhaps my earlier preoccupations were an important and necessary element in my spiritual development. Perhaps in order to evolve into a man of peace, it was required that I understand the horrors of war—an understanding that might have been impossible without some of my former incarnation's experiences being transposed upon my new psyche. Then again, it may just simply be a flaw in the rebirth process. I don't know.

In either case, I am firmly convinced that what happened to me has happened to—and continues to happen to—literally thousands of people around the world. Many quite "normal" people claim feelings of familiarity—a sense of déjà vu—about things from the past, and while some, and maybe even most, may well be purely imaginary, can *all* of them to be explained away so easily? I had an active imagination as a boy (just as I still do today), but so do millions of other children, most of whom do not end up preoccupied with such a narrow range of interests for so many years. As such, the mystery for me remains unanswered and, perhaps, unanswerable.

CONCLUSION

So what is the reader to make of this story? I doubt if it changed any minds about reincarnation: there are enough curious elements in this story for it to reinforce the concept of multiple births in those already persuaded of reincarnation's validity, and yet it lacks the kind of specifics or verifiable facts that might be of interest to the skeptic.

In spite of this, I also believe I am not alone in these feelings of having lived another life. I am convinced that many people have found their personal histories shaped by interests and infatuations outside the scope of what might be expected. Is each curious interest and inexplicable fascination in this present life shaped and molded in some way by the events of an alleged past life? If reincarnation were a fact, shouldn't we *expect* these experiences to manifest themselves in our current lives?

Of course, there are those who might argue that my interest in reincarnation is what may have triggered many of these echoes, and the strong desire to want to believe in the concept simply created the prerequisite elements necessary to realize that wish. While it is evident that there are people who do precisely that, it must be remembered that as a teenager I did not believe in reincarnation (or have much of a belief system of any kind at that point). I would have probably considered myself a nominal Catholic with only the most superficial religious beliefs, and reincarnation was certainly not one of them. Additionally, once I embraced evangelical Christianity in my early twenties, reincarnation was clearly out of the question. Christianity was about resurrection, not reincarnation, and I spent the next twenty years contemptuous and dismissive of the idea. In short, I would not be, in most people's minds, a good candidate for manufacturing evidence in support of an alleged past life. It simply wasn't part of my nature.

So where does that leave the debate? Was it all simply my imagination run amok, or is there more to life than we are aware of? I honestly don't know which it is and must leave it for the readers to decide for themselves. I can only do my best to try and understand my past from various perspectives, of which reincarnation is but one of them; I can only offer reincarnation as a possible explanation, not *the* definitive solution. As far as I'm concerned, I simply don't know. And it is that not knowing that often proves to be both the curse and the blessing of reincarnation.

chapter six

THE CASE AGAINST REINCARNATION

Having looked at the evidences for reincarnation, this book would be shortchanging the reader if it didn't also look at the other side of the equation and examine the main objections to the concept. The goal here is not to undertake an exhaustive examination of each objection, but to highlight and briefly respond to each of the critic's best volleys. I offer it purely as an aid in providing the reader with a more balanced, objective understanding of the issue, for it is my contention that unless and until one's beliefs have been challenged and severely tested, they are not worthy of being embraced. It is only after a concept has "weathered the storm" of doubt and emerges still afloat that it deserves to be firmly held to by any thinking person.

Objections to reincarnation generally fall into two basic categories: rational / scientific and religious / ethical. The category in which one finds his or her most compelling arguments is largely a matter of that person's world view. Objections based purely and solidly in empirical evidence and rationalism appeal to the intellect, and are generally directed toward an audience that is largely secular (or even atheistic) in orientation. Those based on religious/ethical reasons, in contrast, appeal to those who may accept the idea of the supernatural but find reincarnation to be a threat—or, at very least, a challenge—to their own beliefs. Of course, those who approach the question from a decidedly secular/rationalist perspective may also be attracted to some of the ethical arguments against it, while those who find reincarnation to be in conflict with their tightly held religious beliefs may also appeal to reason and scientific objections to bolster their case; yet even then they will generally still remain loyal to one perspective.

This is important, for both groups are fashioning their arguments from very different models of reality, thereby generating their objections from entirely different perspectives. The rationalist, for example, will concentrate the bulk of his or her criticism against problems with methodology and the verifiability of reincarnationist claims, while "supernaturalist" arguments largely deal with questions of fairness, justice, retribution, judgment, and mercy. In essence, rationalist criticisms are generally based on "hard science," while the supernaturalist's will be largely motivated by questions of right and wrong and how a specific belief squares with the teachings of his or her particular religion. This is, then, at least one instance in which both science and faith inadvertently join forces to battle the "threat" that reincarnation poses, though their purposes for destroying it are entirely different.

Since most rationalists are usually materialists by nature,[1] they find reincarnation a challenge to their firmly held skepticism about spiritual matters in general. As such, the rationalists fight the concept because they consider it a threat to the intellectual health of society. Their crusade is to destroy reincarnationist beliefs before they destroy mankind's

---

1 A materialist being defined here as one who believes that matter is all that exists and that there is nothing more to the universe than that which we can perceive with our physical senses or conceive through rational deduction. Therefore, the materialist would naturally reject the entire notion of the supernatural.

capacity to think, thereby returning humanity to the dark ages of super-
stition. Religious people, on the other hand, in addition to finding reincarnation a threat to their long-held belief system, also find within it the
potential to lead people astray from the truth and thus into spiritual
darkness. Their objections, then, tend to be mostly subjective in nature
and are designed to appeal to the emotions rather than to the mind
(though efforts to interject scientific objections are often used to bolster
the effectiveness of a subjective opinions).

Which camp one holds to, then, will define what constitutes a logical
argument against reincarnation. Because of the human propensity toward
allowing one's rationalism to be determined and influenced by his or her
subjective world view, what may appear to be a rational argument from
one perspective will often appear irrational from another. As such, appeals
to logic frequently fail when neither side can first agree on such basic concepts as the nature of reality. This, however, is not true just of a subject like
reincarnation, but of the entire range of human knowledge.

Hoaxes

Probably the first thought that crosses most people's minds when a
good case of apparent past-life recall appears is that the subject is simply
making the whole thing up. Considering the cunning with which some
people operate, the value of a good joke, and the access to information
we have available to us today, such a possibility is always a threat and
must be taken into account.

It is not difficult to imagine a person browsing the Internet and local
libraries in an effort to acquire enough information to create a plausible
past-life memory. A Civil War buff, for instance, could fairly easily obtain
enough data to recreate a very convincing past-life persona. That person's
knowledge of the era, if extensive enough, could even provide him or her
with enough authenticating details to "flesh out" his or her performance,
while a careful perusing of historical records would permit the person to
weave together a verifiable and plausible trail for a researcher to follow. It

could be as simple as selecting the name of a senior officer from a particular regiment one was studying and, with a bit of determination and perseverance, retrace the man's entire family history—a task that would be
made easier by the fact that many senior officers in the Civil War often
came from wealthy families, giving them historical "footprints" to follow.
As long as the hoaxer didn't go overboard and strain credulity by claiming
to have been General Lee or Ulysses S. Grant, he or she might well produce a plausible past-life persona and be able to convince the casual investigator that the past-life memories were legitimate.

That there are individuals who are perfectly capable and perhaps
even willing to pull this off is without a doubt true, though it remains to
be seen how doing so would be particularly beneficial. Of course, there
are those for whom the mere success of their prank would be reward
enough, but if financial gain or fame were the motives, it is a risky path
toward either. Past-life accounts, after all, are not uncommon, and even
the best of them rarely get a person noticed on a national level. Unless
someone were to write a bestselling book or get a Hollywood studio to
make a movie from his or her story, the chances of realizing significant
financial gain off the fable would be minimal. Additionally, if the story
did manage to reach a national audience, the scrutiny that would be
suddenly directed upon the hoaxer would be intense, and most likely
the truth would be discovered eventually (by some intrepid debunker
from *Skeptical Inquirer,* no doubt). How this might impact the hoaxer
legally, professionally, or financially would remain to be seen, but, at the
very minimum, the potential damage to a person's reputation could be
extensive and irreparable (as was amply demonstrated in the Bridey
Murphy case). It could even have legal ramifications.

Of course, there is another category of hoaxer out there as well—
those who might hoax a story not for financial gain or their own amusement, but for "the cause." These are those rare individuals who feel it
necessary to create a hoax for the sole purpose of disproving an idea
they personally find threatening or distasteful. Just as there are people
who will hoax a particularly convincing ghost photo so they might

demonstrate how simple it is to do (skeptic and debunker Joe Nickell of *Skeptical Inquirer* fame is famous for this tactic), so too are there people who, for the sake of "saving" people from their own gullibility, might hoax a past-life persona.

Such a tactic, however, is short-term, for it must be exposed at some point in order to have the necessary educational effect and to permit the hoaxer to feel justified in his or her skepticism. An entire book could be written on the psychology of people who make it their life's purpose to disprove the beliefs of others, but suffice it to say that in my opinion, such individuals actually help the paranormal cause—not by demonstrating that everything is nonsense, but by forcing serious investigators to be aware and, by extension, more careful, rigid, and objective in their studies. It is the awareness that a past-life memory can be hoaxed that makes the careful investigator cautious about accepting anything at face value, thus improving the quality of the evidences he or she uncovers. To the serious past-life researcher, it is only after fraud has been eliminated—and the debunkers are invaluable in demonstrating how it occurs—that the "real" evidence for reincarnation (or any phenomenon, for that matter) can be obtained. As such, far from hurting the reincarnationist's case, debunkers and copycat hoaxers actually provide an invaluable service by keeping investigators honest.

Aside from the would-be hoaxer's motives and risks of being exposed as a fraud, there is the difficulty of fooling those who deal with past-life regression on a daily basis to consider. Any competent regression therapist should be able to differentiate a fabricated past-life memory from an authentic one, regardless of the amount of detail the subject may provide. Genuine past-life memories differ from fantasies and hoaxes in that the subject usually exhibits a distinct change in personality, with often marked differences in temperament, intellectual capacity, world view, and even emotion. In some of the strongest regression cases, the subject is not only capable of relating details of a past life, but often expresses the very emotions he or she felt at the time. For example, a subject who is recounting being tortured will frequently writhe in pain in the therapist's couch as though he or she were genuinely feeling the pain. Such vivid memories are frequently unsettling (even to the therapist) and would be difficult to convincingly mimic by even a professional actor. Additionally, authentic past-life memories often contain more subtle and intimate details than one could reasonably cull from written materials and records. Pet names, geographic sites that have since been renamed, archaic or obsolete language no longer in contemporary use, and other seemingly "minor" details are common—and are the kind of details a hoaxer would be hard-pressed to duplicate. And, finally, authentic past-life memories lack the sheer volume of data a hoaxer would reveal; hoaxers and non-hoaxers, for instance, frequently cannot recall entire segments of their past life, though they may be able to recall some elements with remarkable clarity (much the same way most people's memories operate in real life). Additionally, the memories are not given in any particular order, may be disjointed or incomplete, and often contain superfluous, redundant, and even mundane information. Hoaxers, in contrast, usually recount information in a more orderly fashion, common to what one would expect from someone reciting information and details from rote memory; dates and places may be correct, for example, but lack the kind of subtle details that give them authenticity. Their carefully studied and rehearsed "memories" may be *too* complete to be plausible; the human mind in reality works in a far less orderly or accurate manner. In effect, it is the very gaps in the recalled memory that give a past-life memory its plausibility.

As such, that a person could convince a seasoned therapist (as well as a meticulous investigator) of a contrived tale is remote, though not out of the question. And, of course, there is always the possibility that the therapist, investigator, and subject are all in on the hoax, but that would be another matter (and no more likely to succeed, either; the more people involved in a conspiracy, the greater its chances of being exposed). In any case, it must be remembered that in the end, it is the debunker who has all the advantages in such a situation. A past-life memory is an extraordinary claim that demands, if not extraordinary evidence, at least good, solid evidence from reliable, competent witnesses. If it lacks solid, verifiable facts or the information is not supported by reliable sources, the skeptic can dismiss the entire story as a hoax (or, at best, a self-deluding fantasy). If, however, a past-life memory does contain verifiable information—names, dates, places—that can be verified through documentation, the skeptic can simply claim that if such information is available as a matter of public record, then it would also be available to any determined hoaxer. In either case, the skeptic wins, making past-life claims extremely difficult to verify to the satisfaction of the scientific community, and a hoax almost impossible to get away with.

Finally, there is the question of past-life memories in children. While it is conceivable that an adult might have the ability and motive to concoct a plausible past-life memory, the possibility that a five-year-old child could create a credible or sustainable hoax is outside the realm of serious consideration. Even children who are fantasy-prone lack the cunning to create a plausible story purely from their imagination, nor would they likely be capable of providing verifiable details to support their story. While it is possible that an adult could coach a child into recounting a past-life memory and even provide the child with enough convincing details to fool an investigator, the chances that such collusion would not be eventually uncovered—or that the child would not eventually "break" and confess his or her culpability—are extremely low. Competent past-life investigators not only rely on a multitude of witnesses and evidences to corroborate a story, but check the backgrounds and reputations of those involved in the investigation as well, precisely in an effort to determine how reliable those witnesses, family members, and "associates" might be. Like a police investigation, even the smallest inconsistencies are enough to set off warning bells, especially among those who approach such stories with a degree of skepticism in the first place.

Unintentional Collusion

Closely related to outright fraud—but of a more innocent vein—is the possibility of erroneous past-life "memories" being unintentionally manufactured by a deceased person's family out of a need to believe that a departed loved one lives again (even if in another body). This was a concern of Dr. Stevenson during his extensive interviews of children who could consciously recall past lives; since the children he studied often lived fairly close to the family from their "previous" life, the chances of contact between the two families—and the chance that the children might be influenced, coerced, or coached by members of their "past-life" family into "remembering" personal details that only the previous personality should be privy to—was always considered a real possibility. Such collusion, it is suggested, be it intentional or accidental, is thought by most skeptics to adequately explain the remarkable degree of accurate information these children frequently recount, and remains one of the favorite arguments against past-life recall used by the scientific community.

Basically, the idea is that a five-year-old Indian boy might begin telling stories to his parents of his "other life" when he was a grown man named Rajay living in the nearby town of Mahalabad. The child, of course, is merely role playing or fantasizing about being an adult—a common game among children—and is simply making up names (though the name of the town may be real). His parents, however, being devout Hindus, imagine that the child is telling them of a past life, and take him to Mahalabad to look for a man named Rajay. Sure enough, they eventually discover that a man by that name had once lived in the town, but had died years earlier. Curious now to follow this promising lead, the parents track down Rajay's surviving family and inform them that their son claims to be their reincarnated son/husband/uncle/father Rajay. Excited at the news—and believers in reincarnation themselves—the family regales the child with stories of their beloved relative, which the child—enjoying the attention—readily absorbs.

The story soon makes the local papers and eventually finds its way to Stevenson's desk. Unfortunately, by the time the good doctor arrives on the scene many months later, the child has already had considerable contact with his "previous" family, and so, when Stevenson is taken to meet Rajay's family, it's not surprising that the boy is able to correctly identify various family members and recount other intimate details of his supposed past life. Firmly convinced he is witnessing an authentic past-life memory, the case is then written up as one more inexplicable example of reincarnation, and the scientific community is left with yet another mystery on its hands.

This, at least, is the theory. Anyone who has bothered to study Stevenson's research, however, will very quickly see how tenuous this hypothesis really is. First of all, Stevenson is a careful researcher and does considerable preliminary research on each subject specifically to learn how much, if any, previous contact there has been with the family of the supposed previous-life personality. If it is extensive, the case is considered compromised and filed away.[2] As such, most of the cases he has studied extensively are those in which contact with the "previous life" family was either extremely limited or had not yet occurred by the time Stevenson arrived on the scene, greatly reducing (or even eliminating outright) the possibility of collusion.

Second, the children in the best cases Stevenson has studied recounted extensive details—including the means of their own death (something children would be unlikely to fantasize)—long before meeting their prior family. In fact, it was usually only through the wealth of information the children provided originally that locating the prior life family was even made possible.

---

2 Though having collected data on almost two thousand cases of past-life memories, Stevenson has written extensively on only a few dozen of them, demonstrating how careful he is in his research methods. Even skeptics, if they are honest, admit that he is a hard man to fool.

Third, in many cases neither the child's current family nor the prior life family were particularly happy about the situation. Despite what many Westerners assume, Hindus do not necessarily find spontaneously recalled past-life memories to be a good thing, and frequently are uncomfortable when they emerge.[3] In some cultures, recalling a past life is even considered bad luck and is actively discouraged. Additionally, there is always some concern about motives (especially in cases in which the child recalls being of a higher caste in his or her previous life), which often makes the initial contact between the families awkward and uncomfortable. This would seem to make any collusion between families even more inexplicable, for what possible incentive would a superior caste family have in convincing a lower caste family that their child is the reincarnation of their relative, especially if the subject of financial remuneration might come up?

Additionally, Stevenson has observed that the prior-life family members consistently display shock and amazement at being recognized by a child they do not know, and have even been observed trying to "trick" the child by having family members change identities in an effort to see if the child catches the error. While the child's memory was not always 100 percent accurate and mistakes were made, his or her ability to identify former family members correctly and articulate personal details of his or her past life is far beyond what coincidence or lucky guessing could produce.

In conclusion, in order for collusion to carry the day, the skeptic must conclude that:

- Children as young as four years old are capable of memorizing a tremendous amount of detail and consistently convincing adults that they are the reincarnation of a dead relative without ever breaking character, making a significant error, or growing tired of the game.

---

3 Among Hindus, past-life recall in children is often considered a sign that the child
   will die young, making it unlikely that such memories would be encouraged.

- Stevenson and others who research past-life memories are easily fooled and inept researchers incapable of performing even the most rudimentary preliminary investigations.

- The families involved are gullible and quick to believe everything without question.

- Dozens of family members are willing to corroborate on deceiving investigators—for whatever reason—without anyone later admitting the ruse or "blowing their lines."

While people can be and often are deceived, it is difficult to imagine how one might deceive literally dozens of people and maintain the delusion for any length of time (plus, there is the question of motive). This objection, then, can only be maintained by ignoring common sense and logic in a determined effort *not* to believe.

IMAGINATION, FANTASIES, AND SUGGESTIBILITY

Those who challenge reincarnationist accounts seldom imply that a story is intentionally hoaxed. Instead, it is more commonly suggested that the subjects are unintentionally (or unconsciously) creating these stories out of their imaginations and passing them off to both themselves and their therapists as past-life memories. In effect, they are victims of their own self-delusion and/or the inadvertent efforts of their therapists to induce or cultivate such memories.

The hypothesis works in one of two ways. In one scenario, let's say a female patient who is curious about her past lives (and obviously already a believer in reincarnation) seeks out a regression therapist in an effort to uncover her presumed past. Not surprisingly, once under hypnosis, the subject, likely drawing from a vast number of images stored in her subconscious, "creates" a seemingly plausible past-life "adventure," which, again not surprisingly, happens to correlate well with her preconceived ideas about who she believes she was in a past life. Her belief in reincarnation, combined with her own vivid and likely underappreci-ated imagination, work in unison to provide her with the very "proof" that she has been seeking. It is simply a matter of the imagination creat-ing what the mind wants—or, perhaps, needs—to find fulfillment and self-acceptance.

The other hypothesis maintains that while the subject may be gen-uinely ambivalent about the question of reincarnation (although it begs the question of why she would seek out a regression therapist in the first place), and have no preconceived ideas about an alleged past life, she creates a past-life memory in any case—again, out of her imagina-tion—in an effort to either bring some "color" to her otherwise ordi-nary life or to please her hypnotist by giving him or her what she thinks her hypnotist wants to hear.

Of course, this theory works from the assumption that most people are eager to please their hypnotists/therapists or at least do what they ask even if it means creating a plausible past-life memory from scratch. In cases where the therapist is a strong believer in reincarnation and eager to obtain evidence to support his or her belief, there is also the possibility that the therapist may be unconsciously leading or coaching the subject into remembering a "past life." As such, the therapist may ask leading questions or inadvertently fill in details in his or her zeal to prove reincarnation to be true while the patient, perhaps sensing the therapist's enthusiasm and excitement, simply paints the picture that he or she senses the therapist wants to see. It is a case, then, of the reincar-nationist making the data fit his or her hypothesis rather than seeing if it supports the hypothesis naturally.

The larger problem inherent with all past-life regression lies with the unreliability of information obtained through hypnosis. Most people have never been hypnotized and Hollywood has generally fed erro-neous information about the practice into the public consciousness, so it is necessary to stop for a moment and clear up some misconceptions frequently held by many people, and to examine the subject in greater depth to determine exactly why hypnotism is not generally considered a reliable tool for determining truth.

First, it is a common fallacy that hypnotism puts one to sleep or into a state of unconsciousness. In actuality, subjects are not asleep in the classical sense, but in a heightened (or enhanced) state of consciousness, similar to what one might experience in a state of deep meditation. As such, the widely held assumption that the subject has no control of his or her actions and is completely at the mercy of the hypnotist is entirely fallacious. Subjects are quite capable of refusing to obey a hypnotist's instructions, and can usually pull themselves out of their trance whenever they wish.

Another common but untrue belief about hypnotism is that it is a type of truth serum in which the patient, once in a deep trance state, is incapable of lying, exaggerating, or fantasizing. However, evidence has shown that subjects are perfectly capable of doing the same things under hypnosis that they are capable of doing while fully conscious, such as making events up, misinterpreting experiences, and even imagining things that never actually happened. Hypnotism is not a magical means of acquiring truth, but a means of acquiring information on a deeper, subconscious level than is normally possible to access from a conscious state. For example, if you truly believe you were abducted by aliens, you may well recount that belief under hypnosis—not because it's true, but because you *believe* it's true. In other words, the subconscious is often no more capable of distinguishing fact from fantasy than the conscious mind is, and, being that it is believed on a much deeper level, is often harder to change. As such, if one believes that he or she were Cleopatra in a past life, the subconscious mind is quite capable of producing the necessary imagery to support that belief (information that may well be gleaned from books and movies). As such, it seems unwise to accept anything told under hypnosis as fact, leaving the greatest percentage of the evidence for reincarnation in serious doubt. Additionally, when one considers that there are people who are, by nature, "fantasy prone," information acquired through hypnosis becomes an even more dubious affair.

Of course, all of these points are valid considerations; that there are people who possess what is known as a "fantasy-prone" personality is undeniable, and undoubtedly there are many examples of people unconsciously creating a past life out of their imagination for the reasons noted above, but this theory doesn't take into account one very important point. It fails to address the issue of what one does with the often verifiable information that comes out of these sessions.

Certainly, if one were merely imagining specific details of a past life that had no basis in fact, there should be no such thing as corroborating evidence. For example, if a man is convinced that he was once a tailor by the name of Rothenthal who lived on Third Avenue in Baltimore during the 1890s, and, upon further research, the information proved to be entirely correct, that would be difficult to explain away as pure fantasy. It might be dismissed as dumb luck or a remarkable coincidence (or it might be suggested that the subject had done some historical grave digging), but it would still not diminish its significance. A make-believe story must, by its very nature, be a random collection of thoughts and ideas unlikely to contain more than a trace of historical accuracy. Certainly, it should not contain information that is verifiably true. The fact that many do, then, is important.

Much is made of the fact that past-life accounts, even if they do occasionally contain details that are later found to be true, also usually contain information that cannot be verified, is only partially correct, or is sometimes entirely wrong, thus implying that the "memories" are fantasies that just happen to contain a few verifiable "coincidences" within them. However, this explanation utterly fails to account for how *any* accurate information could work its way into what is supposed to be an entirely fictitious story. Coincidence may explain some things, but it has its limits in terms of how effective it may be in explaining the inexplicable. Yet coincidence is the "Holy Grail" of the debunker and is useful in excusing almost any veridical information, no matter how unlikely that information was to have been a lucky guess. For example, in the well-known Bridey Murphy case, Virginia Tighe—speaking as her nineteenth-century Irish persona Bridey Murphy—recalled the name of two local Belfast merchants she supposedly dealt with; names that were later proven accurate (and were discovered only after much research by a Belfast librarian). Yet if Bridey Murphy was an imaginary person—as the skeptics contend—then how could Mrs. Tighe have guessed the names of not one, but *two* nineteenth-century grocers who operated stores in the immediate area of Belfast in which Bridey lived? Can coincidence really explain such a remarkable feat?

Yet what of the "misses"? If accurate information supports the contention that a memory may be authentic, couldn't the opposite argument—that erroneous information suggests a memory is a fantasy—also be made? While that seems a fair question, it fails to take a few points into account. First, regardless of how much erroneous information a past-life account may contain, the fact that it contains *any* verifiably accurate information—especially of a very specific and detailed nature not easily obtained without considerable digging into historical archives—has to be taken into account. In other words, the "hits"—being so difficult to achieve—should logically carry more weight than the common "misses," and be carefully considered into the equation when determining the authenticity of a past-life memory.

Secondly, it should be remembered that even a genuine a past-life personality is still a flawed human being, capable of error, exaggeration, and even lying, just as all human beings are capable of these things. Therefore, we can't assume that a past-life persona is going to be inerrantly accurate or even necessarily honest in everything it recalls. Past-life personalities may remember things incorrectly or incompletely, and may be just as guilty of recounting things the way they saw them rather than the way they really were—much the same way the still living frequently do. (Certainly, anyone who has had the opportunity to listen to the same incident recounted by two feuding relatives cannot help but appreciate how extraordinarily different two accounts can be.) To return to the

Murphy case for a moment, even Bernstein himself wondered if Murphy wasn't above exaggerating when she described her father and husband as "barristers"—which would have been considered a more prestigious profession at the time—rather than the more common and likely title of "law clerks." Perhaps the human propensity to shade the truth survives death as well.

Finally, it should be considered that past-life memories are being told from the perspective of the current personality. As such, it would be remarkable (and, perhaps, even a bit suspicious) if some degradation of memory did not occur during the transfer of information. This would also, by the way, account for why modern rather than archaic phraseology is sometimes used and why few people speak the language of their past-life persona; the past-life persona is being "filtered" through a modern brain, with its own vocabulary, language skills, and limitations, and so complete and unfettered access to the previous personality may not be possible.

It's also possible that this "mixing" of past-life personas with the current personality could result in information culled from this lifetime being superimposed upon information gleaned from a past lifetime. The debunker's claim—that Bridey Murphy, supposedly having had a neighbor in Chicago by the same name, thereby proving her past-life memories to be bogus—fails to take into account how genuine past-life memories might well be confused with modern experiences. Dr. Wambach, in her demographic studies in the 1970s, discovered that in hypnotizing over one thousand subjects over a ten year period, most of them had difficulty recalling their past-life names, implying that precise recall of such information is unusual; is it possible then that Tighe unconsciously "borrowed" her neighbor's Irish-sounding name in an effort to "flesh out" her nineteenth-century persona?

CRYPTOMNESIA (OR FORGOTTEN MEMORIES)

The skeptic has a ready answer for the mystery of verifiable data, and that is the well-known and documented phenomenon known as *cryptomnesia*. Cryptomnesia (also referred to as hidden, repressed, or forgotten memories) is the phenomenon in which individuals may acquire a bit of information—perhaps from a book, a movie, or even through a conversation—at some point in the distant past, and then completely forget it, only to recall it years or even decades later under hypnosis. Such intimate knowledge, then, can easily be used by the subconscious to paint a credible and historically accurate past-life "memory" and convince others (and themselves) that they did, in fact, have a past life.

That the mind contains a wealth of long-forgotten information is quite true. Apparently the brain is capable of storing far more information than we can begin to fathom; on some level everything we've ever said, heard, or done is stored somewhere within the vast complex of neural energy we call the subconscious. As such, it is theoretically possible to recall very nearly every experience one has had in the course of a lifetime through hypnosis, including those things we have long since forgotten. Such "hidden" memories are, in fact, the driving force behind most psychiatric techniques in the first place, for the mental health professional works from the premise that the experiences of one's past—though no longer consciously recalled—are at the root of most trauma. As such, most phobias and a whole host of other behavioral and emotional problems can often be traced to experiences the patient may have had much earlier in life, but has since repressed (or "forgotten") until the experiences manifest later in life as mental health issues. Sometimes these memories can be obtained through regular methods of induced recall, but often it is necessary to use hypnosis to regress a patient back to a time when a particular problem first emerged so it may be identified and dealt with.

Unfortunately, not only does the mind contain memories of thousands of events that actually occurred, but it seems equally capable of retaining memories of things that never genuinely happened at all. For instance, suppose you read a book about Spain when you were ten years old. Almost every detail in the story is likely stored somewhere in your brain and remains there long after you've consciously forgotten you've read the book. (In fact, many cryptomnesia subjects vehemently deny having read a particular "source" book even after it is proven that they had.) Therefore, the theory goes, under hypnosis it may be entirely possible that the past-life "memory" being recounted is nothing more than the plot of a long-forgotten book, movie, or play. Since many authors routinely include a great deal of historically accurate detail in their writings in an effort to give their story a touch of authenticity, the apparent memories may well be verifiable, not because they are genuine memories of actual events but because the author did his or her homework. However, since the brain cannot always distinguish between fact and fantasy, the information might well take the form of a past-life "memory" to be innocently believed by patient and therapist alike.

This theory is, for the most part, the main weapon in the skeptic's arsenal and one of the most effective, as cases of cryptomnesia are well-documented and have even been proven to explain a number of seemingly very strong past-life memory cases. The Bridey Murphy case is the most well-known of these,[4] but there have been other even more impressive cases of apparent past-life recall that have fallen victim to the skeptic's sword. As a result, cryptomnesia has been largely embraced by the scientific community as the best and most likely explanation for those past-life memories that contain a large degree of verifiable past-life details, while those that contain only a little or none at all are dismissed as pure fantasy. It is touted as the airtight explanation for past-life memories, and as such proves to be a powerful objection to reincarnationist claims.

---

4 See appendix A for a more complete examination of this controversial case and why it may not be a genuine example of cryptomnesia after all.

But there is a twofold problem with the theory—at least insofar as explaining away all past-life memories. The first is that it is frequently difficult to prove cryptomnesia; how does one "prove" to others the books he or she read or the movies he or she watched as an eight-year-old child? Since it is nearly impossible to locate the "source material" for most forgotten memories, the assumption that a past-life memory is based on a movie or book must remain purely speculative. However, for the debunker who does not believe that human consciousness can survive death, it is the only viable explanation. Regardless of how unlikely it is that a person may have read a particular book (what if he or she is illiterate?) or seen a certain movie—or, by extension, had it told to him or her—cryptomnesia *must* be the answer because there is no other explanation available. It's as simple as that.

The other problem with the theory is those cases in which there is no apparent source for the recalled details. Often the details are so obtuse or take place in such a largely unknown or foreign environment that it is impossible to locate a possible source for them. Then there is the problem of recounted past lives that prove to be mundane or commonplace. Even mediocre fiction, after all, usually has some interesting characters or curious plot twists to enliven the story; who writes epics about ordinary and largely uneventful lives?

Additionally, why do we not see past-life fantasies gleaned from other types of literature such as science fiction or fantasy? Undoubtedly many people have read H. G. Wells or J. R. R. Tolkien, yet I have never encountered a case in which a person recalled under hypnosis being a crewman onboard Captain Nemo's *Nautilus* or having been a resident of Middle Earth. If cryptomnesia is the source for all past-life memories, we should find as many genres of false memories as there are genres of fiction, yet such is not the case. It seems that cryptomnesia only occurs when historical novels are read; apparently other types of literature are simply not susceptible to it.

Of course, the source for hidden or forgotten memories need not be a book or television program; it can be something as simple as snippets of an overheard conversation or a forgotten story told around a camp-fire, which are what supposedly fuels the most intimately detailed and picturesque memories that subjects often recount. By way of an example, suppose an uncle visits his five-year-old nephew and regales the boy with colorful stories of living in London during the war; stories the boy enjoys immensely at the time but has completely forgotten by the age of seven. Then, forty years later this same boy, now an adult, "remembers" under hypnotism having lived in London during World War II and provides some impressive details that are eventually verified as being correct. Since such information could only be obtained by someone who had actually lived in London at that time, and being that the subject had never been there and was born many decades after the events he describes, it appears that reincarnation is the only plausible explanation for such vivid and detailed memories. Further digging, however, uncovers the truth—along with the long-since deceased uncle who had inadvertently started it all—and the mystery is soon solved, much to the relief (and confusion) of the subject, who truly has no conscious recollection of his uncle telling him about London and to whom the "memory" seems as authentic and inexplicable as it did to everyone else.

That such scenarios are occasionally played out is undeniable, but there are a lot of "ifs" involved with this explanation. *If* a relative or acquaintance existed who actually had a particular experience and *if* he or she were prone to talking about it and *if* the child was privy to such conversations and *if* the details of the past-life memory were similar to those contained in the story, then, yes, cryptomnesia is probably the best explanation. But what if none of these factors are evident? Or what if only the first one—that the uncle had been in London during the war—were true but there is no report of the relative ever recounting stories to the child and the later recounted past-life "memory" had only a superficial connection to the relative's story? Would cryptomnesia still remain the best answer?

That cryptomnesia occurs and accounts for a percentage of past-life memories is undeniable. That it explains them all is not only a stretch, but more difficult to believe than the theory it is attempting to disprove. There is simply too much information revealed that can be verified only after the most extensive searches are undertaken for cryptomnesia to be the only answer. The identity of the two Belfast grocers named by Virginia Tighe/Bridey Murphy (see appendix A) wasn't confirmed until months of exhaustive research by some dedicated Belfast librarians. Even then, they found the grocers' names listed on the yellowed, curled pages of a century-old ledger discovered in an obscure storeroom— information no one would have been privy to except time or a nineteenth-century personality. Only a tiny fraction of everything that has actually happened in history has ever found its way into either the written record or into the plot lines of novels and movies to serve as source material for a forgotten memory; to imagine otherwise is purely an assumption.

Finally, there is the case of Stevenson's children to account for. How could children as young as five years of age recount details of a past life—details told not under hypnosis but quite consciously—from books and movies, especially when the subjects of their past lives were often neighbors who lived only a few miles away? Unless there is active or inadvertent collusion between the current and "past" family—a question we have already looked at in detail earlier—it is difficult to imagine what might serve as the source for such "hidden" memories. This is especially true when one considers that these children are often illiterate and live in conditions in which television is unknown and, further, began discussing their past lives almost as soon as they were able to talk. Cryptomnesia may be a valid explanation for some hypnotically-induced adult past-life memories, but it is simply too much of a stretch to apply it to very young children growing up in under-privileged environments. It simply doesn't stand up to logic.

The Genetic Memory Hypothesis

One controversial hypothesis sometimes forwarded by anti-reincarnationists to account for especially vivid and verifiable past-life memories that has recently gained some attention, especially in this age of cloning and genome mapping, is the suggestion that past-life "memories" may be genetic "hand-me-downs" passed through one's DNA coding. In essence, the "memories" a person may recall—either consciously or through hypnosis—are not his or her own but those of some distant relative. As such, this theory maintains, if you recall having been a soldier in one of Julius Caesar's Legions, it's not because you really were a Roman soldier in some past life, but because a distant ancestor was. In effect, an ancestor's experiences somehow acquire a chemical "signature" that is encoded into his or her DNA only to be passed along to his or her future offspring and, finally, to you. In other words, you inherit not only your mother's blue eyes and your father's weak chin, but your great-great-great-grandfather's memories of having fought at Waterloo as well.

The first and biggest problem with this hypothesis is that there is no scientific evidence that memories *can* be passed along genetically and no known mechanism that might explain how it *could* happen. Additionally, even if such *were* theoretically possible, it should only affect one's direct descendents, yet few people have past-life memories in which they recall having been a direct family ancestor. Although Stevenson did investigate a few cases of alleged reincarnation occurring within the same family among the Tlingit Indians of Alaska, this is not a common occurrence (and, further, seems to be limited to only certain cultures). However, for this theory to work, past-life memories would *always* have to correspond to that of a direct descendent (albeit possibly an unknown descendent, if distant enough), but this is simply not the observed norm. Only rarely is a past-life persona even remotely related to the present subject and, in many cases, couldn't possibly be related for reasons of ethnicity or other physiological factors.

Further, if such past-life memories were indeed imbedded within a DNA strand, one would expect these memories to surface in one's biological siblings and other close relatives as well. In effect, if I can recall Great Granddad's days working on the Chisholm Trail, shouldn't at least one of my siblings have similar (if not identical) memories as well? Certainly this would do much to confirm the theory, and yet there has never been a case of siblings recalling the same or similar past lives.

The second problem with genetic memories is that in many cases subjects recall their own deaths in their previous lives—often with great clarity. However, for a genetic memory to be transferred to one's offspring, only those memories that had been acquired up to the time of conception should, by all rights, make it into the genetic coding. Any events—and, especially, one's own death—that occur *after* conception could not be passed on for obvious reasons, theoretically making any genetically-induced memory of a prior death impossible.

While genetic memories are an interesting effort to find a physiological answer to verifiable past-life memories, the theory falls on its own sword by failing to take into account how one could remember things that happened to a distant ancestor long after the ancestor's child-bearing years were over. Yet it is an intriguing theory that deserves consideration, especially when one considers the phenomenon of corresponding birthmarks (see chapter 3) and the apparent ability of the soul to impress wounds received in an earlier incarnation onto the developing fetus of a new incarnation. Apparently, the ability of the soul to affect the physiology of the human body may be more substantial than we might imagine, and could well provide more than a few little surprises down the road.

CONCLUSION

It should come as no surprise to the reader to learn that science in general rejects the notion of multiple rebirths. Science may be intrigued by some cases and even perplexed from time to time, but for the most part, it is generally confident that it can explain away most—and, some would say, all—cases of apparent past-life memories as fraud, coincidence, the power of suggestion, the apparent inability of many humans to recognize the difference between fantasy and reality, humanities' capacity to fool itself, and the sometimes inexplicable inner workings of the brain.

However, while science has every right to and, indeed, an obligation to test reincarnationist claims, such tests need to be done in a far more objective manner than has been generally demonstrated so far. Simply challenging the reliability of witnesses or writing everything off as fantasy and coincidence is neither scientific nor a useful means of determining truth. Science does not need to insist that past-life memories be 100 percent accurate in order to be considered viable evidence, nor does it have the right to insist upon standards that cannot possibly be met simply because it is supposedly utilizing the "scientific method" in determining reality. Reincarnationist memories exist within a different realm of "evidence" that is every bit as valuable as that which is normally accepted by science. That anyone can correctly name dates, places, and events from the past that are far beyond his or her capacity to either know or guess—*even if only in part*—is important and must be taken seriously. The question is simply too important to be ignored because certain arbitrary standards of proof are not met, and I fear science may be throwing away what could be one of the most important discoveries of the age by dismissing the subject so casually.

chapter seven

PRACTICAL OBJECTIONS TO REINCARNATION

While the evidence for reincarnation can always be attacked by science on purely empirical grounds, there are other hurdles the theory must attempt to overcome before it can ever be embraced by our modern culture. Whereas up to now we have examined some of the more potent empirical objections to reincarnation, in this chapter we will look at those difficult questions the idea brings up that lie outside the area of easy scientific rebuttal. These are the practical objections one frequently encounters when the subject of multiple lives comes up, and being outside the venue of empirical, testable data, they can be among the more difficult to answer. However, no treatment of the subject would be complete without both examining these issues honestly and attempting to answer them from a logical standpoint. I doubt if any of these answers will satisfy the die-hard skeptic, but they should be adequate to at least give the objective readers some useful points to ponder as they consider whether reincarnation has anything to say to them personally.

The Past-Life Memory Dilemma

Probably the most common objection to reincarnation, and one that proved to be a stumbling block to me for many years, is the question of why we don't consciously and clearly recall our past lives. Certainly, it seems that if reincarnation is to have any value in developing us spiritually, then recalling our past lives would be imperative. What value is there in the hard lessons learned in a past life if we can no longer recall them? For that matter, doesn't the entire process become a waste of time if we end up repeating the same mistakes because we don't remember having made them before?

In a way, this is a valid point, but it fails to understand precisely what reincarnation is trying to do. The purpose of reincarnating is not to simply recall our past errors so that we might avoid making the same mistake again, but to grow spiritually—*even if making the same mistakes over again are a part of that growth process.* As such, it may be *necessary* for us to forget our past lives—along with both their mistakes and successes—so that we may once again acquire a platform upon which to experience life anew. Were we to recall our past lives in perfect clarity, we would not be experiencing a new life but merely continuing a previous incarnation in a new body. So it is important to the process that each time we reincarnate, our memory and, for that matter, our previous personality in toto—with all its idiosyncrasies, quirks, mannerisms, knowledge, perceptions, and a lifetime of memories and experiences—disappear. Much like a chalkboard is erased at the end of each school day in order to prepare for the next day's lessons, so too our "chalkboard" must be wiped clean so we may start our new lessons afresh.

Additionally, consider for a moment how problematic past-life memories have proven to be to those people who claim to experience them. Often they are traumatic memories that require psychiatric counseling to overcome. This is why preincarnate or past-life memories are generally bad—they prevent people from moving toward spiritual maturity until and unless they first deal with their past-life traumas, and this process can be time-consuming.

By way of an example, imagine that a man who was brutally tortured and murdered in a previous incarnation is so traumatized by the event that he lives out his present life in a perpetual state of fear. Terrified of people and unwilling to leave the "safe" confines of his home or interact with others in any meaningful way, he is incapable of moving on to other lessons he needs to learn in this lifetime to grow spiritually. If he is fortunate, he may receive therapy to deal with his trauma, but it may take years before progress is made. Plus, of course, there are those who never seek help at all and so are entirely stymied in their efforts to grow beyond their fearful past. In such cases, a past-life memory has become a hindrance to the growth process and can, in fact, stop it completely if not purged from the conscious memory. The problem lies not in failing to recall past-life memories, but in failing to expurgate our psyche of *all* of them.

The other reason we cannot recall our past lives is more prosaic: we are no more capable of remembering the precise details of a past life than we are of recalling many of the details of our present life with any clarity. In essence, human beings simply aren't very good at retaining long-term memories; instead, the bulk of our life experiences are filed away in some dark recess of the brain where they can only be accessed through hypnosis or brought back to conscious recall by some external stimulus. Additionally, the further back in time the memory is, the more difficult it is to recall—especially with any degree of accuracy—until, in most people, it fades from the conscious mind entirely. If this is true of our present life, then, how much more so will it be true of an even more distant past life—especially if that life was rather ordinary and forgettable to begin with?

Of course, most people will always retain memories of a traumatic or memorable event: their wedding day, the birth of a child, a near-fatal auto accident, the time their home was destroyed by fire, and so on, and will be able to recall them throughout their entire lifetime with relative ease. However, this seems to be true of consciously-remembered past-life memories as well; most people who are able to recall events from a past-life usually remember them because they were traumatic or defining in some way, and so, like present-life memories, they are more prone to "sticking" in the conscious memory. In this respect, our present and past-life memories are similar in that they are both driven by the same stimulus, and manage to enhance or inhibit our lives in similar ways.

Finally, there is also the idea that while we may not retain conscious memories of a past life, we are still retaining the underlying lessons those past-life experiences taught us. For instance, we may not recall the process by which we acquired our patience, but we retain the benefit of that process in this lifetime. Past-life experiences—while absent from our current consciousness—are retained on a deeper "soul level," where they can be carried over from one incarnation to another. While the specific details of each past-life lesson may be lost, it's only because they aren't important; it is the end result that reincarnation is interested in, not the process by which we get there.

The "Napoleon" Syndrome

Another widely held belief among opponents of reincarnation is the idea that most people who believe they lived before profess to have been Napoleon or Joan of Arc or some other noted figure in history, or that they lived in some exotic historical context such as ancient Egypt or Greece. Others have even remembered a past life lived on Atlantis or on other planets, thus suggesting that many of these "memories" are nothing more than fantasies held by eccentric and, in some cases, unstable personalities. Not surprisingly, this has proven over the years to be one of the most formidable objections to reincarnation—not because it's true, but because it so effectively ridicules the idea that people who might be tempted to entertain the notion are quickly cowed into silence.

This is a case where the anti-reincarnation lobby demonstrates its gift for unfounded assumption. Anyone who has bothered to look into the vast number of cases of people professing past-life memories will find very few instances of individuals claiming other than rather ordinary and even mundane previous lives. Most recall lives lived as homemakers, merchants, farmers, servants, soldiers, or some other usually unspectacular occupation, and while occasionally someone will make claims that are a bit exotic, such as that they were once a seventeenth-century Russian ballerina or a medieval count, such cases are rare (as well as subject to how one defines "exotic"—is the revelation that one was once a fourteenth-century Portuguese bandit exotic or mundane?). Some even claim to have engaged in criminal activity or prostitution in a past life—embarrassing occupations few people would be likely to invent to impress others. For the most part, however, the bulk of documented past-life cases rarely include subjects who suggest they were anything out of the ordinary in their past incarnations. For example, of the 1,088 past-life cases recorded by Dr. Wambach in her demographic studies, she recounted only one in which the subject claimed a somewhat famous past-life persona: one woman had a memory—among several she recounted—of having been the fifteenth president of the United States, James Buchanan.[1] Whether this qualifies as a particularly famous person I leave for the reader to decide, but it could be argued that if one wanted to confabulate an entertaining past-life memory, President Buchanan, a generally obscure American president, would not seem to be the best candidate.

It's also interesting to note that even people who are relatively famous in their lifetime rarely claim to have lived noteworthy past lives. Charles Lindbergh, Henry Ford, and Benjamin Franklin all professed a belief in reincarnation, yet none recounted having been anyone famous in a previous incarnation. Even the colorful Second World War general George S. Patton, though a firm believer in reincarnation, never claimed to be a

---

1 Helen Wambach, *Reliving Past Lives: The Evidence Under Hypnosis* (New York: Bantam Books, 1978), 62–64.

famous military leader in the past even though he might have had the pedigree to substantiate such a claim.[2]

As far as claims to having lived in the Pharaoh's court in ancient Egypt or having been a citizen of Atlantis, such cases are somewhat more widespread but by no means a common recollection of a past-life regression patient. However, almost all past-life regressionists have encountered such claims, suggesting that at least some past-life memories may be suspect.

In these cases such memories may indeed be mere fantasies. Admittedly there are people who really are a bit eccentric or given to overactive imaginations, and so this is to be expected. Frequently, however—at least according to some past-life hypnotists—such "memories" may be more akin to guesses or speculations than accurately recalled events from a past life. The idea is that as the subjects attempt to discern the confusing images they may encounter in past lives, some may simply assume they are in a locale manufactured purely from their own subconscious simply because they have no other references from which to work. In other words, a woman who sees herself dressed in a toga-style outfit and walking about the streets of a magnificent, bronze-age city may guess that she is in mythical Atlantis, based purely upon what she has gleaned from books and movies on the nature of the place. Especially if she lacks a strong knowledge of ancient history, any 300 BC–era civilization might be mistaken for "Atlantis" simply because that is how it was portrayed in the books she may have read about it. Atlantis, then, is a guess; the woman may, in fact, simply be standing in a seaside resort in ancient Sparta without for a moment having a clue as to her actual locale. In effect, we are limited in our ability to accurately describe our surroundings by our own level of knowledge.

---

2 There is some anecdotal evidence that suggests Patton may have believed he was the Carthaginian general Hannibal in a past life, but this has never been confirmed. Even if true, however, is the idea that the flamboyant general was once the famous ancient leader really so incongruous?

The same can also be true of people who recall having lived a past life on Mars or some other planet. A lack of astronomical acumen might well result in a wild guess, especially for a person whose knowledge of the universe is limited to the names of a couple of planets and a constellation or two. Additionally, we will take a look later at the possibility that some souls may have actually resided on another planet in a past life, making such claims not nearly as bizarre as some might imagine.

In any case, even if a small percentage of past-life memories turn out to be entirely fallacious and the product of an overactive imagination, that should be no reason to dismiss the entire concept in toto. Every religious, philosophical, or political movement has its "fringe" element, and the occasional colorful character who claims to be the reincarnation of Napoleon no more disproves reincarnation than the psychotic who claims to be Jesus Christ disproves Christianity. The objective researcher looks at the *best* cases of previous-life recall to determine the validity of reincarnationist claims, not the most questionable ones.

The Same Culture Dilemma

The fact that Hindus frequently recall past lives as a Hindu and Westerners commonly recall past lives lived in similar Western cultures would seem to challenge the idea that reincarnation is an objective reality, for if reincarnation were a fact, our past lives should reflect a multitude of different cultures and backgrounds and not be so narrowly confined within the context of our current cultural perceptions. In other words, if reincarnation is true, shouldn't Hindus and Westerners recall having lived as Amazonian Indians and Aborigine tribesmen in their past lives as frequently as they recount lives lived in similar venues to their own?

This appears, at least on the surface, to be a powerful obstacle to the concept in that it clearly suggests that past-life memories—being so culturally similar—are simply fantasies or confabulations created within the confines of an individual's own understanding and cultural awareness.

Researcher Ian Stevenson, who studied conscious past-life memories among the Tlingit Indians of Alaska, noted that their past lives seemed to have been lived out within the same tribe (and, sometimes, even within the same family). Hindu children who recalled past lives also frequently experienced their previous incarnation within mere miles of their current home, again suggesting that their "memories"—in being so culturally similar to their own—may be entirely fictional. In many cases, the argument might be made, it seems that the extent of one's past-life experiences is limited by one's own historical and geographic understanding of the world. In other words, an African tribesman may not recall a past life lived in Tahiti largely because he has no idea such a place even exists, and so is forced to confine his "memories" within the parameters of his very small frame of reference.

This would seem to be a problem at first glance, but once all the data and some thought is put into it, the objection is not as formidable as it first seems. First, it should be noted that while many past-life memories do appear to be culturally consistent, this is not always the case; many people *do* recall lives lived in foreign and exotic environments decidedly different from their own, forcing us to account for these "anomalies" if all past life recall is purely culturally-induced fantasy. Second, most past-life regressions deal with only the most recent past lives; seldom is the subject sent back to even earlier incarnations where cultural "drift" may be more evident. And, third, since past-life memories are effectively filtered through the knowledge and consciousness of the present personality, it is possible that any past-life environments the present psyche is unfamiliar with or unable to comprehend might simply be suppressed or ignored. In other words, do people who cannot recall a past life do so because reincarnation is not true, or is it because their minds are not capable of processing the information and so they, in effect, "draw a blank?"

This might sound like an easy out, but when one takes personal choice within the rebirth process into consideration and factors in a particular person's level of spiritual maturity, it is not unreasonable to imagine that a soul—especially an immature or "young" soul—may opt to repeatedly reincarnate into a society it is already familiar with. As such, when a Hindu dies, his or her soul may be most comfortable reincarnating as a Hindu once again—perhaps even within the same general geographic area—simply because that particular soul finds doing so to be "easier" than starting over in a new and alien culture. Then, once it eventually matures, it may be more willing (or compelled) to widen its horizons and try something new. Could this mean that the more knowledgeable or "worldly" we become, the greater range of choice we will have in determining our next incarnation? Such is an intriguing possibility.

To test this theory yourself, it is only necessary to ask your colleagues which society they would choose to come back to if they were reincarnated. Most would probably opt for the familiar confines of their own (though they may choose to be reborn into more affluent or interesting circumstances) rather than venturing too far afield. Even if they chose another country or culture, chances are it would not be one that is all that different from their own; an American, for example, might opt to be born in Europe or Australia in his or her next life, but it is unlikely that they would choose Niger, North Korea, or Mongolia. Are we to imagine that we don't retain this same ability to choose—at least to some degree—the venue for our next life as well?

As such, the idea that our past lives mimic in many ways our present life should not be surprising and would, in fact, be completely consistent with human nature. We as a species tend toward the path of least resistance; why should it be any different in the spiritual realm?

THE TIME-RECALL CHALLENGE

One phenomenon that frequently crops up during past-life regressions is what I call the "time-recall challenge." Basically, it has to do with how a past-life personality can recall with such certainty the year in which it finds itself, especially if it is remembering a life lived in a culture that used a different calendar or it lived in BC times. In effect, a person recalling a lifetime lived in Baghdad in the eighth century shouldn't know that he or she was living in the eighth century, especially since Muslims use an entirely different means of marking the years (based upon the prophet Muhammed) and the eighth century is essentially a Christian-based measuring system that became internationally recognized and adopted only recently. This problem is even more pronounced when we deal with people who recall lives from an even more distant time when each culture maintained myriad measuring systems to gauge the date. Therefore, if I regress a subject back to 1500 BC or even AD 500 (as Dr. Wambach did in her studies), he or she should have no idea what the date is, for the past personality did not live by our modern calendar.

This, again, could be a fatal blow to the reincarnationist until we take into account that when one speaks with a past persona, he or she is doing so through the filter of the modern persona. In other words, while my past-life personality may not know what the year AD 200 means, my *current* personality does, making it fairly simple to provide the past persona with a modern time meter. Therefore, if a hypnotist regresses a patient back to the distant past and asks what year it is, and the patient replies "300 BC," that is merely the modern intellect (with, perhaps, help from the resident soul using some sort of universally consistent clock) answering. In effect, the year is "calculated" by the modern intellect to approximate the past persona's timeframe by applying modern knowledge about the past to affix a likely date. This is, at least, a reasonable working theory.

This also, incidentally, may explain why a personality claiming to be an eighth-century Arab speaks only modern English and why the twelfth-century Indian girl can't name certain items common to her culture but foreign to our own; the past-life personality is being filtered through the current personality and so is forced to work within its limited vocabulary and understanding. This is also why past-life personalities do not come through as strongly as they might; they are, in effect, "watered down" so much by the current personality that much of the richness and individuality of the past-life persona is lost. Past-life regression is not a "natural" process, and so we shouldn't be surprised if it is far from flawless.

What's important to recognize, however, is the close relationship that each of our personalities maintain with each other, and how the modern personality tries to assist the past personalities in expressing themselves within the context of our current time, culture, and vocabulary. The modern personality does not simply step aside when a past personality wants to communicate, but does everything it can to facilitate that exchange. If one works from the premise that our past-life personas are all a part of a larger soul (an idea we will look at in more depth later), this should not only be reasonable, but expected.

THE POPULATION DILEMMA

One objection often raised by skeptics of reincarnation is the question of world population and how it relates to the potential pool of souls available to be reincarnated. With a world population approaching seven billion, there are far more people alive today than there have ever been before. In fact, it is a common belief that there are presently more people residing on this planet than have existed throughout the course of human history! Yet if past-life regressions reveal that people have had multiple past lives, then where did this population of souls come from? There simply weren't enough people/souls around in the past to account for the staggering number of people/souls alive today, and since more people are born each year than die, the question naturally arises as to how one can account for the fact that more souls are coming into the world than are departing it. As such, how do we account for this population disparity? This argument has proven to be a stumbling block to many and appears to be a potent argument against reincarnation until one looks at the issue in depth and takes the time to do the math, at which point it will become clear that the objection is based on a number of false premises.

The first incorrect assumption this objection makes is that one is reincarnated immediately after death, requiring an instant one for one exchange of souls. However, most literature on the subject suggests that an interval of time passes between incarnations, with periods that may range from weeks to years and even centuries! Like comets, we may all have individual and distinct "orbits" that determine when we reincarnate—orbits that may be determined by our level of spiritual development and experiential desires.

The second erroneous assumption is that it presupposes the number of souls in existence at any given point in time to be a fixed number. However, the fact is that there is no way of knowing how many individual souls exist. Considering the immensity of the universe—with its billions of galaxies each containing billions of stars (many of which probably possess planets with sentient beings like ourselves)—the total number of souls could be, for all practical matters, infinite. In fact, we might speculate that the nearly seven billion people alive on this planet today may in fact constitute only a tiny fraction of the total number of souls in existence.

Further along this vein, it is an error to assume that souls can only incarnate on earth. The possibility that there may be—and likely are—sentient, morally conscious creatures elsewhere in the universe who also possess souls adds infinitely to the number of "available" souls exponentially. While it is possible that some souls may prefer to reincarnate repeatedly and exclusively on earth, this may well be a preference rather than a requirement, much like choosing to stay in the same school or university rather than transferring to an entirely new school each semester. Perhaps changing venues, like frequently changing schools, is as detrimental to the spiritual growth process as it would be to the learning process.

The third incorrect assumption is that new souls cannot be or are not being created. Why this is presumed is curious, however, for there simply is no particularly compelling reason why new souls can't come into existence (or "wink out" of existence, for that matter) all the time. After all, souls have to emanate from somewhere and at some point in linear time to begin their spiritual journey. In fact, such an idea corresponds neatly to the teaching within reincarnation that suggests there are both "young" and "old" souls (a concept we will look at later) as well as other souls returning to the Creator once they have completed their journey (or reached full maturity). As such, from a purely linear perspective, souls may be emanating from the Creator while others are returning to it at the same instance as part of an immense, eternally ongoing process.

Another false premise is the assumption that all people have past lives. While it seems that past-life memories are common, very few people have ever been regressed to reveal past lives. As such, there is no way of knowing if a particular person has had a hundred, a dozen, two, or no past lives at all. In fact, if we work from the premise that there are newly emerging souls coming into physicality all the time, it would make sense that some (and perhaps many) people alive on earth today are on their "maiden incarnation" and so would have no past lives on their "spiritual resume."

The final and most egregious assumption is the belief that there really are more people alive today than have existed throughout human history—a belief that has taken on an air of scientific authority but is, in fact, little more than an oft-repeated but utterly fallacious urban legend. In actuality, when the numbers are properly "crunched" we find that the vast number of people currently residing on this planet today constitute only a tiny fraction of all the humans who have ever lived.

Unfortunately, population statistics are notoriously difficult to quantify due to factors such as infant mortality rates, life expectancy, wars, famine, and disease, and, as such, any numbers that might be used must be considered educated guesses at best. It is also entirely possible that population estimates from the distant past may be badly underestimated, as there is very little data to go by. The fact is that gauging prehistoric population levels is pure guesswork based entirely on certain presumptions about the ancient past. In any case, even if we stick with the most conservative estimates, according to some experts, and using the United Nations' own estimates, the number of human beings that have existed throughout history may be many times higher than the current number alive on our planet today.

Consider that modern man—Homo sapien—is generally thought to have emerged on the planet around fifty thousand years ago (some anthropologists place that date even further back to nearly one hundred thousand years ago). Using the more conservative estimate, however, and using a minimalist approach to population growth by starting with just two people fifty thousand years ago, it is estimated that it took almost forty thousand years for the world's population to reach five million (during which time over a billion people lived and died as well). That number grew exponentially, however, as civilization took hold, until by AD 1 the world's population likely stood at around three hundred million, a rate that was to remain relatively constant for the next fifteen centuries. It finally reached one billion inhabitants early in the nineteenth century, and two billion another century after that, and today it stands at its present population of around 6.5 billion. To achieve such a population growth rate requires a birth rate of around eighty births per one thousand (before the first century AD) and about sixty births per one thousand after that period (up to around the eighteenth century), and thirty births per one thousand since then. Taken together, then, we find that, conservatively speaking, over one hundred billion people may have been born on planet earth since Homo sapiens first appeared, and that our current population of 6.5 billion constitutes less than a tenth of that total.[3]

As such, the "pool" of available souls is well within the capabilities of historic versus modern birth numbers. Even if we consign all souls to an exclusively earthly venue within which to incarnate, and further presuppose that there are no new souls being created (or migrating from other planets), we have no problems coming up with a "soul pool" large enough to permit every human being alive today to have reincarnated

---

3 Much of this information is taken from a *Population Today*, November/December 2002 article by Carl Haub, along with statistics provided by the United Nations' publication on "Determinant and Consequences of Population Trends." See www.prb.org for more information.

potentially dozens of times. So the "population dilemma" that is frequently touted as reincarnation's Achilles' heel is in fact no dilemma at all, but simply the result of faulty assumptions and poor math skills.

chapter eight

ETHICAL/RELIGIOUS OBJECTIONS
TO REINCARNATION

Having looked at some of the more potent arguments against rein-carnation from a scientific/rationalist perspective, it is now neces-sary to turn to those ethical/religious objections that any belief dealing with issues of life after death is guaranteed to produce. Unlike scientific arguments against reincarnation—which work from the premise that the soul (or personality) does not survive death—ethical/religious arguments normally assume that there is an afterlife. They also tend to look at the issue from the perspective of deeply ingrained religious and cultural beliefs that reincarnation threatens, which is why these objections elicit more of an emotional response than do scientific-based arguments. After all, the issue of postmortem survival—whether in the context of reincar-nation or not—is an intensely personal one that strikes at the heart of humanity's fears, hopes, and beliefs. It would be surprising, then, if people didn't attack the concept from the very same emotional level.

There is a second point to consider where reincarnationist beliefs are considered within the context of Western religion. While the scientific community has little to lose if reincarnation should ever be proven (and, indeed, much to gain in terms of acquiring a means of accessing historical knowledge from the past), Western-style religion would have much to lose. It would mean nothing less than a rethinking of thousands of years of orthodoxy, and so it should come as no surprise that some of reincarnation's most formidable attacks come from the religious community. To many of the faithful it's not merely a question of testing a hypothesis, but of keeping order. So firmly entrenched in Western theology is the concept of the single life and final judgment that there is the fear that reincarnation might well overturn the whole apple cart, so to speak, and threaten the very mechanism by which Western religion functions. Without a fear-based theology to maintain the religious hierarchies of Christianity and Islam (and, to a lesser extent, Judaism), control over the faithful could well be jeopardized, and presumed chaos would follow. Missionary work would grind to a halt if the natives ever got wise to the fact that they could "repent" in the next life, and, by extension, it was always imagined many a church pew would grow cold if the congregation caught similar wind of the idea. In effect, if reincarnation were ever to be proven true, it would mean nothing less than the death of traditional Western religion as taught over the last two millennia.

Lest anyone accuse me of overstating the case, I can still recall with great clarity the disgust I held for the concept of reincarnation when I ran with the fundamentalist crowd. Western religion works around very clear-cut understandings and expectations of what is true and what is false, and those who do not operate in the "truth" are doomed to eternal separation from their Creator, never to be redeemed. Christianity is a "one chance only" affair that cannot work—or, at least, work as efficiently—within the context of reincarnation, with its many chances to repent. Reincarnation gives second chances—and third, fourth, and fifth chances, for that matter—which simply will not do.

Of course, there are those who object to the concept on entirely nonreligious grounds as well, though I submit that most such objections are still, at least in part, religious objections dressed in secular garb. Immortality is an emotional issue for many people, and even the most objective people can't help but approach the question of reincarnation without some inherent emotional baggage at their side. Such is not only natural, but to be expected, and, hopefully, is accounted for in these objections.

I've also approached this material in a different manner than in the previous chapters, preferring to lay it out in a simpler question-and-answer format, which I believe to be the most effective method for moving through the material quickly (as well as simplifying the process of locating one's own objections easier). Just as with the previous chapters, much of what I write here is largely speculative, but I believe it remains internally consistent and will provide the open-minded skeptic with some reference points from which to work. Further, my responses are, not surprisingly, crafted from a predominantly Judeo-Christian perspective, and consist chiefly of those objections to reincarnation that I've personally encountered from the faith communities with which I'm familiar. As such, I recognize that those from other traditions might well imagine objections I have not thought of. This is, unfortunately, an unavoidable oversight, but not one, I think, that will detract from the overall value of this material.

If Reincarnation Is True, Why Isn't the World a Better Place by Now?

If souls are slowly moving toward "enlightenment" in each incarnation—the skeptic may well ask—shouldn't the world be a significantly better place by now? After all, if we gain new insight and wisdom through each incarnation, shouldn't there be a positive cumulative effect upon the entire planet? Yet we see a world of war and hatred and the potential for great misery just as we have throughout human history, so how is reincarnation helping, and, indeed, is it helping at all?

First of all, it is generally believed by mystics and New Age purveyors that humanity is still in its infancy, spiritually speaking, and, as such, what growth we might see is still in its earliest stages and therefore not easily perceived. Reincarnation's value to society is gradual and often imperceptible in the short term. It is akin to a slow but steady infusion of clean water into a filthy pool; the cleansing effect may not be obvious for a very long time, but one day the last of the impurities will be fully flushed out and humanity will at last be able to look upon its reflection in the water with pride. Perhaps when we look back upon the world of today a century or even a millennia from now, we will be surprised by how far we have come, spiritually speaking, and the benefits of multiple incarnations will be more apparent.

But what of those who imagine that the world is actually growing worse? With overpopulation, pollution, and the perceived decline in traditional morals and religious beliefs, many argue that we are actually going backward spiritually, completely rendering as nonsense the idea that reincarnation fuels spiritual advancement.

Of course, that many people perceive the world to be growing increasingly worse is a matter of opinion. Judging the spiritual state of a particular culture or society is highly subjective, so determining whether our culture is more or less spiritually advanced when compared to its past is often a matter of personal perspective. Additionally, we also tend to see things within the limited context of the recent past and so remain largely ignorant of what things were *really* like in the "good old days." However, a look at the broad scope of history (beyond just the last century) can be enlightening and, in many ways, provide some reason for hope.

That there are still multitudes who live out their lives in grinding poverty and hopelessness is undeniable, but then poverty, deprivation, and want has always been a part of the human equation. The question we need to ask ourselves is not whether there is still hunger and poverty, but whether the *percentage* of people who live in these conditions is the same, greater, or less than it was a century ago, or two centuries ago, or a thousand years ago. Clearly, the percentage of human beings living in poverty is going down (if not in actual number, at least proportionally) while the world is seeing the birth of a small but growing middle class emerging in even the traditionally poorest countries. This is a fairly recent innovation in the human condition and, I think, a positive and important one.

Consider also that human justice has improved considerably, even over the last century. Slavery is not legal on the planet today and, for the most part, people cannot be worked to death, beaten, or summarily executed for petty crimes, as their ancestors often were. The rights of women, children, and minorities has also improved substantially—especially when contrasted to the conditions of even seventy-five years ago—until today truly repressive societies, while still in existence, are growing less common and sustainable. Of course, there are exceptions: child labor laws are sometimes lax in Third-World countries and exploitation by the wealthy is still common (and, in places, prevalent), but the point is that such behavior, when exposed, is routinely prosecuted, whereas a century ago such behavior was common, expected, and tolerated. While still far from realizing a utopian world, it would be difficult to maintain that humanity is not collectively becoming increasingly aware of the rights of all human beings. Humanity is not as willing as it once was to exploit the weak for the benefit of the wealthy.

Even our government institutions have demonstrated tremendous (and usually positive) changes in just the last sixty years. Immediately prior to the Second World War, there were no more than a dozen functioning democracies in existence on the planet. Today between half and two-thirds of the world's people live under some form of democracy or benign, constitutional monarchy that guarantees individual liberties and freedoms. Further, largely as a result of this democratization process, war as an almost natural and expected instrument of foreign policy is growing increasingly unpopular and uncommon. Though small-scale conflicts still rage in some isolated spots around the world (and are usually confined to nondemocratic nations), really big wars are growing increasingly rare, demonstrating that today nations are far less willing to resort to violence to resolve their disputes. Certainly the recent conflicts in Iraq and Afghanistan—regardless of how one feels about their necessity—are potent reminders to the world that war as a tool of foreign policy is indeed losing its luster, if not its effectiveness.

Yet what of the two great wars that ravaged the twentieth century, the horror of the Holocaust, Stalin's brutal gulag, the proliferation of nuclear and biological weapons, and the more immediate concerns about rising crime rates, terrorism, and international drug trafficking? Couldn't it be said that modern history argues far more persuasively for a humanity in moral decline than for a world on the verge of a golden age of enlightenment?

The atrocities committed in this century *seem* so much worse than those in the past only because we have both conveniently forgotten that past and because the technology exists today that permits a single evil man to do far more damage than his predecessors. It's not whether there are more evil deeds and criminal acts being committed today than in the past, but whether there are *proportionately* more. The real question, then, is not "Do bad things happen?" but "Are we, as a society, safer, healthier, and generally more enlightened than our ancestors?"

Those who hold to the disintegrating society theory are unlikely to be impressed with these examples, but I submit their gloomy outlook can only be sustained by determinedly ignoring the judgment of history. While in many ways we are still a very brutal planet just one mindless act away from exterminating ourselves, we are at the same time far less tolerant of those who diminish the value of human life, rape the environment, or practice injustice. Perhaps this is the result of numerous incarnations, or maybe it's simply that we're naturally, albeit slowly, advancing as a species (or perhaps it's a case of one leading to the other). Whichever the cause, the case for increasing spirituality and enlightenment on a political, social, and religious level around the world can be denied only if one insists on keeping both eyes firmly shut.

Since One Can Always Come Back and "Do It All Over Again," Doesn't Reincarnation Encourage Spiritual Apathy?

This common objection may be a valid one, but it is no more valid within the context of reincarnation than it is within life in general. Reincarnation is no more an encouragement toward spiritual apathy and laziness than is the misplaced belief that people can always "get right with God" later in this life after they've "had their fun." In effect, if people delay learning their spiritual lessons in this lifetime, they will not evolve spiritually regardless of whether they believe in reincarnation or not. They will remain, by their own choice, in a spiritually primitive state not because reincarnation encourages it—it clearly does not—but because apathy is the truest reflection of their spiritual state.

The ultimate goal of reincarnation is for the soul to evolve spiritually, and it never ceases its efforts to move a person toward that goal. While some people may choose to ignore the soul's urging throughout their entire lifetimes, eventually they will tire of their fight, and, like a bit of brackish water temporarily stalled within an eddy of a slowly moving river, they will ultimately rejoin the inexorable march toward their own spiritual evolution. Whether it takes two, ten, or a thousand lifetimes to achieve progress, eventually each soul will acquire the maturity to recognize that it needs to take advantage of every opportunity it's being given to advance and move on, for one never knows what hardships and trials the next incarnation may hold. In fact, once people recognize that the next incarnation might not afford them the opportunities this one does, reincarnationist beliefs might even serve as an *incentive* toward spiritual growth.

On the other hand, it can be argued that spiritual growth occurs in every life regardless of how "lazy" or "unevolved" one may appear to be. Since spiritual growth is an ongoing process, even those incarnations we judge by our human standards to be "failures" may in fact be an important part of the growth process. For that matter, the soul may choose to experience what we might consider a "wasted" incarnation precisely so it may learn from that experience and use that knowledge to advance in the next incarnation. Even within the most hardened criminal's life, we can't always be certain of what's occurring on a spiritual level, but must trust that the process itself knows what it is doing. For all we know, the soul may be setting the stage for a tremendous growth spurt to be realized in the next incarnation, a spurt that might be made possible only by experiencing the world from the confines of a prison cell in this incarnation.

Doesn't Reincarnation Allow One to Escape Justice?

The idea that all humans must be held to account for their earthly life, with the deeds of each person being carefully weighed and measured in an effort to determine his or her final estate for all eternity, is common to all Western faiths and is a core belief within Christianity and Islam. As such, it isn't surprising that so many Westerners perceive reincarnation as simply a means of avoiding being held responsible for their earthly crimes. This demonstrates, however, a certain ignorance on the part of anti-reincarnationists, as well as a tendency to assume much.

Reincarnation *does not* disagree with the concept of judgment per se, but while the Western world sees it as a single—even historical—event, reincarnationists see judgment as a recurring (and, in some ways, ongoing) and necessary part of the growth process. Additionally, while Western religious concepts of judgment are generally seen as punitive in nature, reincarnationists see these "reviews" as essentially instructive. It is a time when the soul—not God—judges itself in order to determine what it needs to experience in the next incarnation in order to continue its forward progress. While this self-assessment can be unpleasant (as confronting one's own flaws and errors always is—even in this life), it is not designed to punish, but to simply point out where a soul has digressed from the true path so it may "repent"—that is, "change course"—and find its way back to its own divine nature.

Of course, this self-appraisal between incarnations might prove more hellish in souls that have lived on a very primitive spiritual level; the process of being stripped of the facade of moral certitude and superiority and having the diseased state of one's inner soul revealed for all to see may be a torturous process, especially to the sensitive soul. Though designed as a means of demonstrating how far the soul still needs to go before it can finally realize its perfected final estate, its inadvertent effect on some people could be very unpleasant indeed. Ideally, however, this review should become increasingly less severe as one progresses spiritually, until eventually very little "purging" is required.

But doesn't such a process make a mockery of justice, as well as render our evil acts on earth meaningless if they do not have permanent consequences? Additionally, what of those who have committed heinous crimes while in the body? Surely justice is not served if their sins are merely "pointed out" and they are allowed to return to the flesh once again?

While a very human response, it is not a divine one. Justice is not served by condemning a soul to eternal torment. Reincarnation does not seek to punish, find fault, hold accountable, or otherwise condemn a soul for its own ignorant foolishness and selfishness, but instead it seeks to heal it. It is humans, not the Creator, who demand that the celestial scales of justice be balanced through retribution.

Yet the idea that the deeds done while in the flesh are not offset in some way after death, and that even the most brutal, vicious, and selfish person on earth might "get away" with a crime, is unacceptable to most people. We expect and, in fact, *insist* that evil be judged and punished, with hell being the preferred method of balancing the cosmic weights of justice. In fact, retribution for sin is one of the foundational principles upon which all Western religion is based, for it is unimaginable that God would not be as deeply offended by sin as we or that God would not punish it as severely as we would.

In that respect, then, the surface it does appear that reincarnation gives us a "pass" on our transgressions, though there are several perspectives on this that need to be carefully examined. First, it should be noted that among many reincarnationists, reincarnation *does* punish past transgressions through the law of karma, which teaches that one reaps in the next life what one sows in this one. As such, a wicked person might be born into a lower caste or, in some cases, he or she might reincarnate as an animal (or even an insect) as retribution for past misdeeds. While karma differs from Western concepts of punishment in the respect that the punishment is both temporary—a person may "work off" his or her karmic debt and return the next time to a better life—and is realized in the flesh rather than in the spiritual realm, it works along the same principles of making atonement for one's sins. However, it is thought to be a fairer system than the Western belief in an eternal hell in that the punishment is more proportionate to the crime and only temporary. We will discuss karma in more detail later, but for now it is enough to realize that among most reincarnationists, retribution is factored into the equation, rendering erroneous the complaint that the evil get off scot-free.

Of course, not all reincarnationists accept the idea that some form of punishment or retribution must be meted out to the wicked in order for justice to be realized. Some look at the question from the opposite point of view and ask how justice is served by punishing a person at all— whether it be through the mechanism of karma or through eternal torment in hell. Obviously, some people seem to be born "unlucky" in that they incarnate into circumstances that are almost guaranteed to result in a hard and brutal life. For example, many people are born into thoroughly dysfunctional families and realize a bad start from the beginning, while others are born into abject poverty where crime is often the only means of survival. Should people who are born into a brutal and vicious world and are essentially "trained" to become brutal and vicious be punished for the consequences of an unfortunate venue? Where, the question might properly be asked, is the "justice" in that?

Additionally, exactly how does punishing a person for his or her sins offset the consequences of those sins? In other words, if we send Hitler to hell for his role in the slaughter of millions of Jews, how does that balance the scales of justice? It doesn't undo anything he's done; none of his victims return from the dead to go back to their families and resume their previous life, nor is a single tragedy or trauma removed from the collective psyches of the survivors. In other words, no amount of punishment can make up for the enormity of his crimes, so what is the point in punishment at all (beyond the natural human thirst for vengeance)?

It could be argued that "sin" is a necessary ingredient in the process of spiritual growth, and those whom we call "wicked" actually have an important role in leading us, both individually and collectively, toward enlightenment. After all, we cannot realize goodness, compassion, or kindness at all without also experiencing cruelty, selfishness, and evil, for the one cannot exist in the absence of the other. Just as we could never really appreciate a nice day if the weather were perfect all the time, we cannot realize goodness without evil. Therefore, to punish the evil is to declare an element of the entire process flawed when, in fact, it could not function at all without both the good and the bad. In effect, it is the darkness that brings us to appreciate the light.

Additionally, it should be remembered that even if a person is not specifically punished for a particular crime in the afterlife, there are still consequences inherent to every action to be realized within both the earthly and the spiritual realms. Criminals commonly end up dead or imprisoned, adulterers often end up in divorce courts, and the selfish and arrogant frequently live out their lives alone and embittered. Even those who are never caught for their crimes usually spend a lifetime looking over their shoulder, preventing them from ever genuinely enjoying the freedom they imagine themselves to possess. In fact, nearly everyone has known of people who, through their own stubbornness and poor decision-making processes, live in a kind of self-imposed hell and manage to keep themselves confined there for years. The human capacity to unwittingly punish oneself is easily observable and even, to a degree, predictable. It is as if there is something within the human psyche that prevents one from ever truly and completely enjoying life once they have done something they know in their heart is wrong.

Of even greater punishment than the guilt and remorse of a life lived selfishly is what one loses in the process. In choosing to live a life entirely dedicated to the self, a person is cut off from the very source of love that permeates the fabric of time and space itself. To live a lonely, joyless existence is, from the perspective of eternity, more than sufficient punishment for even the most heinous of crimes. Frequently the worst suffering is not imposed from without, but from within.

Reincarnation, then, sees the people we would call "wicked" as being "soul sick," and, as such, it would seek only to heal such a wounded soul, not punish it further. Such a soul is already in agony; there is no purpose served in prolonging its pain, and it is outside the venue of a truly loving God to do so in any case. Reincarnation is about restoration of the human spirit, not retribution for the actions of an injured and angry soul.

Doesn't Reincarnation Essentially "Rob" One of Going to Heaven?

Similar to the objection that reincarnation permits one to avoid judgment and punishment is the complaint that it deprives one of going to heaven as well, and since an eternity in paradise (however one defines this magical realm) is the great hope and promise of many religions, it appears that reincarnation "robs" people of their heavenly reward by "making them" return to the flesh—and sometimes to a very unfortunate and difficult life at that.

The problem with this objection is that it perceives heaven as a "place" where one goes to enjoy eternal bliss. In actuality, however, heaven is not a place but a state of being that one realizes. In effect, all souls live in heaven eternally; it is only our misconceptions, limitations, and illusions about the world around us that keep us from experiencing it as such.

While this can be somewhat difficult to grasp, one can begin to get some idea of this truth by observing those rare individuals who seem to be able to constantly maintain a positive and upbeat disposition regardless of the difficulties they encounter. Even in poor health or in dire economic straits, they frequently manage to find joy and peace in even the most trying times, and appear to positively affect everyone they encounter through the sheer force of the positive energy they constantly put out. Such people are uncommon, to be sure, but one would be hard-pressed to deny that they seem to bring heaven with them wherever they go (in precisely the same way some people bring hell with them wherever they go). As such, from a reincarnationist perspective, heaven is not something we attain but something we recognize as already existing around us.

On a purely practical level, the reincarnationist would also question the value of an eternal heaven to spiritual growth. After all, if one spends eternity in a state of perfect peace without a worry in the world, what is that person really experiencing? Without challenges to overcome, heaven becomes a sort of beautiful seaside resort in which one simply lounges on the beach between thrice-a-day massages before gorging on a gourmet feast. While such would be a wonderful environment in which to rest or recover from some terrible trauma, eventually it would take on a mind-numbing sameness that would result in the soul becoming increasingly restless. Even if the soul were capable of constantly changing the heavenly scenery, so to speak, that still would not fix the problem, for the soul would know that none of the scenarios it has imagined would satisfy it completely or eternally.

Life is about experiencing the vast range of human dramas and growing closer toward the God that lives in each of us. It is not about resting forever in some beautiful garden. Just as is true with any ideal vacation spot, it is the temporary nature of heaven that makes it heavenly.[1] In effect, while heaven might be a nice place to visit, one wouldn't want to live there.

That being said, it is important to realize that to the reincarnationist heaven does exist—both within the context of the spiritual realm and within the physical—as a natural element of reality. However, it is only possible to experience it as such if it is contrasted against what it is not.

---

1 Of course, "heaven" exists as a part of the spiritual realm, and so it is naturally eternal. As such, it cannot be temporary in reality, though the "experience" of heaven can be temporary (as are all experiences).

In effect, it is hell that makes heaven so heavenly, just as it is hunger that makes a T-bone steak so delicious. If you gorge on a favorite food day and night that food will eventually become a torture to swallow; it is only in its absence that it retains its appeal. So it is with heaven: keep a person there eternally and it becomes a prison; allow a person to visit it between incarnations and it resumes its role as the paradise it was meant to be.

Isn't Reincarnation's Teaching That One Must be Punished in This Life for the Sins of a Past Life Unfair?

The idea that reincarnation is an oppressive belief system is a common objection deeply held within Western cultures. In many people's eyes, the idea that millions of innocent people could be doomed to live out their lives in abject poverty or blind from birth as a result of some evil committed in a previous lifetime is the epitome of inequality and a damning indictment of the entire concept, and it is often rejected on that basis alone.

Actually, what the Westerner is railing against is not reincarnation, but one element of it known as *karma*. We will look at karma in more detail later, but for now it is enough to understand how the concept is understood in the East. Among the world's nearly one billion Hindus, it is generally believed that a person accumulates both positive and negative karma within each lifetime. However, unless the positive karma (often referred to as *dharma*) offsets the accumulated moral debt, it is thought necessary that one be born into a more trying and difficult life in an effort to "balance" one's negative karma and offset a seemingly perpetual sin debt.

The greatest example of this injustice is seen within India's caste system, where one's caste (social/economic status) is determined by how much negative karma one has to work off, with those possessing greater moral debts being born into a progressively lower social strata. The result is the creation of a socio-economic system that effectively freezes one into a particular social strata from which that person is to "work off" his or her sin debt, keeping millions trapped in squalor and poverty until their karmic debt is paid off. Since one's station in life is a reflection of one's last incarnation, then, no effort has traditionally been made to redress these inequities or improve the lives of those in the lower castes, resulting in a vastly unequal and frequently cruel and unjust society. It is this system, which has been in operation for almost three thousand years, that is often pointed to by opponents of reincarnation as evidence of the teaching's detrimental effect and, by implication, proof of its inferiority to Western religious concepts.

Of course, this socially unjust system does nothing to either prove or disprove the validity of reincarnation. What it does demonstrate, however, is humanity's propensity toward using religion to justify and perpetuate inequality and protect social privilege. Even the institution of slavery was maintained for centuries by appealing to certain religious dogmas and traditions. As such, before we in the West point a finger at the inherent injustice of India's caste system we should look carefully at the class distinctions evident within our own societies first. While the caste system may be a result of errant religious beliefs, is it any worse than the natural tendency within all countries to consign individuals from birth to a lower economic class because of political, racial, gender, religious, or economic distinctions? Yet few people hold Western religious concepts responsible for these injustices, nor do they suggest that such inequalities are evidence that a particular faith structure is false; therefore, why is reincarnation condemned because of a single erroneous belief about it?

That some religions use reincarnation as a means of justifying oppression is undeniable, yet ultimately irrelevant. The willingness to oppress one's fellow citizen is a human failing; it should not serve as the litmus test for a particular religion's authenticity, but instead merely serve as a reflection of a particular society's level of spiritual development.

Doesn't Reincarnation Invalidate all Religions?

This objection works from the premise that if reincarnation is true, it doesn't seem to matter what religion or belief system one embraces since one is fated to reincarnate into another body—and probably another faith structure—anyway. Therefore, the question could be asked, "What value is there in affirming any particular belief system?"

While it's true that reincarnation doesn't require one to adhere to any particular faith or creed for it to work, that's not to say religion doesn't remain an important element of the process. Since the purpose of reincarnation is to evolve spiritually, those religions that affirm and enhance one's spirituality are of vital importance toward achieving that goal. Multiple rebirths allow one the opportunity to learn from many different traditions, thereby pulling from each those elements most needed at that point for spiritual development. To completely eliminate religion, then, is to retard the work of the soul.

However, there are two points to consider. First, not all religions or belief systems are conducive to spiritual growth—some, in fact, can be positively detrimental. Therefore, it is important that one find a religion or faith system that operates from the perspective of love rather than fear. Love-based religion is affirming, tolerant, forgiving, compassionate, inclusive, and seeks to heal; fear-based religion, in contrast, is intolerant, authoritarian, secretive, and exclusive, and seeks to divide people into warring camps. The religion that someone seeks out in this life will not only impact that person's spiritual development, but will serve as a barometer that gauges where he or she already is—spiritually speaking—in this life; people who are basically loving and kind will usually be drawn toward belief systems that affirm that nature, while those who are, by nature, angry, suspicious, judgmental, and condemning will seek out and embrace those elements within each tradition that speak to that "dark side." In essence, one's religion does not always shape one's spiritual development, but may instead be a reflection of it.

The other point to consider is that spiritual development can proceed even outside the context of an established religion. Religious belief is not required for spiritual growth to take place (though it is frequently helpful); the soul may even choose to practice its own inherent moral code completely independent of all religious trappings so it might understand morality in an entirely different context. Therefore, even a compassionate atheist can move toward higher spiritual ground—albeit unconsciously, thereby demonstrating that spiritual growth is often a mysterious and complex process that frequently lies well beyond our capacity to understand.

Doesn't Reincarnation Deny the Teachings of the Bible, the Koran, and Other Religious Books?

To most people in the West, the fact that reincarnation is not clearly taught in their sacred writings is tantamount to denying that it exists. Therefore, if the Bible, the Koran, or any other holy book is silent on the subject, some people believe that it seems foolish to consider it at all and outright heretical to embrace it.

However, simply because a particular religious text does not address a specific issue does not mean the subject is nonexistent or false. Neither the Bible nor the Koran, for instance, say a word about human cloning, abortion, or euthanasia, yet that doesn't mean these subjects are not serious moral and ethical dilemmas that face us today. Holy books are products of their environment and shouldn't be expected to contain everything there is to know.

Second, it can be argued—successfully, I think—that holy writings that may have referred to reincarnation have been subsequently suppressed or destroyed over the centuries because influential religious leaders couldn't—or wouldn't—accept the idea. There is good evidence to support the belief held in some circles that early Christianity may have had a strong reincarnationist vein running through it that was later suppressed and exorcised from its later teachings.[2] Therefore, one can

---

2 See appendixes C and D.

never be certain if a book is silent on the subject of reincarnation because it does not believe it, or whether it simply didn't survive its opposition and make it into the "official" canon.

And, finally, Western religious texts might be silent on the subject not because it is a heretical belief, but because it wasn't important to what the religious writers were trying to say. It could simply be that the concept was omitted because the ancient prophets were not interested in the last life or the next one, but only in *this* one! Reincarnation, then, may have been considered a distraction to their basic message, which was meant to help people in the here and now achieve spiritual growth, and was left out as irrelevant and redundant (especially if presented within a culture in which the concept was already accepted).

Finally, it should be realized that even though reincarnation is not taught by Western religion, reincarnationists generally do not discount the validity of these ancient texts. Spiritual growth uses all paths, and finds useful spiritual information contained within all holy books, as well as what is taught by all the great spiritual teachers. As such, reincarnationists generally affirm the truth behind all ancient wisdom writings while insisting that none of them are exclusively true.

Doesn't Reincarnation Deny the Christian Doctrine of Resurrection?

It is undeniable that reincarnation is at odds with the Christian doctrine of the resurrection as that concept has been traditionally taught. However, from a metaphysical perspective, it need not necessarily conflict with the doctrine at all. In fact, resurrection could be viewed as an integral part and ultimate goal or purpose of the entire process; it's all in how one defines "resurrection."

Resurrection as the resuscitation or reanimation of the human body after death is clearly incompatible with reincarnation, which teaches that the soul is repeatedly reborn into a completely new and different body (with the old body being discarded and reclaimed by the elements). However, if resurrection is defined as the joining of the soul with the Creator as the final, ultimate estate the human spirit seeks, then it is not at all in conflict with reincarnation or the Eastern goal of achieving reintegration with the universal spirit. However, this is not the traditional Christian interpretation of resurrection, which is generally clear about it being a physical reunion between soul and body, which is at odds with Christian tradition.

At least reincarnation manages to avoid having to account for certain questions that traditional resurrection theology has to grapple with. For example, what happens once a corpse turns to dust and is scattered across the face of the planet (as has already happened to the bodies of most people—including Christians—who have ever existed)? And if it is reassembled from the "dust of the earth," in which way is it still technically a "body" in any real sense of the word? Additionally, what if one was born with a physical deformity, or had a propensity toward obesity? Does that person spend eternity in the body he or she had on earth regardless of what state or condition it was in? For that matter, does one remain a particular sex, race, and age in the same way Jesus was resurrected in his final earthly form as a young Jewish man?

These are all problems that reincarnation manages to avoid. It does not assign such value to the human body, which is perceived as merely a temporary vessel within which to experience physicality. Humans are pure spirit in nature and in essence, and find the body—any body—to be a severe limitation to realizing its natural form; humans take bodies only out of necessity. The spirit may enjoy the experience of residing in the body, of course, but only for a time and only until it is necessary to move on to the next incarnation. As such, the reincarnationist would see no value in returning to a previous body and, in fact, would see it potentially as a detriment to spiritual growth.

Could Past-Life Memories be Evidence of Demonic Delusion?

This is a popular objection to reincarnation proposed by the more fundamentalist factions of Christianity (and, for all I know, Islam and Judaism as well). The idea that Satan and his army of demon followers are out and about deceiving people into accepting false ideas is as old as Eve and the Garden of Eden, and frequently one of the most difficult to dispel.

Essentially, the idea is that demons—which are presumably fallen angels—are extremely clever and unusually intelligent beings capable of great mischief. Additionally, being essentially invisible to the physical senses and capable of interacting with the natural world puts them in the perfect position to "suggest" (probably through some form of clairvoyance) all sorts of erroneous ideas to the unwary and naive, thus further thinning the ranks of those who would be saved from eternal judgment.

Apparently, the theory goes, demons accumulate information about an actual person (perhaps someone they once possessed) and then pass that information along to some unwary person, who assumes the information to have been internally acquired rather than fed to him or her through an external entity.[3] Since that person repeats clear and often verifiable memories of having lived another life in the distant past, he or she naturally assumes that reincarnation is the explanation and embraces the concept, thereby presumably abandoning any Christian beliefs in the process, much to the detriment of his or her eternal soul.

Of course, this entire premise is based upon a few major assumptions, the first being that there really are such things as demons. It is beyond the venue of this book to explore this question in any detail, and it would be difficult to persuade those already convinced of their existence in any case, so I will not press the issue. For now it is enough to simply remind those who hold to this position that using demons to explain reincarnation is simply an appeal to one mystery to explain another.

Worse, from the perspective of acquiring knowledge and objectively studying an issue, the belief in deceptive demons is detrimental in that it

---

3 This belief is one reason fundamentalist Christians are frequent critics of hypnotism. It is thought that when a person is put into a trancelike state, demons have their greatest access to the subject, and are able to pull off their greatest deceptions.

makes the issue a question of faith versus disobedience. To many people, reincarnation is an occult concept and, since contact with the occult is expressly forbidden by scripture, it makes even a healthy inquiry into the subject not only potentially dangerous to one's eternal soul, but an act of rebellion against God himself. In effect, then, to even consider the evidence is a sin that must be avoided, immediately slamming shut the doors of knowledge through the presumption of inerrancy in one's own beliefs.

Another assumption about reincarnation that has repeatedly proven to be erroneous from a fundamentalist Christian perspective is that to embrace the concept is to reject one's faith (and, by implication, to be led deeper into the darkness of the occult). The reality, however, is that there is no evidence that a belief in reincarnation alters one's basic religious beliefs at all. People who believe in God or Jesus or Muhammed or Allah before embracing reincarnation usually still believe in these figures afterward. In fact, according to the 1999 Harris poll I referred to in the introduction, a quarter of all professing Christians maintain some kind of reincarnationist beliefs, and yet most seem to manage to maintain other elements of their traditional faith in the process. While it is true that some former Christians who have adopted reincarnationist beliefs are no longer active in their church, that is not reincarnation's fault. Some people leave the church over doctrinal disputes while others leave because they no longer agree with the church's politics or find the atmosphere increasingly intolerant or judgmental. Some even leave simply because they've grown bored with it. In effect, people leave the church because it no longer fills some need in their lives. Some may try alternative spiritual traditions (of which reincarnation may be one) while others will abandon all organized religion entirely, but the point remains that reincarnation is no more likely to induce a person to abandon his or her faith than anything else is. Indeed, the evidence suggests just the opposite: it is quite possible for people to believe in reincarnation and remain active in their traditional congregation (assuming they are not too vocal about their opinions on the subject). Therefore, it's difficult to see what the "payoff" is for the poor demons who have to go through so much work to deceive others. It seems that rather than trying to persuade their victims that they have lived before, their efforts might be better served convincing religious folks to vilify those who are different or maintain positions that are doctrinally different from their own; that, at least, would bring some real disruption to the unity of believers.

Finally, from a more technical perspective, there is no evidence of "demonic" activity within the lives of people who remember past lives, nor does the belief in reincarnation seem to result in the sort of emotional or psychological damage that fundamentalists believe happens to people when they participate in occult activities. In fact, the belief in reincarnation has frequently proven to be a spiritual boon to many people—providing them with a more hopeful context from which to ponder eternity—and, in the case of regression therapy, has even proven to cure many deep-seated and debilitating phobias. It's difficult to understand how a person could be in such intimate contact with a demonic entity without suffering all sorts of psychological and spiritual problems, yet most people who claim past-life memories seem to go on about their business none the worse for wear. If demons are as dangerous as they're made out to be, that simply doesn't make sense.

The belief that reincarnation is a demonic teaching is nothing more than a dogmatic assertion based purely on subjective opinion. It is, however, a remarkably effective tool in the fundamentalist's bag of tricks, which, perhaps, is all it was ever meant to be.

Doesn't the Possible Existence of Ghosts Run Contrary to the Idea That the Soul Reincarnates?

Some have seriously suggested that the existence of ghosts constitutes evidence that reincarnation cannot be true, for if we reincarnate, how can we also manifest as ghosts?

Assuming that one believes in ghosts and that one considers them the disembodied spirits of the recently deceased, there is still no reason to discount reincarnation as a viable postmortem possibility. As I wrote earlier, few reincarnationists maintain that one is *instantly* reincarnated at the moment of death or that they even reincarnate at all. There may well be a period of time—even a very lengthy period of time—during which the recently departed have the opportunity to acclimate to their disembodied existence. Also, as stated earlier, there may be a period of spiritual rest between incarnations in which souls have the opportunity to review their previous experiences, potentially be purged of some "negative energy" they are still burdened with, and generally prepare for their next incarnation. Additionally, some people may be so linked with family and friends left behind that they are reluctant to break those ties— even for their own good—while others may have suffered such horrific deaths that they are initially too traumatized to make a clean break with their earthly existence (credible stories of ghosts often involve people who die violently or unexpectedly). I think it is significant that hauntings consistently and rarely last more than a few decades at most, suggesting that eventually even these "lost souls" find their way to the light and ultimately into the flesh once again.

CONCLUSION

I would not be surprised if the reader came up with several more objections to reincarnation. Clearly the subject is a complex one and prone to so many misinterpretations and misunderstandings that an entire book dealing with just the perceived problems with it could easily be penned.

I don't deny that there are difficulties with the idea, just as there are with all belief systems. Yet I am also firmly convinced that reincarnation, as a postmortem possibility, possesses an inherent internal consistency that is difficult for other belief systems to match. Once it is thoroughly understood and the data carefully and objectively examined, it is a persuasive concept that can be denied only out of a stubborn refusal to accept any possibility of a post-mortem existence or a mindset that will not permit objective examination of any idea that lies outside the realm of one's already firmly entrenched bias. For those who are looking to make sense of life, however, it has much to offer.

chapter nine

JAMES THE SUBMARINE MAN: A CASE STUDY

Having looked at the evidence both for and against reincarnation, it might be helpful to put a real-life example of a past-life memory to the test and examine it within the context of the material we have covered so far to see how well a "good" case stands up to careful scrutiny. Unlike most books on reincarnation that deal with multiple examples of past-life memories, aside from the Bridey Murphy material alluded to earlier, this is the only documented case I'm going to present in this book. The reasons for this are twofold: first, I am not interested in simply compiling another volume of intriguing anecdotal stories about past-life recall, as there are already numerous books of that nature on the shelves; and, second, I am less concerned with the details of a life past-life memory than I am with examining the way the human mind works in perceiving and attempting to answer the perplexing questions these stories bring up. In other words, this chapter is not about a particular past-life memory per se, but about how the reader should examine every plausible reincarnationist account using logic and a carefully maintained objectivity. Only in this way can the natural human tendency to either blindly believe or automatically reject be, at least to some degree, kept at bay.

THE SKEPTIC'S COMPLAINT

In most cases of past-life recall, objective verification of people, places, and dates are often impossible to achieve due to a lack of written records or living witnesses to affirm the statements. Further, when details of a past-life memory can be verified, the skeptic will often object that if the information is obtainable by the researcher, it should be just as available to anyone determined to fabricate a credible past-life memory, thus creating a scenario in which the skeptic wins either way. Even when hoaxing is eliminated as a plausible explanation, it is understood that innocently acquired information can and does frequently disappear into the recesses of the brain only to re-emerge years later in the form of "lost memories." Further, the charge is frequently leveled that pro-reincarnation investigators themselves are partly to blame because they lack the necessary objectivity to weigh the evidence in a balanced and impassive manner and/or are overly trusting. It seems, then, that there are always ways to explain away even the best evidence, giving the reincarnationist little hope of ever persuading the hardened skeptic of anything.

It should come as no surprise then that when a past-life memory account appears that contains verifiable evidence—places, names, dates— that is capable of being corroborated, and when hoaxing seems unlikely, and where there is no apparent source for any hidden or lost memories, the scientific community becomes extremely suspicious. One such case emerged in the late 1980s that manages to challenge even the most ardent critics and still entices them into taking a second look to this day. What gives this story a better "pedigree" than most reincarnationist accounts and makes it an especially compelling test case is that the subject's alleged past life took place recently (within a generation of his birth) and left a significant paper trail that has endured the most careful scrutiny. Additionally, it has the advantage in that some of the "memories" are capable of being verified by witnesses who were still alive at the time. Considering that most of the best past-life cases recount lives lived in the distant past when record-keeping was spotty at best and there are no living witnesses to verify the details, the fact that this story has both official government documents to back up many of its claims and eyewitness testimony—albeit dated—to verify some of the more personal and intimate details is a rare combination and makes for some powerful corroborating evidence.

For the purposes of understanding how an objective examination of a past-life case should work, we will examine this account from the perspective of a skeptic[1] to see how well certain facts stand up to scrutiny, for if one can find more prosaic explanations in the best cases of past-life memories, reincarnation as a postmortem possibility becomes increasingly unlikely. As such, I lay this case on the debunker's altar to see if reincarnation can survive as a plausible option for humanity, or if it will fail every test the skeptical community can throw at it. Only in this way can we hope to acquire some practical idea of what a test case would look like, and what obstacles it must overcome before it may be considered powerful evidence for reincarnation.

This account was originally printed in the *Journal of Regression Therapy* by Rick Brown,[2] a certified hypnotherapist from Glendora, California, and former Vice President of the International Regression Therapy Association. The story was also featured on an episode of *Unsolved Mysteries* in

---

1 A "skeptic" being defined here not as someone who necessarily refuses to believe in reincarnation, but one who looks for natural explanations to solve apparently paranormal claims.

2 Rick Brown, "The Reincarnation of James the Submarine Man," the *Journal of Regression Therapy*, vol. 5, no. 1 (Dec. 1991), 62–71.

1993, and was recounted in greater detail in a book written by Mr. Brown himself.[3] It is recounted here in greatly condensed form.

James the Submarine Man

In 1987, a thirty-four-year-old Glendale, California man by the name of Bruce Kelly sought help for severe cases of hydrophobia and claustrophobia. These fears—which he had experienced to some degree all his adult life—had grown increasingly serious to the point that they were beginning to interfere with his ability to perform his job as a traveling sales rep, a problem that proved to be especially serious whenever he was forced to travel by airplane.[4] He found that being enclosed within the fuselage of an aircraft induced severe anxiety that didn't begin to subside until the plane had been airborne for some time. Even more debilitating was his fear of water, which was so acute that complete immersion in any body of water was impossible, and even partial immersion in a bathtub, pool, or hot tub would result in irregular breathing, dizziness, nausea, trembling, and cramps. Additionally, he exhibited idiopathic chest pains that defied medical explanation and further contributed to his difficulties.

As Kelly's symptoms worsened, and having exhausted all traditional medical techniques in an effort to find a cure, he began exploring various metaphysical concepts in an effort to find relief. Though he was an evangelical Christian, he became intrigued with the idea of reincarnation and approached Brown about the possibility of undergoing hypnotic regression in an effort to get at the root trauma that was responsible for his

---

3 Unfortunately, Mr. Brown passed away in October, 2002 before I had the opportunity to contact him about further details of this case. As such, I was forced to put this story together based exclusively on his book and details from the *Unsolved Mysteries* segment the case generated.

4 Kelly did not exhibit a fear of flying per se, but instead a fear of being inside the enclosed fuselage of the aircraft, making his phobia more akin to claustrophobia than aviophobia (fear of flying).

problems. After carefully explaining to Kelly what was involved in the procedure, Brown successfully regressed him back to a time when he first experienced his fear, and what was uncovered proved to be a fascinating and astonishing story.

Kelly claimed, under hypnosis, to have acquired his fear of water—as well as the related fear of being in enclosed spaces—due to his death by drowning onboard an American submarine in the opening months of the American involvement in World War II. Identifying himself as a sailor by the name of James Edward Johnston, Kelly recounted being trapped within the hull of the ship—which he identified as the USS *Shark*—as it rapidly sank as a result of a Japanese depth-charge attack, killing him and all fifty-eight men onboard in a matter of minutes. Apparently this event proved to be the source of his traumas, and once it was identified, Kelly's symptoms, at least according to Brown, eventually faded, to the point where they no longer had a significant effect on his life.

Intrigued by the remarkable story, both Brown and Kelly agreed to do some further investigating and were able to confirm a number of details that had been recounted in the session. A quick check at the local library revealed that there had indeed been an American submarine named USS *Shark* that sank in the opening months of the war and, according to the crew manifest, that there had been a man by the name of James Edward Johnston onboard. (The manifest also contained the names of two other crewmen Kelly had named who had died with Johnston.) He also correctly identified the *Shark's* home port (Manila) along with several other submarines the *Shark* operated with, and provided credible information regarding the nature of the attack on the vessel and a historically accurate date for the sinking (February 11, 1942).[5]

Finding Kelly an especially good subject and hoping to acquire more verifiable information, Brown hypnotized him several more times, eventually regressing him back to an earlier point in his past life before Johnston

---

5 A more complete history of the USS *Shark* and the possible causes for its loss are discussed in detail in appendix B.

had joined the Navy. In these sessions, Kelly claimed to have worked at one point for the Civilian Conservation Corps (a depression-era federal recovery program that put unemployed Americans to work building roads and clearing forests) in California and Alabama, and he recalled a number of personal memories from his boyhood growing up in a small town in Alabama. This information proved to be so detailed that Brown thought it useful enough to make further investigation feasible.

True to Kelly's/Johnston's account, the information he recounted was verified after a careful search of government archives and personal correspondence. A later visit to the Alabama town in which Johnston had lived proved to be consistent with the subject's memories, including the location and layout of the house he recalled having grown up in. Still-living acquaintances of Johnston also confirmed many of the idiosyncrasies Kelly remembered about Johnston, such as a preference for the heels from a loaf of bread and the fact that he always entered his house through the back door. He also successfully recounted the death of his mother when he was twelve years old along with other details not widely known outside of the Johnston circle of acquaintances. In all, Kelly was able to recount over a dozen specific pieces of information about the life of Johnston—a man who had died eleven years before Kelly was born—that proved to be verifiable and accurate, making this account one of the best cases of an alleged past-life memory on record.

But was it a real past-life memory, or are there other more prosaic explanations for the remarkable incident? This is where the skeptic enters the picture to test what seems to be an "open and shut" case of reincarnation.

HYPOTHESIS #1: THE STORY WAS A HOAX

The amount and quality of verifiable details in this story naturally leads one to question both Kelly's and Brown's credibility and honesty, especially in light of the fact that both later reaped some benefits in terms of money and "fleeting fame" for their story. Both men appeared in a segment of *Unsolved Mysteries* in 1993, and Brown penned a book on the incident,[6] leading some to immediately suspect not only collusion, but outright fraud.

Clearly, the fact that such a story *could* be hoaxed is not out of the question. Information that is verifiable via public records is also information that can be acquired by someone intent on constructing a plausible past-life memory. For instance, the crew manifest of the USS *Shark,* along with a few details of the ship's brief and tragic war record, are easily obtainable from several sources. (In fact, it is far easier to obtain a crew manifest for a vessel that was lost in the war than for one that wasn't. Websites often serve as electronic memorials for ill-fated vessels.)[7] Further, Kelly's considerable knowledge of at-sea submarine operations—recounted during his earlier sessions—could have been acquired through studying books written by naval historians. Finally, details of the ship's internal layout could be provided from schematics of the ship itself or by visiting one of several similar vessels on display around the country today.

Obtaining information about Johnston's life before the Navy would have proven more difficult, though not impossible. With a bit of digging into naval archives and some luck, it would have been possible to match a service record to one of the crewmen on the *Shark's* manifest, which would also provide a gold mine of pertinent information for a would-be hoaxer. Most useful would be the sailor's "home of record" (usually the man's home town), date of entry into the service, naval bases he trained at, and other useful corroborating information, all of which would provide a hoaxer with a starting point from which to weave his tale. Locating a person's former home might be more difficult but doable for a determined hoaxer, and having witnesses whom one can "pump" for information about the deceased person would be an added bonus, especially if they were talkative. As such, with a great deal of time and determination,

---

6 Rick Brown, *The Reincarnation of James the Submarine Man* (self-published, 1990).

7 The Internet was still in its infancy in 1987, so it's unlikely that Kelly used it as a source of information.

along with a bit of luck, a credible hoax might be perpetrated and foisted upon an unsuspecting and highly suggestible therapist, or an alliance might be formed between patient and therapist in an effort to acquire some publicity and/or financial gain.

To some debunkers, since this scenario is *potentially* possible, that is usually enough to discount it in toto. That, however, would not only be premature and presumptuous, but would fail to take into account a number of mitigating factors.

First, it fails to examine the men involved: what are their reputations, both professionally and personally? What do friends, family, coworkers, and acquaintances have to say about their character and ethics? Are they known as people who are highly suggestible and easily deceived, or are they usually thought of as more careful and objective? Second, how much information could two men—assuming they were working together— really acquire about their "submarine man" to make him credible? While some of the most basic details about Johnston's life may be a matter of public record, how easy would it be to find the necessary personal details to make him viable? Plus there is the matter of keeping the preliminary investigation secret; certainly, if either Kelly or Brown had met with Johnston's surviving acquaintances earlier in an effort to obtain personal details about his life, are we to really imagine that such a fact would not have eventually surfaced (or are we to assume the townspeople were in on the scam as well)? One can acquire only so much information about a person from public records; personal details—especially on a man who lived and died over half a century ago—would be almost impossible to obtain without a great deal of cooperation from those who had actually known him. The fact that no such collusion was discovered prior to the *Unsolved Mystery* filming is significant.

Also, these men had far more to lose from being exposed as hoaxers than they might conceivably have to gain by being successful with their scam. Neither man realized significant financial gain from the experience (in fact, Brown had to self-publish the book he had written on the incident, which is costly and rarely financially lucrative), and, especially in the case of Brown, a professional reputation—along with certification credentials—were on the line were he to be exposed. Clearly, the risks in this case were hardly worth the potential gain, and it seems unlikely that simply perpetrating a hoax for the sake of a good laugh would have proven enough incentive for either man.

Finally, it should be recognized that if this account was indeed a hoax, it was good enough to fool the producers of *Unsolved Mysteries,* who were known for carefully investigating the claims made in every story before committing themselves to filming and airing a report. In working with law enforcement agencies in an effort to solve crimes and disappearances, they understood the need for their information to be as accurate as possible, especially as the reliability of their stories directly impacted their reputation as a law enforcement aid. Had they uncovered problems with the story early on, it is difficult to imagine that they would have aired it.

As such, the hoaxer theory, while not impossible, seems unlikely. There is simply no evidence of collusion having taken place between either Brown or Kelly and the surviving acquaintances of James Johnston, nor is there evidence that either man's character would have made them likely candidates to attempt such a hoax. Further, there was little of substance to gain from fabricating such a story and, indeed, a great deal to lose in terms of professional credibility and credentials. (They also would have faced general ridicule and a possible lawsuit from the producers of *Unsolved Mysteries.)* Finally, the story has never been disproven, nor has any evidence surfaced since it first emerged to contradict any elements contained within it. While none of these points prove the story *couldn't* have been hoaxed, when combined they do present an imposing obstacle to the idea.

HYPOTHESIS #2: THE STORY WAS A FANTASY SUPPORTED BY A BIT OF COINCIDENCE

This theory, like the hoaxing hypothesis above, presumes that Kelly, despite his denials to the contrary, may have had more than a passing interest in submarine history and possibly used that knowledge—albeit unconsciously—to fantasize the submarine story, potentially as a contrived mechanism to deal with his fears. In other words, to effect a cure for a clearly unpleasant and disabling phobia, Kelly's own subconscious, working from information stored deep within its "lost" memory archive and/or fed by a healthy imagination, contrived the submarine story as a means of accessing the underlying trauma by creating a more comfortable scenario (a past-life drowning) from which to safely play it out. The fact that there really was a man named James Johnston onboard a real ill-fated submarine named the *Shark,* then, was either a huge coincidence or a "lost" memory Kelly had inadvertently acquired earlier.

But what of the pre-war details of Johnston's life that Kelly later recounted? Could they also have been another series of coincidences or was the information unconsciously gleaned from Brown's later inquiries? In effect, once Kelly (and Brown, for that matter) became convinced of the validity of Kelly's past-life persona and had learned a few things about the man's earlier life, could that information have been inadvertently accepted as a memory rather than recognized as a newly-learned fact? In effect, could either man have been so eager to believe the Kelly/Johnston link that information later unearthed about Johnston was enthusiastically embraced as a retrogressive memory, especially by the time the story emerged some years later?

While it's difficult to imagine how anyone could confuse a newly-learned fact with an already known one, the desire—indeed, even the *need*—to believe can sometimes be strong enough to make the believer unconsciously reorder the sequence of learned facts to conform to a preconceived notion. This could also be done by the therapist asking leading questions of his or her patient in an effort to get the patient to "confirm" the information he or she had only recently acquired, and the information is innocently recalled later as a "revealed" memory.

Finally, as far as accurate memories about Johnston's boyhood home are concerned, this might be written off as a series of coincidences as well. The home he described in such "uncanny" detail, for example, could have described any of a dozen similar homes in a small Alabama town, and the later confirmation of some of Johnston's alleged idiosyncrasies as a boy (entering through the back door and preferring the heel on a loaf of bread), while apparently significant on the surface, might be explained away as "planted" memories eagerly confirmed by curious and overly helpful acquaintances *wanting to believe* that Kelly was indeed the reincarnation of their long-dead friend. By the time Kelly met with those who remembered Johnston, he had been dead over fifty years, which is plenty of time for memories to fade and inaccuracies to creep in as "facts." Even if they couldn't clearly recall key points about the man's teenage years, who wants to deny an obviously sincere young man his corroborating evidence in front of a national audience, especially when they can't be *entirely certain* that Johnston *didn't* sometimes enter the house through the back door or eat the heels off loaves of bread?

So where does that leave the Kelly story? Could it all have been nothing more than a fantastic combination of fantasy, wish-fulfillment, unconscious coaching, and a bit of coincidence that all came together in such a way as to create a very plausible and seemingly inexplicable past-life memory?

While such a scenario is theoretically possible, it seems highly improbable. First, consider the remarkable chain of coincidences that would have to be realized for it to come to pass. Not only would Kelly have had to unconsciously name the proper submarine and the most likely date for its sinking, but correctly name at least three of the crewmen who had died onboard. The chances of guessing the name of even *one* crew member on any particular submarine lost in World War II—by his or her full name, no less—is astronomical;[8] to name three men would be beyond chance and explainable *only* through hoax, cryptomnesia, or reincarnation.

The second problem comes from the details culled from Kelly's later sessions. If we are to accept that Kelly correctly recalled his pre-Navy life working in the CCC (Civilian Conservation Corp) *before* the verifying data had been uncovered, the chances of guessing that correctly would be many billions to one. Further, correctly "guessing" Johnston's home town in Alabama *before* Brown had acquired Johnston's military service record and then correctly identifying a number of personal details about Johnston's teenage years would be beyond chance. There are simply *too many* remarkably good guesses for coincidence to be a reasonable explanation; even if some of the facts proved to be incorrect or unsubstantiated (and few of them were) it would *still* be too great a coincidence to be sustainable. While there *is* such a thing as coincidence, it can be considered a reasonable explanation *only* when it does not strain credulity to the breaking point, which is clearly not the case here.

Finally, the idea that data acquired later could be erroneously recalled as hypnotically revealed facts is countered by the fact that Brown tape-recorded each regression session, giving him a time meter by which to gauge when he received corroborating information. His personal correspondence while attempting to verify certain details of Johnston's life would also have been dated, making it even more possible to reconstruct a data-gathering timeline.

---

8 Especially considering that the name "Johnston"—with an added "t"—is less common than the name "Johnson." To correctly name a "Johnson" on a manifest of just fifty-eight men would be difficult enough; to correctly name a "Johnston" would be remarkable, and to further correctly guess the first and middle name as well would be beyond the realm of chance.

Hypothesis #3: Bruce Kelly Was Recalling Forgotten Information

This is the popular cryptomnesia explanation in which Kelly was suppos-edly recalling information while under hypnosis that he had acquired at some earlier point in his life but had later forgotten. In effect, Kelly may have inadvertently skimmed the crew manifest of the ill-fated *Shark* years earlier—perhaps while browsing through books on submarine his-tory at the library—and unconsciously appropriated one of the names from the list and built an entire and completely imaginary life (and death) for the man in a textbook example of cryptomnesia.

Yet if we are to take Kelly's word that he had no prior interest in sub-marines and had never read a book that might have contained the *Shark's* crew manifest prior to his regression session, what are we to make of this? Either he is lying (see hypothesis 1) or he had read such a manifest and had simply forgotten he had read it.

This latter point, however, seems unlikely. A submarine's crew mani-fest is not the kind of information one inadvertently stumbles across in the course of one's reading; it is a very specific type of information use-ful only to history buffs (or the descendents of the crewmen) that takes a bit of effort to uncover. While it's not difficult to find, it is something one would have to intentionally look for; it is not likely to be contained in books on submarines, nor is it something one would be likely to for-get having read.

Further, most confirmed cases of cryptomnesia find their source in his-torical novels or movies and television programs, but such stories are rarely generated by genuine historical events and seldom do they deal with the exploits of a real person. Even in those cases in which a novel uses a genuine historical event as a backdrop, the characters and the events of their lives are almost always entirely fictional. Unless one is recalling a past life as some famous personality such as Napoleon or George Washington, the past-life persona arising from a cryptomnesia-induced memory should be entirely fictitious and absent from any and all historical records. The chances of a man named James Johnston being a character in a novel or movie concerning the sinking of a fictional submarine named the USS *Shark* is beyond chance and outside the venue of logic. Additionally, if such a book or movie did exist, why has it never been identified? One would think that with the wealth of detailed information Kelly provided about the vessel and its exploits, locating the corresponding movie or article he got the information from, either consciously or unconsciously, should not be difficult.

Even if Kelly's knowledge of submarines and the crew manifest of the *Shark* were unconsciously acquired and retained in some recess of his brain, however, what of the rest of Johnston's past? What material could Kelly have inadvertently come across concerning the man's childhood and experience in the CCC that might have served as the source for these memories? If Johnston was nothing more than a name retained from a page in a book, Kelly's memories of Johnston's prewar past should be ambiguous at best, or, more likely, entirely absent. The cryptomnesia theory is dependent upon some kind of source material being at the heart of the hidden memories, but what could possibly serve as the source in this case? The cryptomnesia proponent, if he or she is honest, can only admit to a dead end at this point, and either give up the inquiry entirely or revert back to the hoax theory. There is simply nowhere else to go.

Hypothesis #4: Bruce Kelly Was in Contact With the Spirit of James Johnston

While the first three hypotheses that attempt to explain Kelly's uncanny ability to recall the biography of a man who had died eleven years before he was born are based on rationalist arguments, for those who accept that a supernatural realm exists and are inclined to look for a paranormal explanation for reincarnation, this last hypothesis is basically the only "show in town" left.

According to this hypothesis—one favored by some parapsychologists, occultists, and a few religious pundits—past-life memories are the work of disembodied spirits that somehow have acquired the ability to relay information about their previous mortal existence to some unsuspecting person, who then interprets these "memories" as his or her own from a previous incarnation. The idea is that a hypnotized subject—being in a particularly agreeable state of mind—might be receiving communications from the disembodied personality of a deceased person, which the subject innocently relates to the hypnotist as a past-life memory. (This would also explain why so much of the information is verifiable in nature, for the disembodied personality *did* exist and *does have* a personal history.) In effect, the subject is not recounting his or her own past life, but is simply serving as an inadvertent conduit through which a disembodied spirit is reliving its own past and, with it, its own personal traumas (which apparently impact the living host as well). As such, Kelly didn't really die in an American submarine in 1942, but the spirit of Johnston, who really did die on that vessel, convinced him that he had, and, believing it himself, he unconsciously manifested the symptoms of Johnston's trauma—hydrophobia and claustrophobia—to correspond with that belief. Therefore, what is actually nothing more than a ghost recalling events of its life on earth is inadvertently interpreted as a past-life memory, further confusing things in the paranormal and physical realms.

The chief advantage of this explanation is that it does account for Kelly's vivid memories and the wealth of detailed information. Certainly if one accepts the premise that the personality survives death, the notion that disembodied personalities (often referred to as ghosts) may be able, under ideal conditions, to communicate with people who are still living is not beyond the realm of possibility. In fact, it is the stuff that seances and psychic readings are made of, and part and parcel of the channeling and medium trade.

While an interesting argument from a reincarnationist perspective (and who knows how much ability a disembodied consciousness may have to communicate with the physical realm), the theory has a number of flaws. First, judging by the large number of past-life regressions performed over the years, it would require the cooperation of myriad spirits, all eager to recite their personal biographies through hypnotized people (without ever managing to tell the same story twice through two different people). When one considers that over the course of a single ninety-minute regression session a subject may recount several independent and distinctly unique past lives, the idea that this is the result of multiple disembodied entities lining up in an effort to tell their tale becomes increasingly problematic. Additionally, if past-life memories are simply the memories of deceased people, why do they always manage to die prior to the date of their host's birth? In other words, if I can pick up telepathically generated information from a person who died prior to my own birth, why can't I also occasionally pick up information from a spirit that died more recently as well? In effect, shouldn't I be occasionally recounting memories from time eras that existed within my own lifetime along with those that predate me? The timelines should stumble all over themselves, yet past-life memories are nothing if not careful about maintaining a sequence of past lives. Either past-life memories are sequential lives lived through the experience of a single soul or the spirits are remarkably adept at keeping good records so as not to step on each other's toes or repeat themselves.

Finally, since some people maintain debilitating phobias supposedly as a result of a past-life trauma (as was the case in Kelly's situation) it's not clear how the disembodied personality's own personal traumas could have manifested themselves within its living host's life for years before the regression therapy even began. Such a degree of telepathic empathy goes well beyond simple thought transference, and borders on the realm of possession (an entirely different phenomenon).

From the perspective of parapsychology, the theory also poses some problems as well. It's not that the psychic researcher discounts the possibility that disembodied souls may be able to communicate with the living—even to the point of the living not realizing that their thoughts are being directed from some outside source—but that the type of information being obtained is entirely different from what one usually gets from a past-life memory. Kelly wasn't simply relaying facts during hypnosis, but *feeling* very real emotions—fear, panic, confusion, anger, and so on—as well. It takes a high degree of empathy for the listener to feel the same emotions that the storyteller feels. Anyone who has ever listened to a person recount some terrifying event can attest to this; even though we can appreciate the fear another person may have felt, we cannot literally "feel" it in the same way he or she does. Could anyone who has never been trapped within a dark, flooding compartment of a sinking submarine *really* imagine how that feels and, even more so, be able to convincingly express those feelings, even under hypnosis? While I suppose there are those gifted professional actors out there who might be able to mimic such emotions, that's not the same as *owning* them yourself.

As such, while the disembodied-spirit hypothesis remains a distinct possibility, it seems unlikely. Communication obtained from a disembodied personality via a medium, channel, or through a direct seance is usually disjointed, dispassionate, and clearly external to the contactee. In this case, however, the Bruce Kelly/James Johnston link is too seamless to be anything but a past-life memory as told from a first person perspective. While I agree that there is good evidence to suggest that telepathy and other psychic phenomenon exist, and can also see how a disembodied personality might want to communicate with the living, it seems unnecessarily cumbersome to use ghosts to explain away reincarnation. They appear from all outward evidences to be two very different phenomenons, and while both (or neither) could be true, the one does not need to destroy the other in order to survive.

CONCLUSION

Either Bruce Kelly and Rick Brown are lying (or, at best, badly mistaken) when they recount the sequence of events in this case, or Kelly had knowledge about a man who died years before Kelly was born—knowledge he received through some means beyond the normal understanding of science. Occam's razor maintains that whatever explanation, *no matter how unlikely,* that takes into account *all* the known facts in a particular case *must* be the correct explanation. If the story of James the submarine man as recounted by Rick Brown is accurate, it is not explainable through coincidence, wish-fulfillment, fantasy, or cryptomnesia, leaving only reincarnation (or, perhaps, some other psychic mechanism beyond our current understanding) as the only possible explanation, no matter how unlikely that may seem. That this may be difficult for science and the rational mind to accept is not an indictment against reincarnation, but a flaw within the empirical sciences' unwillingness to explore new ideas in an objective fashion. The evidence that reincarnation may be a fact is abundant enough for any honest, objective researcher to affirm; that one refuses to even consider the possibility is less a statement about the nature of the universe than it is about the human propensity to see the world through a single set of lenses. It is not faith versus knowledge, but knowledge versus knowledge and, to a great degree, faith versus faith.

Part II

The Mechanics
of Reincarnation

IT HAS BEEN MY EXPERIENCE THAT DETRACTORS OF REINCARNATION ALMOST exclusively look to the empirical evidence in their efforts to refute the concept of continual rebirth. Past-life memories are something that can be weighed and judged for their historical accuracy; birthmarks are a curiosity that can be examined under the lens of scientific and medical scrutiny, and the veracity of each case can be closely examined under the harsh glare of a skeptical audience. But what is rarely examined by the skeptic is the underlying rationale behind reincarnation, the "mechanism" that makes it work. This is a point I find most curious, for it is upon the mechanics of reincarnation—its rationalism, methodology, and function—that the concept ultimately stands or falls. Just as it is not necessary to attack the fossil record if the process of evolution itself is irrational, attacking reincarnation on the weight of the scientific or veridical evidence is pointless if the underlying premise that drives the idea remains illogical.

Further, I've noticed that many critics of the concept genuinely are unaware of the superb rationalism that drives the process. Much as young earth creationists often appear to remain oblivious to the inner workings of evolution, so too do the critics of reincarnation often seem to remain obstinately unaware of what the process is trying to accomplish. In doing so, they are merely attacking the facade without doing any real damage to the inner structure.

As such, having looked at the evidence for and against reincarnation from an empirical, religious, and logical perspective, it is now necessary to leave the world of what can be known and delve into the world of what can only be surmised. This section will look at how reincarnation supposedly operates, and will discuss the rationale behind (along with the inherent strengths and weaknesses of) each position. It will also deal with questions concerning the nature of God, the definition of the soul, and ideas about time and space as they relate to the spiritual realm, along with a number of other issues that frequently arise when any discussion of postmortem survival is attempted. The ideas discussed here are not designed to convince the reader of any particular perspective, but merely offer various opinions to be pondered. It's likely—in fact, it's a certainty—that there are other ideas or hypotheses that I have overlooked or dealt with in a manner that is too superficial for some people's tastes, and for this I apologize. Unfortunately, in dealing with a subject of such an esoteric nature, there are naturally many ways of looking at how the process might work, not all of which I may be either familiar with or understand sufficiently to discuss intelligently. Hopefully, this shortcoming will not prove detrimental in presenting a good, comprehensive foundation from which to explore the question of reincarnation further. I only offer it to the thoughtful reader who wishes to understand the concept better; my goal is to show that reincarnation is not intellectually or rationally void, nor does it lack internal consistency. It is, in fact, quite logical once one can get past the notion of postmortem survival and view the universe through the lens of new possibilities and fresh perspectives, which is the only way genuine learning can take place.

chapter ten

WHY WE REINCARNATE

W hat is the purpose of life? This may seem like a simple question, but it has proven to be among the most difficult for human beings to answer—at least with any degree of certainty or conviction.

Some suggest that the point to life is to be happy, and I have no argument with that, as far as it goes. Yet how does one define happiness? Is it determined by the type of work one does, the size of home one owns, or by the amount of money, power, sex appeal, or even "fun" one has in life? Is life nothing more than simply filling our days with worthwhile pursuits (and, again, however we define "worthwhile") while avoiding pain and hardship, and then dying a quick and painless death after many years of living a rich, full life?

While there is certainly something to be said for this philosophy, I personally find that it leaves me empty. If there is no more to life than simply enjoying ourselves and hopefully being a little lucky, I wonder if it is worth all the trouble. We live our lives, we die, and in a few centuries from now (and, in most cases, probably far sooner) we will be forgotten. Everything we've learned, experienced, enjoyed, thought, dreamed, achieved, and imagined equals exactly nothing. As the writer of the Old Testament book Ecclesiastes put it, "All is a meaningless chasing after the wind" (Eccles. 2:11).

But what if life does have a greater point than merely the things we do with it? What if we are here to achieve something larger, something this brief earthly experience is only a small part of, and that's the case, what could it be?

Perhaps in the greater scheme of things a life lived well is sufficient in and of itself to realize life's purpose, but there is something within the human spirit that seems to strive for more. We are creatures of change, and that need and desire to change is always tugging at us, even if we aren't aware of it. There is a palpable desire in most people to be more than they are; to grow beyond themselves, so to speak, in an effort to become something bigger and better than what they already are. We may have achieved considerable success both professionally and financially, have a loving family and fine home, and have acquired myriad friends and hobbies to occupy our free time, but even then there is often still this sense that we are incomplete—an uncertain and often inexplicable discontentment that frequently leads to a feeling that we need to do or be more. It is this need to be *more* that is the sound the soul makes when it grows restless.

While the human personality tries to find contentment within the confines of each day's twenty-four hours, the soul is not so easily amused. It wants more than mere entertainment, and so it is always urging us on with a quiet insistence that points us in the direction of spiritual growth. Reincarnation is the mechanism that allows us to experience that growth and permits us the means to push beyond our current station in life, to explore new possibilities and realize new and never-before-imagined dramas, challenges, and dreams. It is this quest for spiritual evolution that fuels the rebirth machine, keeps us going, and gives significance to everything we do.

Actually, "evolution" is an unfortunate term to use here because it retains so many scientific ramifications. Within science and biology, evolution simply means adaptability; that is, the process by which a species will adapt in an effort to fit into a new environment. While sometimes this change results in the introduction of what might be considered a more "advanced" organism, this is only a by-product of evolution and not the point of it. It is actually designed to weed out those species, regardless of how "advanced" or "primitive" they may be, that are unable to adapt and allow to survive those species that can make the necessary alterations. As such, evolution, in the naturalist sense, is neither enhancing nor diminishing but a neutral process that rewards a species only if it is able to adapt to its new environment. It is not technically attempting to take the species to a higher plane of existence or specifically turn it into a more complex or advanced life form; it is simply finding a way for life to survive.

Within the realm of the spiritual world, however, evolution is more than simply changing or surviving, or, for that matter, even necessarily becoming smarter, wiser, or more compassionate—although these are inevitable byproducts of the process. Instead, it is realized in becoming more aware of one's divine nature and allowing that nature to experience new incarnations through which it may find its fullest expression. As such, a better term for the process might be "spiritual maturation" rather than "evolution," for, indeed, that is what reincarnation is attempting to achieve: the maturing of the soul. Just as a human goes from infancy to childhood to adolescence and, finally, to adulthood, the soul too is making the same journey, yet it realizes the process not over the course of a single lifetime but often imperceptibly over the course of dozens or, potentially, even hundreds of lifetimes. It is how the soul, in effect, "grows up."

This implies, of course, that certain people are further along in this process than others, and that would be correct. However, to be further along does not mean one is better than those who are not as far along. In the same way that it is no better to be a college student than a kindergartner, it is no "better" to be a spiritually advanced soul than a less advanced one. Each soul is moving at its own pace and according to its own timetable, following its own unique path toward its eventual maturity. There is no "right" way to proceed, or, for that matter, no "wrong" way. Each path is proper in that all of them are leading toward the realization of one's own divine nature.

That's not to say one path may be easier or less burdensome than another. Each path has its own consequences and rewards built into it. To be further along—that is, more "aware"—may be to experience a greater degree of peace and joy in one's life (though not necessarily fewer hardships) while to be early in the process is frequently to live in darkness and fear. One may be easier, at least by human standards, but "better" is a purely subjective opinion. It is all simply a matter of perspective, as well as a question of precisely what the soul is attempting to achieve.

But why does the soul need to mature at all, one might ask? Even if one is willing to accept the premise that the soul is a reflection of the divinity that animates it, why not simply accept it at whatever level of maturity it finds itself upon death and remain within that state? After all, if it is not better to be an advanced soul than it is to be an immature soul, what is the point of growing up? In effect, why not stay a child forever?

The human soul "grows up" because it will never settle for only a partial life experience. It is the very nature of the divine and, as such, the nature of the human spirit, to experience all there is to experience, and that is possible only by being put into a range of venues from which to observe and experience life. It may sound like fun to remain a child forever, but eventually the soul would grow bored with that single experience and long to experience more. Anyone who has ever watched children at play will notice how they usually take on "grown up" roles in their make-believe world, as if they are practicing at being the very adult they will one day become. For example, a girl may be content to cuddle her doll for the time being, but a part of her anticipates one day being a real mother with a real child to nurture. It's not that she's unhappy being a child pretending to be a mother; it's just that even she realizes her childhood is only fleeting and an incomplete expression of life. She longs to one day take on the mantle of adulthood even while she wiles away the hours at play because a part of her understands that to stay a child forever will not make her truly happy. By the time children mature into young adolescents they are often chafing at the opportunity to take on adult roles and responsibilities, along with all the benefits and even the consequences that doing so may entail. It may seem frightening to some degree, and a few children will delay it for as long as possible, but even the most pampered and timid teenager eventually understands that he or she must move on in order to have a full life experience.

But couldn't this spiritual maturation process be realized within the spiritual realm entirely without the need for repeated incarnations? Isn't heaven a place in which this process might be accomplished without all the inconvenience of coming "into the flesh" once again, to essentially start the process over and over?

While undoubtedly spiritual growth can be realized within the purely spiritual realm, it is difficult to imagine how one might realize the fullest range of experiences available to him or her without the context of the physical realm within which to play out an infinite number of roles. It is like saying that one can learn everything he or she needs to know about archeology in college without participating in hands-on field work; surely, even an encyclopedic knowledge cannot substitute for the experience of getting one's hands dirty on an archeological dig, nor is one going to make any significant new discoveries from within the halls of academia. Archeologists who have made a name for themselves and are universally recognized within the field are not sedentary but are often to be found covered in the layers of dust and grime acquired from many hours of digging and sifting dirt at some isolated, windswept and sunbaked dig. They may return to the museum to catalogue and study and evaluate what they've found, but eventually they are driven to return to the dusty digs once again in the never satisfied quest to learn more.

And so it is with the soul. It may have access to all the knowledge of the ages from within the timeless confines of the spiritual realm, but it is all purely academic and conceptual. The soul is looking to experience life, not imagine what it is like, and that requires some hands-on field work that only an incarnation into the flesh can provide. If we work from the assumption that heaven is a place of perfect love and peace and joy, how is it possible to truly experience any of these things without the hardship of our earthly incarnations to compare them with? It is only when subjected to a world of obstacles, trouble, and hard work that peace, rest, and joy acquire their significance; it is only when subjected to raw hatred, anger, and rage that love, compassion, and forgiveness demonstrate their true value.

The soul, you see, is on a journey back to its "source," which we call God, and the reason the soul moves toward God is twofold: first, it does so because it is naturally drawn to the Divine as a result of being a part of it, and, second, as it learns (or actually "relearns") that love is the only path to eternal bliss and the Creator is the source of that love, it looks to reunite itself with the source of all love. It does this, paradoxically, by experiencing what it is to be without love, for the soul can only experience love by putting itself in situations where it does not experience love, and that experience ultimately propels it toward the source of all love—that which we call God.

The best analogy I can think of is a child who does not understand why he or she cannot touch a hot stove. No amount of lecturing will help the child understand precisely what the danger is. It is not until the child's mother turns her back and the rebellious child places his or her hand on the heated metal that the child, at last, understands what "hot" means. In the same way, the soul (and, by extension, God) needs to experience hate to understand love, sadness to understand joy, and selfishness to understand selflessness. It may understand these concepts conceptually, but until it experiences that which it is not—namely hatred, sadness, and selfishness—it will never experience or understand these things in the practical world of absolute reality. And it must experience these things in order to exist in any meaningful context or else all of existence is realized purely on a theoretical level.

However, since there is such a vast range of experiences to realize, in the course of a single lifetime no one person (or "piece" of God) could begin to experience even a tiny fraction of all there is to perceive. We are all born into a specific set of parameters—a particular gender, class, religion, race, and so on—and provided with definable characteristics, skills, limitations, and flaws that will dictate the range of potential experiences we may encounter within the course of a single lifetime. Yet since these parameters all have tremendous limitations as well, we are able to sample only one small aspect of what it is to be human. It is akin to having only a single food to eat; no matter how good or nutritious the food may be, it is only one tiny taste of all the foods there are to sample. Therefore, in order for the soul to experience the fullest possible range of experiences—experiences that may be, for all practical purposes, infinite—it is necessary for us to undergo many incarnations, if not on earth, then as some sentient lifeform elsewhere in the universe.

Think of each cell in God's body being sent forth to experience the entire range of human emotion, and then each unique experience being added to those of the other cells to form a complete picture of what it is to exist. Each soul is one of those "cells" sent forth repeatedly to experience more and then return to the whole to enhance the total cumulative effect. We are, then, God's "experience sensors," providing God with the means necessary to experience itself.

The second reason we reincarnate is somewhat more prosaic: we reincarnate because there is nothing else we may do. It's like being a water molecule; we cannot choose to fall to the ground, to seep into the soil, to be swept up in the currents or tossed about by the waves, or even to evaporate beneath a warm sun, for each is the very unchanging nature of water itself. We are what we are, and what we do is experience life, within the context of both the physical and the spiritual realm.

That is the purpose of reincarnation. It is not something we do because it might be an interesting experience; it is something we do because there is nothing else for us to do, and in so doing we have an eternity to do, be, realize, and experience *everything*.

Painting Like One of the Great Masters

By way of an illustration, imagine that once there was a young man who dreamed of painting like one of the great masters. After years of admiring their work and studying their techniques, one day he decided to attempt to be a great painter himself. Obtaining all the necessary supplies when he felt he was finally ready to begin in earnest, he sat down to a fresh canvas and went to work.

He labored for months on his piece, painting and repainting as required and even reworking entire sections until finally, after great effort, he felt he was finished. He was happily admiring his work when one of the great masters he was attempting to emulate entered the room carrying a canvas of his own under one arm. Without a word, he sat his painting on an easel next to the young artist's and quietly took a seat next to him.

The young man was crestfallen by what he saw. He had imagined his painting to be on par with those of the greatest artists of the age, but now that he could compare the work side-by-side, he could see how amateurish and inept his painting was. Distraught, he poured out to the master how badly he had failed, how his sense of perspective was askew, how the composition was sadly lacking, how his use of color was entirely inadequate. The great master simply smiled and patiently waited for the young man to finish his damning self-critique.

"Do you wish to try again?" he asked gently.

The young man blinked back tears and stared at the old man. "I don't know," he answered uncertainly. "I want nothing more than to be a great painter myself, but I don't seem to have it in me. I've failed."

"No," the master gently chided. "You did not fail. You simply have not succeeded at achieving your goal yet. But be aware that a great painter already lives within you, waiting to emerge. You simply need to let him out. You must try again."

With that the master went on to encourage the young man, to point out his successes and review the things he had learned even through his failed attempt. Finally, the master offered him a fresh canvas and encouraged him to try again.

"Only do not paint the same picture," he instructed him patiently. "Try a completely new scene, a different landscape, another palette. Do not forget the lessons you have learned, but apply them to this new work."

Encouraged, the young man eagerly set about producing a second painting, enthusiastically applying the lessons he had learned from his earlier piece. After many months and several false starts, he finally managed to produce a second work that even he could clearly see was far superior to the first. Just as he was busy admiring his newest creation, the master walked in with his own freshly painted canvas once again, this one carrying a scene reminiscent of the one the young artist had painted. He placed it on an easel next to that of the young novice's for comparison.

Again, the young man was discouraged. Though he could see that this new painting was better than his previous work, it was still far from matching the master's skills. The young man discussed its flaws and inadequacies, and the master encouraged him to try again. The novice agreed, not only because of the master's unwavering patience and encouragement, but because he recognized he had indeed improved and believed he could do better if he tried again.

So for a third time the novice, who by now had been striving toward his goal for many years, started a new painting. Again, after several false starts, he finally produced another work, this one his finest to date, and once again, no sooner had he applied the final brushstroke than like clockwork the master appeared once again with his own similar piece for a comparison. This time, however, the young man was not so crestfallen. He could see he was still not at the level of the master's work, but he could also see, as the master pointed out himself, that he was getting close.

A fourth, fifth, and sixth canvas followed, and each time the young man refined his work until it began to mimic that of the great master himself. One day, after many years of laboring on his greatest piece, the master again appeared to examine the work, placing his own painting alongside the new piece. This time, however, the two pieces were equally perfect, though not identical. Neither the student nor his teacher could find anything that required refinement.

"You have no need to paint any longer, my student," the master said quietly. "You are now a master yourself."

The aspiring painter at first wept tears of joy at the fact he had at last achieved his goal, but then stopped abruptly. "I have no need to paint anymore?" he asked, somewhat confused. "But why? Now that I can paint like one of the great masters, why should I stop?"

"Because there is nothing more you can learn. You have achieved mastery."

"But what shall I do?" he asked. "I have worked all my life for this moment. What else can I do?"

"Indeed," the master replied. "What else can you do? You have three paths open to you. You may stop painting and simply rest in the knowledge that you have achieved the mastery you always sought and labored for, you may continue to paint masterpieces until you have filled the world with your beauty, or you may choose the most difficult road and show others how to paint as a master yourself. Each path is equally good noble. Which shall it be?"

The artist thought hard for a moment. "I choose to show others."

The old master smiled and nodded, pleased that the new master understood.

That's how it is with reincarnation. Each incarnation is a fresh canvas upon which we place the brushstrokes of life. Sometimes we choose to begin again with a new canvas. Sometimes our canvas is destroyed before we've had a chance to complete it, though usually we manage to finish the piece, and, when we die—or leave this current incarnation—we have the opportunity to appraise our work and judge for ourselves what we have placed upon that canvas. Quickly we see where we have "failed" and, conversely, where we have succeeded by judging our own piece against the perfect canvas we call God. Eventually, once we are ready to try again, we will receive a fresh canvas and begin once more. The old painting is forgotten and buried; in fact, so intent are we on painting this new picture, we scarcely recall the old one at all. Even so, the lessons it provided remain within us to become an element of this new creation.

Finally, one day, our personal masterpiece is finished. That's when we will decide whether to stop painting and break the wheel of multiple rebirths, to go on painting vastly different landscapes on a new canvas through numerous incarnations, or to teach others. The choice will be ours, just as it has been from the beginning and always shall be.

chapter eleven

DEFINING THE SOUL

I suspect that most people believe they understand what the soul is—even if they may not personally believe they have one themselves. However, it is my discovery that, like the term "God," it tends to be defined in many different ways, so for the benefit of this study it will be necessary to "nail down" a single definition so that we may understand the process of rebirth in a more consistent manner.

In basic terms, the soul is the energy of our essence or, more simply, our true self. It is that part of us that exists outside of and apart from the body, and it is both inherently immortal and eternal. It is that element of ourselves that transcends our human experiences and at the same time reflects those experiences back into each new personality we take on. It is more than mere intellect and personality, but is, in fact, the very heart of who we are as people, with all our dreams, wisdom, humor, compassion, and love intact. The soul is who we are on the inside, not what we want others to see on the outside—the true us stripped of all pretense and role playing.

While most people are probably willing to allow me this definition, that is where agreement usually ends. The problem becomes that even if we can agree that the soul is the nonphysical aspect of ourselves, that still doesn't tell us precisely what it is. Where does it come from? What is it made of? Is it a created thing, or is it a part of something much larger than itself?

Within Western religions, the soul is generally considered a created "thing" that is brought into existence by God to animate his creation. As such, it is not usually considered eternal (that is, it has not always existed) and, according to some philosophies, it may not even be necessarily immortal, though this is the minority view. Normally, it is generally thought to exist in either a state of eternal bliss (heaven) or within a world of darkness and regret (hell) after leaving the earthly plain, though there are also those who believe that the disembodied soul exists within a type of perpetual, unconscious limbo world or perhaps within some sort of dream state. Some even imagine that it remains tied to the physical realm in some capacity, at least for a time, to exist as a type of ghostly entity. In effect, there are as many opinions of what becomes of the soul after death as there are religions.

Within Eastern religions, however, the soul is not simply some ball of created, conscious energy floating about in linear time and space somewhere, but an integral part of something larger and far more vast than we can begin to imagine. To the Hindu and the Buddhist, the soul is part of a much larger "super soul" in much the same way that a single, tiny tongue of flame is an element of a much larger inferno. In some traditions, this larger soul might be better understood as another term for what we might call God, making the soul, in effect, nothing less than a part of God. In fact, it *is* God, collectively speaking, in the same way that all the water molecules in the sea collectively make up the greater ocean.

Of course, to the Western mind such a position would be considered untenable. The soul may be similar in nature to the Creator, but it is still considered a separate element apart from God, which, while being formed "in the image" of God, would not be considered an integral part of God, much less God in both essence and nature. That would be taking the definition too far, at least to some people's way of thinking.

However, to understand reincarnation it is necessary for the soul's relationship to the Divine to be firmly established, for it is this relationship between the soul and God that is the rationale and, indeed, the mechanism behind rebirth. To divorce the soul from its source is to miss the entire point of the exercise. While it's entirely possible for a created, individualized soul of the Western variety to reincarnate—perhaps for the purpose of purging itself of the last vestiges of sin so it is at last worthy of being in the Creator's presence—it is understanding the soul from the Eastern perspective that pulls the concept together in a more coherent, cohesive manner. As such, before we can go any further with our discussion, it is first necessary to rethink how we define God, for since the soul and the Divine are intricately linked, to understand the one is to understand the other.

I am aware that I am treading on sacred ground here, and the concept of God I introduce in these pages may be entirely too alien for many to accept, but even those who are unwilling to accept the Eastern definition of divinity can still come away with a good working knowledge of how the process is supposed to work, and that, at least, might prove beneficial down the road. At a minimum, it should at least give one an appreciation for how varied and diverse the definition of God can be, forcing us to appreciate the rich tapestry of tradition that makes up the belief systems of this planet's seven billion residents.

DEFINING THE DIVINE

Perhaps one of the most remarkable aspects of reincarnation is that one doesn't need to believe in God to believe in reincarnation. For example, the Jainists of India, a sect of Brahmanism, do not believe in God at all, but simply imagine that souls perpetually move in and out of physicality with no particular purpose in mind. To them, the soul has always

existed and always will, and requires no originating source nor a particular purpose behind reincarnation beyond simply being the process by
which we exist.

It's probably safe to say that most reincarnationists do believe in God,
though, like the word "soul," how they define this entity, being, or "force"
may vary widely.

There are two basic ways of perceiving God that most people on the
planet who consider themselves theists generally adhere to. The first, and
the one most comfortable to the Western mindset, is known as the
"watchmaker" God. In this concept, God is perceived as transcendent, that
is, a spirit or "personality" who exists outside of and apart from "his" (God
is invariably thought of as male in Western traditions) creation like some
great benevolent monarch overseeing a vast kingdom. He is thought to be
a conscious, moral agent of unlimited power and intellect who, though
existing entirely apart from time and matter, uses both in his ongoing
quest to create and, when necessary, destroy. He is "first cause" or, more
concisely, that from which everything else emanates, and there is nothing
that exists that he did not first conceive of and create through the sheer
power of his will. To the watchmaker God, the universe was brought
into existence in the distant past and will end at some future date, at
which point time will come to an end and the great "experiment" will be
concluded.

The second concept about God held by a substantial percentage of
the world's population is that which might be known as the "evolving"
God. From this perspective, to speak of "God" (if one were to use that
term) is to refer to all that is, all that has ever existed, and all that ever
will exist. God is not a someone or something that creates things out of
nothingness, but rather God *is* the creation itself. Every molecule, every
cell, and every atom in the universe is part of the vast and infinite
"body" of God. It is eternal and immortal, has always existed and will
always exist, without beginning or end. To the Eastern mind, then, God
does not "bring forth" the universe and all within it; "it" *is* the universe
and all that is within it.

The most frequent objection to this perspective is that if God is not a conscious, unique, and separate being with human characteristics and tendencies, but rather a force of immense energy (in fact, energy itself), this makes God not a "person" as we might understand the term, but, in effect, an "it." Aside from sounding a bit insulting (at least to some people's way of thinking), this is tantamount to saying that God is nothing more than an energy force, something like gravity or perhaps cosmic radiation, and to worship such a God would be akin to worshipping the sun.

Such an objection is, of course, quite valid, but also demonstrates a marked lack of understanding of Eastern concepts of divinity. What the Westerner is railing against here is but one ancient concept about God known as *pantheism,* a perception that does hold God to be simply an impersonal, amoral force that permeates everything and gives it life. In fact, it *is* life itself, broken down into its most basic elements, but existing codependently and eternally as part of a greater whole, and as such, it is not something that can be related to personally in any real sense. Yet there is another perception of God held to within Eastern thought that does allow for the existence of a type of divine personality, which is closer to what I am suggesting here. Known as *panentheism,* it is similar to *pantheism* in perceiving everything as a part of God, but it also believes that this force *does* have consciousness and is fully capable of being interacted with. The *panentheist* works from the premise that thought is a form of energy and assumes therefore that if all energy exists as a single unit, it stands to reason that all conscious thought does so as well, forming a type of "collective" or universal consciousness we all tap into, either consciously or unconsciously, as a byproduct of our existence. In effect, it makes the universe itself a conscious organism, and it is this consciousness that we label "God" that serves as the source from which the individual soul emerges.

Which concept one embraces becomes vitally important in understanding the nature of the soul as well as the rationale behind reincarnation. From the perspective of the "watchmaker" God, the soul is not a part of God, but a creation of his, much like the universe itself. At best, we reflect his divine nature in some ways, much as a painting will reflect the skills of its painter or a son will reflect the personality of his father, but for the most part we are things apart from God. To the evolving God, however, the human soul is an emanation of itself—a molecule, if you will—of the greater consciousness that permeates all matter and energy throughout the universe. It is not something that God creates and then sends on its way, but something that exists and has always existed as part of God itself. As such, a soul can be neither created nor destroyed any more than God itself could be, for the one is an integral part of the other. In essence, just as a tree could not exist without each molecule that makes it up, so too God could not exist without each soul. They are inseparable.

The implications of this are profound. Since the universe itself is in a constant state of change, then God too must be constantly changing, making God, in effect, an evolving personality that uses reincarnation to realize this continual process of growth (in marked contrast to the unchanging, transcendent watchmaker God of Western religion). Which position one takes on the nature of God will go far in determining whether he or she can embrace reincarnation as a valid belief system, or whether he or she must discard it as, at best, an unnecessary appendage to understanding the nature of reality. To the person who believes in a God that exists apart from and separate from its own creation, reincarnation seems wholly impractical—at least insofar as traditional Western religion is concerned. Yet for the person who can imagine a God that is thoroughly integrated into the very essence of all life, reincarnation is not only reasonable but almost a requirement. In fact, it would be difficult to imagine it not being a major part of the equation, when one considers the nature of immanent divinity itself.

The Illusion of Separateness

Before leaving the issue of defining God, however, it is first necessary to go off on a short tangent in an effort to clear up some confusion. Basically the problem is that if each of us is inherently a part of a greater divine soul, then why does God *seem* to be so separate from ourselves? Clearly, God seems to be interacting *with* his creation, not as if it were a *part* of himself, but as if he were external to it. As such, the argument might be made that the belief in the unity of all life is purely an illusion and that in fact we are actually all unique and individual creations emanating from the same source, thus bringing the entire need for rebirth into serious question.

So how do we deal with this disparity? In fact, we don't, for the truth of the matter is that both perceptions are, in a way, correct. We are all a part of a much larger universal essence yet we perceive ourselves and God for that matter as separate because it is the very perception of separateness that provides us the opportunity to understand the true singular, all-encompassing nature of the Divine. The illusion of a God who exists "out there" is a necessary fantasy we must maintain due to our limited ability to comprehend "him" or "her" in a way that we can intellectually fathom. To put it crudely, we must turn God into little "bite-sized" pieces because we aren't capable of digesting him/her/it whole.

It might be argued that this piecemeal approach to God results in confusion and a multitude of contradictory and sometimes unsettling images of the Divine. For instance, while one person may perceive God as kind and loving and faithful, another may perceive him as angry, cruel, and judgmental; yet how can he be both at the same time? Doesn't this tendency to want to craft God in our own image reduce our understanding of the Divine rather than enhance it?

To some degree this is true, but our understanding of God is determined by our own level of spiritual maturity, which is the reason for such a wide range of perceptions in regard to the Divine. We simply craft God in *our* image and will continue to do so until we might grow beyond the need for such images and move toward a more mature understanding of the Divine. But this is not entirely a bad thing, for in permitting us the luxury of crafting God in our image, he allows us to see the underlying sameness that permeates all images of God that we maintain. This is not only to be expected, but could even be considered an important part of the process of understanding the vastness of the Divine, who truly can be all things to all people.

Yet simply because we are often unclear and even contradictory in our definition of God, that does not mean that our perceptions are entirely wrong. The analogy of light is a perfect—and apt—means of expressing this truth. If we were to perceive the full range of the spectrum of light as it really is, it would appear as a single point of brilliant white light. There would be no reds or blues or greens, for when mixed together they appear as white. Through the prism we know as separateness, we have to break the white light down in order to make out the various colors of the spectrum before we can perceive any single color. As such, even though red is but one part of the original white light, once we can see it as a separate color we can then appreciate it as a unique individual element of the greater whole, and even compare it to all the other colors in the spectrum.

As such, while recognizing that God is the sum of all, we are compelled to "break" him/her/it down into smaller parts in order to perceive it. This is the reason for the multitude of religions on our planet; God is simply too big to be seen in his entirety and so our natural inclination is to personalize the Divine into something we can understand and comprehend. Enlightenment, then, is simply the ability to perceive the "light" in its totality and recognize that one can learn from any of the various hues or colors into which it's been broken down. The colors, then, are not truly illusions, for they do exist within the greater whole, but they are isolated simply so we can perceive them within the context of our limited perspective. We need the illusion of separateness, then, in order to have some context within which to understand unity and, with it, the Divine.

RECOGNIZING OUR INHERENT DIVINITY

It may be overwhelming to consider that each of us is, in essence, divine, but without that realization, reincarnation has no real point. We reincarnate in order to experience life in all its facets so that the Divine within may experience life in all its facets as well. This is not to diminish God by making his experiences dependent upon our own, but to enlarge God to encompass the vast range of human life (and, no doubt, all sentient life) experiences. Nor is it blasphemous to declare our own divinity, for in doing so we simply understand our source and purpose for being here. In fact, the danger to humanity lies in failing to embrace that reality and so diminishing the divine in the process. It is only when we consider ourselves separate from the Creator that we live in darkness. Recognizing our oneness with the source of all life—not as an artificial construct of the Divine but as a vibrant, living element of it—is what gives us the power to experience the love and joy that is God. Teach people that they are born a sinner apart from God and they will live down to that level; tell them they are children of the Divine and they will invariably rise to the occasion and realize the light that lives within. Anything less would be to dishonor the Divine and ourselves in the process.

If it is necessary to perceive God as something separate from ourselves in order to comprehend any element of his divinity, then it stands to reason that it is also necessary that each soul see itself as a separate and unique element apart from all other souls in order to appreciate the experience of life itself. Therein lies the great paradox that Eastern mysticism speaks of: just as the need to imagine God as a separate thing from ourselves is necessary to truly begin to perceive God in his completeness, so too do we individualized souls require the same illusion of separateness to understand and experience what we are, both in essence and substance. In effect, while we are a part of each other, it is essential that we forget that fact if we are to experience anything outside of a purely conceptual basis. It is this very illusion of separateness that permits us—and, by extension, God—to discern what we call good from evil or right from wrong, for each can be understood and experienced only within the context of *what they are not*. Without the illusion of individuality to work from, good and evil, for example, could only be understood conceptually. But in order to experience the full range of existence, with all its infinite benefits and consequences, life must be not merely conceived, but realized practically. This is why we need separateness. We simply cannot experience anything without it.

And that is what the soul is and does. It is an individualized part of the Divine that exists purely to experience life in all its many facets. Who we are, then, is merely a reflection of what facet of himself God wishes to experience. We are "spirit stuff" on an adventure; the Divine Spark on holiday setting out on that remarkable journey we call physicality or, more simply, life itself. That is the machine behind the process and the very point of reincarnation, as well as the rationale behind every step we take and every path we choose to explore. It is God experiencing himself through us, and it is the adventure of a lifetime or, in the case of reincarnation, many lifetimes.

chapter twelve

Soul versus Personality

E ven if we accept the notion that our soul is an element of the Divine, that still doesn't answer everything. For example, if the same soul takes on a completely new and different personality each time it reincarnates, what happens to that part of us that doesn't "come back?" In effect, what becomes of the personality once it is no longer required and the soul moves on?

Before we go further, however, it is first necessary to carefully define precisely what a personality is and how it differs from the soul. We still tend to think of the soul and the personality (or ego) as interchangeable terms, yet that is where the confusion starts. The soul and the personality are *not* the same thing. Though personality is a reflection of the soul that animates it, the soul is more than merely another term for the personality. This is especially apparent when one considers that within the context of reincarnation, the soul apparently is capable of exhibiting myriad personalities over many lifetimes, many of which are frequently quite different from each other in terms of basic nature and disposition. It is this fact that leads us to the assumption that the personality is a temporary construct of the soul, albeit a construct that perfectly reflects the host soul that animates it. As such, whatever exists within the furthest reaches of the soul, be it love, kindness, compassion, or the more base elements of human nature such as selfishness, greed, jealousy, and hatred, the personality will reflect it. Each personality, then, demonstrates where on the spiritual journey the soul is, or, more correctly, reflects its level of spiritual maturity in much the same way a thermometer tells the ambient temperature of the room that one is in.

Yet that is only one part of the personality's role in the process, and not even the most important one. The personality is what gives the soul the ability to experience life within the physical realm of time and space. Without a manifest personality, the soul is unable to interact with the world, for the physical plane of existence is a foreign country to it. In a way, the personality is like a diving suit that permits the swimmer to descend deep beneath the waters without being crushed or drowned; a feat that would be otherwise impossible without such a device. In effect, the soul simply can't manifest itself on our plane of existence without an "ego suit" within which to roam about.

Of course, one might ask the question of how, if the soul is a part of the greater divine soul and, as such, presumably a thing of light and love, it can manifest the occasional negative or "wicked" soul. In other words, if our personality is a reflection of our soul's level of spiritual maturity and our soul is a part of God, how can we be anything other than what God inherently is? As such, where would traits such as anger, ambition, lust, greed, or hatred come from if our personality is simply reflecting the soul within us?

The answer is that while the base nature of all souls consists of love and light, in younger souls[1] that nature can be suppressed and indeed must be occasionally suppressed, for the fullest range of human experiences to be realized. In other words, a soul might move into darkness

---

1 We will examine the issue of soul "age" in more detail in the next chapter.

simply to experience what darkness is, and manifest a dark personality as a result. This might be either intentional or purely a result of the immaturity of an especially young soul, and may be affected by other factors such as environment, upbringing, culture, and personal soul temperament. As such, while souls may be inherently things of love, they may forget (or purposely choose to forget) that fact, so they may have a wider range of experiences (and they may also fully interact with other souls in their journeys).

What's important to recognize is that it is the soul that powers the personality, and the personality then becomes a reflection of the soul that is animating it. The two aspects work hand in hand to form a complete and total life experience, be it positive or negative, in a symbiotic and mutually beneficial dance of life.

Perhaps the best analogy is that of a light bulb. In and of itself, the light bulb is a fairly useless (and quite fragile) object. Once it is plugged into a light socket and energized by electricity, however, it becomes a very useful and, indeed, an almost indispensable item. In the same way, electricity in and of itself is not very useful (and, in fact, is even highly dangerous and destructive), yet once it is harnessed it becomes extremely valuable. As such, the electricity and the light bulb need each other for both to be of any practical use. Despite the fact that neither has much in common, however—the one is purely physical and the other exists as pure energy—when combined they form a perfect merging of matter and energy.

The soul and personality work together in a similar way: the soul is the divine current that courses through the universe powering everything; the personality is that which the soul energizes. The difference between the soul and personality and electricity and the light bulb, however, is that unlike electricity, the soul is a conscious entity (in fact, it *is* consciousness itself) and the personality is, unlike the light bulb, immortal. Even though it appears that the light bulb has a very short life span from the perspective of linear time, both essentially exist forever from the perspective of eternity. It is all simply a matter of one's point of view.

But what exactly is the difference between personality and the soul? Which is really "calling the shots"?

Imagine that the personality is like a CD that the soul is using to record a lifetime of experiences. It starts out blank and is, over the course of maybe eighty years, filled to capacity with a lifetime of events, memories, thoughts, dreams, and experiences. Yet these things are happening to the personality—to the CD—while the soul is simply using the CD to record the experiences; in effect, trapping each experience within linear time. This is necessary because the soul itself exists outside of time and cannot genuinely experience anything until it enters into linear time, which it does through the personality. The personality, then, is simply collecting data that the soul will process and learn from throughout the course of each incarnation.

What is interesting about this is that through each experience manifesting itself within linear time and space, the soul is impacted by every event, experience, and person that comes into its frame of reference. It is shaped by the culmination of a lifetime of experiences and a host of environmental factors that align themselves to determine the soul's adventures and define its personality type while in this incarnation. However, the resultant personality, while influenced by environmental factors and certain experiences, does not depart from the primary characteristics of the soul that energizes it. In other words, a soul that is basically caring will remain so despite whatever negative environmental factors it may encounter in any given incarnation. As such, a "'good" person in this life is a "good" and wise soul; a "bad" person is a reflection of an immature soul that has only begun its adventure. It's not the personality that is good or bad, but the soul that empowers it that makes it one or the other.[2]

---

2 In truth, there is no such thing as a "good" or "bad" soul; I only use these terms because they are embedded within our cultural understanding. In reality, there are only souls that have come a long way in their journey and souls that have just started out.

The "Death" of the Personality?

So what becomes of the personality—the "recording device" of the soul—upon death? Does the soul, as some believe, separate from the personality and move on while the personality, like the body within which it was encased, is discarded and disposed of? Or does it live on forever in some way, intact with its lifetime of experiences?

Western religion generally maintains that the soul and personality live on together throughout eternity in an unchanging and unchangeable state, while Eastern religion, and reincarnation, maintain that they separate upon death, with the soul manifesting another entirely fresh and unique personality and the old personality falling by the wayside, which is felt to be necessary for the soul to continue its spiritual progress. This is thought to be necessary because the external personality, being largely artificial and contrived in any case, can often impede spiritual growth, and, so that the soul may mature, it must be left behind in order for the soul to be truly set free, like a butterfly that has outgrown its need for its cocoon. To retain complete memories of a past life would not only hinder the process dramatically, but keep us living in a past that no longer exists in linear time. As such, all memories of a past life must by exorcised from our present consciousness in order for the process to proceed.

Unfortunately, by declaring the personality (or ego) to be a temporal aspect of a soul to be discarded upon death while the soul continues on to its next incarnation is to kill the experience of a life just lived. As such, the personality must live on in some capacity in order for the soul to maintain the life lessons that personality experienced. But how can it exist once it is separated from the soul?

Repeater versus Feeder Souls

There are two theories to consider. The first teaches that the soul is distinctly separate from the various personalities that emanate from it. While the single soul may produce countless personalities that incarnate into the flesh, it is larger than any single one of them and is, in fact, far more expansive than we can begin to appreciate. In effect, while a single soul may manifest many personalities, no single personality is the complete reflection of the larger, underlying soul. For the purposes of this discussion, we will refer to this idea as the "feeder soul" concept in that the soul is the source or "feed" for all the various personalities that emanate from it, yet without being uniquely identified with any one of them.

In the feeder soul concept, we have the analogy of a tree that is constantly putting out a new outcropping of leaves, each of which represents an individual human personality. Just as a regular tree has leaves that serve the purpose of providing the tree with the much needed photosynthesis it requires to grow, so too does each personality provide the soul with the life experiences it needs to grow. The "leaves" of each personality may be eventually shed, but the experiences each leaf provided went into enhancing and maturing the "tree" of the soul itself. As such, even if the individual personality no longer exists, the essence of what it was and what it experienced during its brief sojourn on earth remains an integral part of the main tree.

A good way to imagine this is to see the tree as a library, with all the individual books on its shelves the cumulative knowledge acquired by hundreds of personalities over the ages. As each new personality is introduced into the realm of the physical universe, it "writes" another book that is eventually stored in the main library and will remain there long after the original author is dead. Therefore, the complete essence of what that personality was remains eternally inscribed within the pages of the countless volumes lining each shelf, and in that sense it exists forever.

If the soul and personality do part ways, however, this does not mean that the conscious personality that the soul previously manifested must necessarily dissipate. It is possible that the essence of that previous personality may continue to live on within the context of the spiritual realm, perhaps existing in a state of timelessness (much like a long-deceased movie star continues to exist forever on celluloid). In other words, the personality, with all its conscious memories, knowledge, and abilities, and no longer shackled by linear time, may simply exist outside of time within a world of the eternal "now." This need not be an unpleasant existence, for how we experience this state may be largely an element of our nature; if we are generally happy and content, this state will reflect that and the experience may well be a pleasant one. If, on the other hand, one is by nature cynical and judgmental, this "limbo" state could be unpleasant, but no more so than the former life itself proved to be. Which it is depends on the person. Additionally, it is entirely possible that this disincarnate personality may continue to grow in this environment just as it did on earth, providing hope to the "wicked" personality that it may be healed and restored to its natural state of love and light.

As for conscious memories of friends and spouses in past lives, this would seem to be a problem, for we would all like to be reunited with loved ones after we die. Whether we may interact with the disincarnate personalities of those we have known before or are simply responding to memories of them is unclear, however. Certainly, it would seem that within the realm of pure spirit all personalities exist as one and are quite capable of interacting with each other. Given that such interaction is occurring outside of the confines of linear time, they might well be eternal in nature, at least from the perspective of each individual personality.

The curious thing about this scenario is imagining what becomes of each of our past-life personas. It seems that if all human personalities exist within the single moment of "now" within the spiritual realm, each of our past (and future?) personalities should "bump" into each other and even interact in some ways in a single point of time. If this is the case, however, is it possible that all of these personalities could be ultimately integrated into a complete and utterly astonishing "super ego" made up of literally hundreds or thousands of personalities? Imagine suddenly remembering everyone you ever knew throughout the course of a thousand lifetimes or every thought, experience, and scrap

of knowledge acquired over twenty thousand years, purified and sancti-
fied, and now subject to instant recall with no more difficulty than it
takes to recall one's current phone number. The possibilities stagger the
imagination.

The other theory, known as the "repeater soul" concept, works from
the premise that the soul and personality do not separate at death, but
each personality becomes an embedded "memory" of the soul itself. In
other words, unlike the feeder soul, the repeater soul does not simply
reproduce various personalities and send them to experience physicality,
but instead it experiences the physical realm personally and individually.
In this concept, we remain essentially the same person through all of
our incarnations, even though we may reincarnate into a different gender or race. As such, if your basic nature is essentially giving and compassionate, that would manifest or "print" itself onto each succeeding
personality, making it possible for one to reincarnate with a similar personality each time (though a part of that would be determined by environment and experiences). In essence, in your next incarnation you may
be much like the person you are in this one—older and wiser, it is
hoped, but essentially you will still be the same person.

This concept corresponds more closely to the analogy of an actor
who takes on many roles, learning and growing with each new part
while discarding one role and taking on the next in quick succession.
While "the actor" may start out weak and uncertain, as it (the soul)
takes on more roles (that is, incarnations) it grows in knowledge and
wisdom until it eventually becomes a talented performer. In the same
way we all change roles throughout our lives—from infant to child to
adolescent to adult to spouse to parent—so too does each role come
and go, and, while the individual roles and most of the lines that were
spoken have long since been forgotten (or, more correctly, cast off), the
actor behind the roles continues to live on. Just as we are no longer the
person we were thirty, twenty, ten, or even five years ago, so too does
the soul change as it moves on to new and more challenging parts, leaving the old roles—as instructive as they may have been—in the past. It is

a thoroughly forward-looking soul who is seeking only to grow closer to the Divine, and sees each role it plays in that process simply as stepping stones along the way.

The problem with the repeater soul concept, however, is that it elicits confusion. For example, if I were John in eighteenth-century England, Sasha in nineteenth-century Russia, and Carl in twentieth-century America, which is the *real* me? In the feeder soul concept, they would all be unrelated expressions of the real soul that I am, but with the repeater concept they are all related expressions of me that, in effect, supersede each other. In other words, with each new incarnation I reinvent myself, effectively erasing the old chalkboard that contained my previous life and writing a new life on its recently cleaned surface. As such, John, Sasha, and Carl no longer exist except within my memories, and even then only within those memories I choose to access.

Conclusion

I don't know if this has been more useful than confusing, but no one ever said that the mechanics of reincarnation are simple; only that they are useful to understanding the nature of reality. Which notion the reader finds more personally useful is, of course, a matter of preference. I personally believe the repeater soul concept more closely corresponds to what we see played out in regression therapy, for the current personality seems much more likely to be affected, either negatively or positively, by a previous personality only if the two are one and the same. With the feeder soul concept I find it more difficult to explain how a trauma that impacts one personality would easily be transferred onto another entirely new and separate personality. While it makes sense that the feeder soul might well acquire considerable knowledge from its many personalities and then shape the next incarnation from these experiences, it seems to me that one would risk suffering from numerous traumas experienced by multiple past-life personas if this were the case. However, this may only be a limitation of my understanding, and I will not insist on either concept being the correct one. I would not be surprised, either, if in some strange way both concepts were true to some degree, especially since we're dealing with that which takes place outside the venue of linear time and space and resides within the mysterious world—from our perspective—of the spiritual realm.

chapter thirteen

How Souls Interact: Old Souls and Soul Mates

After all of this talk about being individualized "bits of God" masquerading about as human beings, one question remains: "How is it that we can't seem to get along with the other 'bits of God' out there?" It seems that if we are all a part of the larger cosmic consciousness we call God, we should get along considerably better. The fact that we frequently don't seems to argue against the notion.

As discussed earlier, the reason some souls seem peaceful, loving, and compassionate while others appear cynical, selfish, and hateful lies not in their basic nature, but in their spiritual age or maturity level. Just because we are all elements of the Divine doesn't mean we are all on the same level of maturity. It's all a matter of how many incarnations or life experiences we've lived and how we've chosen to incorporate the lessons those experiences have taught us into our present personalities. As a result, we have the issue of what we commonly refer to as "old souls" and "new souls" to consider; these are terms we will now examine in some detail in an effort to better understand why the world is the way it is.

Actually, the term "old soul" is not an unfamiliar one, even within cultures that do not embrace multiple lives (in which case it is usually used as a term when referring to a wise or knowledgeable person). Within reincarnation, however, it generally refers to a person who possesses a "seasoned" soul that has been around for a while and seems more spiritually mature and wiser than most.

But how could one soul be "older" than another? If all souls emanate from God and God is, by definition, eternal, there can be, in reality, no such thing as a new or an old soul. All souls are technically the same age.

Obviously, it is not a question of chronological age, but of spiritual maturity. Clearly, there are those who are further along in their quest than others; those who have made more journeys into physicality than most and are more experienced or practiced in their spiritual understanding and awareness. This, however, is as one would expect, for in order for God to experience all aspects of life, it is necessary for God to see through the eyes of both the wise and the frightened with equal clarity. Anything less would be to see only in one dimension and miss the point of the exercise entirely.

Voyage to the Bottom of the Sea

To better illustrate this process, we might imagine the sky to be a metaphor for the spiritual realm and the ocean a metaphor for the physical world of linear time and space.

Within the sky exists all manner of various gasses that collectively make up what we call air. The air exists everywhere and is not confined to one part of the sky; in fact, since it is air that makes up the atmosphere in its entirety, the air exists as a single unified entity without beginning or end. For our purposes, we will also imagine that this air has always existed and will always exist, making it is indestructible and eternal in all respects.

However, for the air to experience itself for what it is, it must separate from the sky for a time and, in essence, become that which it is not naturally. It must be apart from what it is in order to experience that which it is, and it does this by choosing to enter the depths of the great ocean (that is, the world of physically) where it will no longer be light and free and unified, but will experience heaviness, limitation, and aloneness. Driven by a massive pump through high-pressure hoses to an outlet on the sea floor thousands of feet below the surface, there the soul emerges in the cold blackness of a sunless, airless world in the form of a bubble. Leaving the hose under great force (the birth experience), the air, now encased within its own bubble, immediately begins making its way back to the surface, which it does naturally as a result of being lighter than the surrounding water and naturally buoyant. Apart from the fact that it is naturally drawn to the surface, it also chooses to make the journey to the surface because it desires to return to the freedom and pure ecstasy of sky and sun.

However, before it can reach its home, it must first pass through many thousands of feet of inky blackness, during which time it will experience its separateness from the sky above and, indeed, from the thousands of other bubbles traveling alongside it toward the surface. In this unfamiliar and uncomfortable state, it will experience what it is to be utterly alone within its tiny bubble, and so, for the first time, know fear and hopelessness.

It is not an entirely unpleasant experience, however, for eventually, as the bubble continues to rise toward the surface, it begins to notice the darkness melt away as sunlight begins to penetrate the depths. Further, as its surroundings brighten, the air trapped within the bubble begins to understand its true nature and soon realizes that it no longer requires the limiting, encumbering bubble that has surrounded it all its life. Eventually it comes to look forward to shedding its restrictive though not entirely unpleasant prison and returning to its natural state. Perhaps as a result of this realization, the air within the bubble notices the water begin to shimmer with beautiful shafts of azul green and turquoise as the surface rapidly approaches, and for the first time the bubble begins to appreciate the breathtaking beauty of the ocean around it.

Finally the bubble reaches the surface and, its shape no longer determined and maintained by the weight of the water pushing at it from all sides, bursts and releases the air inside of it. At last free of its encompassing bubble, the air rejoins the rest of the atmosphere in joy and jubilance, excited to be home once again, its long journey from the depths of the ocean complete. Eventually it may choose to make the journey again, but for the time being it is at peace and enveloped in a world of love all its own.

Of course, this isn't a perfect analogy, for even within the atmosphere air is made up of individual atoms of various gases, and these are separate from each other, but for our purposes I think it adequately illustrates my point: each "bubble" or soul starts its journey in darkness and fear but eventually finds its way to the light of the sky, growing in awareness and joy, through multiple incarnations, as it gets closer to the surface. The other point is that the "pump" is constantly pulling air into the long hose arching toward the ocean's bottom, releasing new "soul-bubbles" all the time. Therefore, while the air inside each bubble may be the same age, the age of each bubble is not—some are newer bubbles that have just begun their ascent, and some are older bubbles that have been making their way toward the surface for a very long time. Also, since the size of a bubble determines its degree of buoyancy, some bubbles move toward the surface much faster than others, reaching "home" sooner than many of the bubbles that were released before them. Yet all will eventually reach the surface, even the smallest among them, to complete their journey.

It is these older bubbles near the surface that we often refer to as "old souls," and they are a natural and important part of the process since they are the ones who are to help the younger souls reach the surface. They are the seasoned veterans of the spiritual realm who are not only willing but in fact eager to help others on their journey, just as there were those who were eagerly willing to assist them in their earlier journey.

So how does one identify an old soul? That's a good question, for they are not always easy to spot. At the risk of being presumptuous, however, I would postulate that old souls should possess certain common characteristics that set them apart from younger souls. Seasoned by dozens of lifetimes of toil and tribulation, they have learned tremendous patience, are peaceful and not easily perturbed or flustered, and most of all know how to love and laugh and live in joy. They are those people one sometimes encounters who have a perspective on life that is different from most people's; they are individuals who have a calmness, an inner peace, and a wisdom about them that seems well beyond their years. They are rarely fearful, worried, or angry, but instead have a built-in resiliency that seems almost otherworldly. They may not be well educated or wealthy or even particularly religious; in fact, they are frequently simple, plain folk who live rather ordinary lives. Yet in the midst of life's trials and disappointments, they possess an inner peace and steadfast calmness that emanates from them like a lighthouse beacon. They truly enjoy life as much as they enjoy people, and seem capable of being entirely at peace whether they live in a mansion or a mud hut. I have met people like that, as you probably have as well. They are the end result of many lifetimes of hard "spirit building" work. They are the ones we look to as reminders that the long journey through the darkness into the light may not be an easy one, but they teach us that no matter how frightening the journey may sometimes appear, it is one well worth taking.

The Role of "Old Souls" in the Evolution of Humanity

Aside from simply being more mature souls, old souls serve a vital function on a macroscopic scale as well, for they are the impetus behind every great forward stride humanity has taken toward its collective enlightenment. For example, the abolition of slavery may not have been possible until enough old souls jointly decided that slavery was no longer an acceptable way to treat human beings and, through the sheer force of their will alone, were able to convince enough young souls to follow them and abolish the hated practice. As such, some of the greatest abolitionists in history may have been old souls (despite their shortcomings in other areas). Human rights activists, peacemakers, political dissidents, spiritual teachers, civil rights leaders, free-ranging physicians and caretakers along with a whole host of those who strive to make a more peaceful, just, and compassionate world are often old souls who are determined to make a difference and alter the face of society.[1] Many may give their lives in the process; others will sacrifice careers, family, wealth, and even safety in the effort to drag society a little further along the road toward enlightenment. Old souls do not look to escape the brutalities of this world but instead seek to change the world so that brutality disappears from its face. Though old souls often fail and are sometimes crushed beneath the heel of a dictator's boot, their capacity to shape the direction of society—while frequently imperceptible—is relentless and inexorable, and is frequently seen only in hindsight many centuries after the fact. But their effects *are* felt and will continue to be appreciated in the coming centuries as humanity strives to pull itself out of darkness and into the light of its own divinity. That is only one of the positive byproducts of reincarnation, but one of its most important.

DEFINING AND UNDERSTANDING SOUL MATES

One last issue to look at before we move on is the popular notion of "soul mates" that has become such an element of our social consciousness. Even among people who do not believe in reincarnation, the idea

---

1 However, not every great social, political, religious, or spiritual leader is necessarily an old soul. Some people gravitate to positions of authority out of a thirst for power, fame, or even financial gain, and may, in fact, be among the most immature souls among us. Where they are spiritually is reflected not in what they say, but in what they do, and, especially, in what they are willing to do without.

that there exists within the universe one person designed specifically for them is more than just grist for romance novels, but an accepted idea within our culture, despite finding its basis within Eastern reincarnationist beliefs.

The idea works from the premise that if we accept reincarnation as a fact, it is likely that we have closely interacted with literally hundreds or even thousands of people over the scores of incarnations we've experienced, and, as such, it should be of no surprise if we occasionally encounter one of these souls in this present life. Therefore, when we form a particularly close friendship or relationship, it is often romantically imagined that we do so because we "knew" this person in some past incarnation, and our natural bond with him or her today is simply a continuation of that past relationship. Some even take this to the point of imagining that most, if not all, of their present relationships—including their relationships with siblings, spouses, parents, close friends, and, on occasion, even business partners, colleagues, and employers—continue to move from incarnation to incarnation with them, much like a flock of geese making the same trip south each winter. In essence, some imagine we reincarnate in "packs" through countless incarnations, and it is these fellow sojourners to whom we are most naturally attracted.[2]

The reason many people have no trouble accepting this idea is because we have all shared the common experience of meeting someone for the first time and being immediately and inexplicably drawn to him or her for no apparent reason. This isn't merely a question of sexual attraction (love at first sight) but something deeper: an almost instant rapport and easy familiarity that seems already firmly established even though we have only known the person briefly. The friendship and attraction, in other

---

2 However, not every "soul partner" may appear in every one of our incarnations, even as we may not be a part of each of theirs. As a rule, however, most of them are generally a part of each incarnation, though they may take on vastly different roles. For example, one who may have been your son in one incarnation becomes a close colleague in this one, while your current spouse may have been your parent in a previous incarnation.

words, is not only instantaneous but "feels" extremely natural, as if you have been reintroduced to an old friend you haven't seen for many years and are simply picking up where you left off.

That we are likely to encounter familiar souls from previous incarnations seems reasonable, and that souls might travel in packs is not without some logic. The problem is that most people understand the concept from a purely positive perspective; yet if there are "soul mates" (or, as I prefer, "familiar souls"), this should work in a negative context as well. For example, we have all suffered through difficult relationships at some point in our lives, from an adulterous spouse to a traitorous coworker to an unreasonable and demanding boss. Therefore, it is reasonable to imagine that we may encounter some of these same souls again just as easily as we may encounter those with whom we shared a positive relationship in a past life, and, further, that they may well incur the same kinds of negative feelings in this incarnation as they elicited in the last one. As such, just as most of us have encountered people we felt an immediate affinity for, most of us have likewise met people we immediately took a disliking to for no apparent reason. This instant dislike is more than a result of a person's arrogance or condescending attitude, but is enmity for no obvious reason. Further, it is often felt far more strongly and intensely—sometimes even to the point of hatred— than one would reasonably expect to feel toward a person who is simply unpleasant, uninteresting, or otherwise unlikable.

Is it any less likely, then, that they may have been protagonists from previous incarnations? After all, if we do travel in "packs" through each incarnation, we must assume that at least a few of our fellow incarnates are people with whom we've had negative dealings in past incarnations.

Ironically, if true, these "dark souls" may be, in some ways, more important partners in our spiritual quest than those we count as "light souls," for they possess the capacity to refine us far more sharply and quickly than those positive souls from the past whom we meet again. For example, we can only learn patience with someone who tries our patience, so those negative souls we've known from past lives may be more useful than we might imagine. Further, we may be useful to them in their spiritual development as well. In fact, we might be someone else's nemesis from a previous incarnation without our even being aware of it. Consider this the next time you have a boss who is more than you can handle, or a mousy, conniving coworker whom you can barely stand to work with; you both may be helping each other toward spiritual maturity without even realizing it!

While the concept of soul mates is an interesting idea and, to some degree, a valid one, it is easy to overdo it. With the huge number of people we encounter over the course of a single lifetime, we do not require souls from the past to make our experience in this lifetime any more challenging or fulfilling. Though it is possible and, for that matter, even likely that some souls form bonds that transcend each incarnation—just as there are lifetime friendships capable of withstanding the test of time—we should not assume that everyone with whom we have some significant dealings is a past-life acquaintance. Spiritual growth is about encountering a wide range of people in order to realize the fullest extent of experiences possible; a repeat relationship from a previous incarnation might even prove an impediment, especially if it only serves to reinforce certain attitudes and feelings from a distant past that are no longer beneficial to our spiritual progress. Sometimes the past can come back to haunt us, and that is the last thing the maturing soul needs.

chapter fourteen

Two Worlds

Reincarnation cannot be entirely appreciated without first making some decisions concerning the nature of the universe itself. While it is possible to move through the process of spiritual maturation without a clear understanding of how the universe is actually constructed (just as it's quite possible to be an excellent driver without a clue as to how a combustion engine works), it is equally true that once one understands the nature of time and space, the entire process becomes a little easier to fathom. Only then can reincarnation be appreciated for the intricate and complex machine that it is, and the first inkling of what eternity really means move within our ability to grasp. It is, in fact, nothing less than the road map to immortality.

While it may appear presumptuous to assume that one can reduce the cosmos to an easily understood equation, it is still helpful to consider some ideas if only in an effort to develop some basis from which to work. Just as mountainclimbers work their way toward the summit through a series of pre-established camps, it is likewise essential for us to construct a "base camp" from which to start our journey if we hope to make more than a half-hearted thrust toward the top. While, admittedly, my camp may not be entirely adequate to meet all our needs, it is still better than being trapped out in the barren and windswept open. As such, what I write here will be, by necessity, partially speculative and largely theoretical, and quite possibly entirely erroneous. I believe it is, however, at least internally consistent with what we understand of the process of reincarnation and, as such, a good place for us to begin our study.

The first thing that is important to examine is how we, especially in the West, understand the nature of reality (outside of a purely materialistic sense) and, specifically, the realm of the spirit. Most of us understand life to exist on two separate planes—the supernatural and the natural, or, if you prefer, the world of spirit and the world of physicality. They are, from most people's perspective, separate and impassable, like two great continents divided by a vast body of water that any attempt to bridge them must be, by necessity, one way only. Additionally, it is generally taught that the one—the world of physicality within which we reside—is a largely artificial construct that was produced or created from within the realm of the spiritual world. In other words, the spiritual realm existed prior to the physical, with the latter being the product of the creative energies of the former.

However, it is a myth that the spiritual realm and the physical realm are separate. They are, instead, intricately interwoven aspects of the same thing—namely, existence. There is no "spiritual" world that exists alongside the "physical" world; both are a part of a single "world," which we might collectively call the "natural" realm. Neither is a construct of the other, nor are they genuinely opposites of each other. They are more like two sides of the same coin that coexist eternally.

Yet how is this possible? Doesn't the Big Bang and logic itself tell us that the physical world must have had a beginning, just as it must ultimately have an end?

While this idea is certainly common among Westerners, it is a largely foreign concept to the Eastern mindset. To the Hindu and the Buddhist (as well as a few others) the physical universe is eternal and indestructible. It did not begin one day, nor will it likely end one day. In effect, it will always be because it has always been.

The problem is that we are looking at the equation from a very limited perspective safely ensconced upon our perch in linear time. Can we really be so sure that the present universe came into existence only 13.7 billion years ago and that it will one day simply slide into complete entropy and cease to exist? How can we be so certain that there are not immense gravitational forces or some other as yet unknown processes at work now that might not only ultimately stop the universe's expansion, but begin to pull all the matter in the universe back into itself, causing the Big Bang to reignite a hundred billion years in the future to begin the whole process over? Do we live in a constant-state universe—one that explodes, expands, and finally dies out, or could we be living in a cyclical universe that explodes, expands, contracts, dies out, and then repeats the process not once or twice or even a hundred times, but forever? Could our 13.7 billion-year-old universe, then, be not the first or last, but only the *most recent*?

Science doesn't accept the idea of a cyclical universe, mainly because we haven't acquired either enough data about our universe or had the opportunity to explore it in all its glory, and science cannot and, indeed, should not, accept that which it cannot perceive directly. However, it must be acknowledged that the cyclical universe model does have the advantage of not having to account for how all the matter in the universe got here in the first place. It simply maintains that it has always been here, though there have been vast eons of time when it was largely unusable as a stage upon which to allow souls to play out their sentient dramas. Eternity, however, does not care if it takes five million or five billion years to form the first livable planets from the dust of an interstellar blast of energy. It will wait patiently because it has all the time in the world or, for that matter, all the time in the universe, at its disposal.

While I don't wish to belabor the point, it is entirely possible that we live in an eternal universe, making it every bit as old as the spiritual realm that it emulates. And this makes sense from the standpoint of logic as well, for what does it mean to have a "spiritual realm" if there is not also a "physical realm" from which to differentiate it? Without the one the other is meaningless. Just as the color red becomes meaningless in a world in which everything is red, it is the existence of other colors that allows for there being anything we would call color at all. As such, there can be no spiritual realm if there is not also a physical realm, for the two are but opposite sides of the same coin, and just as one side of a coin cannot preexist the other, one realm cannot preexist the other. Either both are eternal or neither are, and if the latter, one has the difficult task of determining how either—and both—realms came into being. Nothingness makes poor material from which to produce everything.

This doesn't mean that the two worlds are mirror images of each other, however. They each operate by different laws—the physical universe within the context of linear time and space and the spiritual realm apart from it. In fact, it is this difference that makes the one world indispensable to the other. Without a physical universe of set laws that operate within the context of time and space, spirit cannot know anything experientially, and yet human consciousness cannot know immortality without the presence of a universe that exists without a clock. The one is essential for the other to be realized, giving each a codependent, symbiotic relationship. This allows us, once we grasp this principle, to understand that the two worlds are not separate but instead exist as a single unit. They are also constantly interacting with one another, spirit moving into the physical realm and the physical moving back into the world of pure spirit, in an unending cycle of pure experience.

If we accept the notion that souls reincarnate, we can see this interaction between the two realms played out very clearly. A soul, seeking to experience things on a level other than the purely theoretical, moves from one realm into the other in the form of a newborn child. At almost the same exact moment, an old man halfway around the world takes his final breath and his spirit, now freed from the limitations of the physical realm, wings its way back toward the total freedom of spirit. One enters just as another exits, much like a kind of eternally revolving door.

Riding the Universal Subway

To better visualize this, imagine a subway car coming to a stop at a station and, as soon as the doors open, scores of people disembarking while another two dozen people who had been waiting patiently on the platform step onboard. Hundreds still on the train do neither, but simply remain seated patiently waiting for their stop further down the line. And thus the train moves on eternally, constantly dropping passengers off and picking up new ones, making a massive circuit around the city forever.

The train, of course, represents the physical world of time and space that we are all subject to as long as we remain onboard. The station is the spiritual realm from whence we came and where we will eventually return. Therefore, both the train and the station serve vital functions in the neverending cycle of existence.

This implies that there's not much that separates the two realms, and indeed that would be correct. The only thing that prevents us from seeing the other realm is our inability to perceive things that exist in a multisensual context. In effect, we sit within subway cars with smoked-glass windows that make it impossible to see either the embarking or departing passengers clearly (if at all) while those on the platform can peer into the interiors of the trains only with great difficulty. Those sitting inside the train and those outside may catch glimpses of each other, but what they can see is not clear. Some might have better vision than others, and on occasion a few of the passengers and some of those standing on the platform might manage to communicate with each other, but for the most part they have only minimal contact, just as one would expect. After all, the embarking passengers, once they are onboard, have no real reason to keep in touch with those on the platform while those disembarking have places to go and things to do; keeping in touch with those they have left behind on the train is not high on their list of priorities. Besides, both those embarking and those disembarking know they will run into each other down the line again (and perhaps decide to ride together for a time).

So what does all this mean in terms of our spiritual journey?

It means that ours really is a journey in the truest sense of the word, and once we realize that we can finally begin to relax, for, at last, we know what's happening. Too many people approach their own deaths terrified of what it will mean if they have to leave the train, uncertain of what they'll encounter once they step onto the platform and watch the train pull out of the station. Will they be robbed or assaulted in the dark, shadowy confines of some deserted waiting area? Will they get lost and stumble about for an eternity looking for someone to help them? Will there be anyone there to meet them as they had hoped, people who know the area and are prepared to help them find their way around? For people who have spent years riding the train and have no memory of having embarked, it can seem frightening to leave its familiar surroundings. Yet spiritually evolved individuals, like the seasoned travelers they are, know there's nothing to be afraid of. They understand the purpose of the train and know when it's time to get off. They see it not as a place of security (for, indeed, the train is the more dangerous place to be) but as a simple mode of transportation designed to take them from point A to point B (and, ultimately, all the way to point Z), and it is this knowledge that permits them to begin to enjoy the ride.

This analogy, however, while helping us begin to understand how the two worlds operate together, does not by any means cover the entire concept. What's not clear is how much one world might directly influence the other. It also doesn't touch upon the idea that there may be numerous "trains" running on many different tracks on journeys to an infinite number of stations, or whether it's possible for two of the trains to collide (and what that would mean for those onboard if they did). Further, my example makes it sound as though the train is moving along at a steady rate of speed, but the reality is that what we perceive as progression may in fact be nothing of the kind. The train is simply moving—not through time but through an inter-dimensional matrix—toward an infinite number of potential destinations along an infinite number of routes.

If all of this begins to get a little confusing and unnecessarily obtuse, it is better to leave it alone. It is only necessary to understand that everything that exists, be it in the physical realm or the spiritual, is intimately interconnected and dependent upon the other for its existence and function. Only in understanding this does our purpose in constantly entering and leaving the physical plane make any sense or serve any apparent purpose. However, it is only *helpful* to try to understand the process—it is not vital.

The Role of Time in Reincarnation

Perhaps the element of all of this that can be most confusing is how time works within this dual existence of the spiritual and physical realms. As such, no study of this subject would be complete without taking a look at this curious aspect of the equation as well, for it is the single element that makes spiritual maturation even possible.

Most people rarely consider time as a function of our existence, but as a fleeting commodity that so relentlessly drives our lives, and not something we normally stop to think about. But what is the purpose of time? And, more important, how does it figure into our quest for spiritual maturity?

Time is that which allows spirit to experience things on a practical level, and reincarnation is the process that spirit uses to put itself into time. It is the mechanism by which spirit lives, breathes, grows, and dies, all of which it cannot do—except on a purely conceptual basis—outside of time. Therefore, in a way, the spiritual realm *needs* the physical realm in order to exist as much as the physical world *needs* the spiritual realm to sustain it. They are mutually dependent upon one another, and time is the element that binds them together, despite the fact that only one of those worlds exists within the context of linear time.

Unfortunately, the tendency is to imagine that since the spiritual realm exists outside of time, there can be no concept of time within that realm. While the spirit realm does not operate with a clock on the wall, however, it would be only a partial understanding to assume that there is no concept of time per se. In fact, in being so closely entwined within the physical world of time and space, the spiritual realm is intimately involved with time even though it has no use for the stuff itself. While this may sound like a contradiction, it is not. Perhaps another analogy, which I personally find very useful to understanding paradoxes, is in order.

Imagine watching a movie and realizing that though neither the character in the movie nor you know what's going to happen next from the perspective of the movie's producer, director, and distributor, what happens next has already happened many weeks or even months ago. Therefore, while from our perspective we don't know what's coming next, from a larger perspective "what's coming next" already came; we simply aren't aware of it because of our fixed perspective within linear time. We might imagine all kinds of potential scenarios ahead while watching the figures flickering on the screen in front of us, yet regardless of what we think *might* happen, what *does* happen is already preordained.

We can begin to get some idea of how "timelessness" works when we watch the same movie a second time. Then, instead of imagining what might happen next, we already know what is just around the corner and it's the *character* (not the actor, but the character the actor's playing) who is still trapped in ignorance of his or her own future. In fact, each time you watch the movie you'll notice that the character *never* figures out why he or she shouldn't investigate the strange noise outside, and the character repeatedly suffers the same horrific fate each time because of it. From our now expanded perspective, we know what the character should or shouldn't do, but he or she remains eternally clueless, trapped within his or her illusory celluloid world.

This is, of course, exactly the same situation we find ourselves in as long as we exist within the physical realm. We are a character acting within a movie who has no idea what's in store. We might recall what's happened up to now, but for the most part what's next is a mystery. The character in the play, then, is the equivalent of the incarnated personality; the actor playing the role, however, who has already read the script and knows what's going to happen to his or her character, is the soul, who dutifully plays the role even knowing what fate awaits and yet makes no effort to change it. The person watching the movie, then, is the Divine Spirit or cosmic consciousness of the universe, who also manages to be the character, the actor, and the audience all at the same time.

However, even though the movie's producer and actor are not operating within the timeframe of the character in the movie, that doesn't mean they aren't aware that the movie itself has a time meter, or that they can't work around it to get other results. In other words, they are aware of time without being affected by it, which is, I believe, true of the spirit world as well. The spirit world may see us within time, yet it does not experience time the way we do, nor is it bound to it in any way, yet the spirit world remains aware of time and takes it into account when making decisions.

Even more interestingly, just as the movie director can make many movies run simultaneously or sequentially to each other, so too are the "movies" of our various reincarnations running in no particular order—at least from the "director's" point of view. He or she can view them repeatedly or even watch them all at once if he or she so chooses. From the director's point of view, they are in no particular order, though they may appear very precisely ordered from our perspective. That is the illusion created by time, albeit an important one if we are to gain the benefits of multiple incarnations. We need to run the movies sequentially for them to make sense to us, which is why we generally assume that when we reincarnate, we do so in some chronological order. This, however, is all a part of the overall illusion; in fact, from the perspective of the spiritual realm, all our various incarnations are taking place simultaneously in the eternal "now."

This sense of chronological incarnations has other effects on our frame of reference as well. For example, it causes us to presume that we cannot incarnate as two individual personalities that coexist side by side within the same span of linear time. Instead, we assume that each incarnation exists only within its own niche of time, utterly exclusive of all previous and future incarnations. Yet if time is not a consideration from the perspective of the spirit, there is no reason we couldn't exist within the context of two individual personalities simultaneously. Further, if time is nonexistent from the context of spirit, we should not only be able to remember a past life, but a future incarnation as well. Even though the future, at least from our perspective in linear time, has not occurred yet and does not exist, if we work from the premise that time is not linear within the realm of the spirit, then the idea that we can look into our future should seem no more remarkable than our ability to look into the past. Yet it is the very illusion of sequentiality that makes it even possible to experience anything, past, future, or present, in the first place.

Personal Choice

So what does this have to do with reincarnation? Nothing per se, but it does explain one of the more difficult aspects of the concept, which is the idea of personal choice. New Age writings consistently refer to the idea that the soul decides what is to happen next and that therefore there are no such things as "accidents," since everything that is going to happen is effectively chosen beforehand by the soul. Therefore, if my plane crashes and I am killed, that was not an accident but part of the overall plan hammered together by my soul before I was even born.

Somehow I found that less comforting than some insisted I should. Why would I choose such a morbid fate? For that matter, why would I choose to get cancer, get fired from a job I loved, lose a beloved child to SIDS, or get a really bad haircut? Clearly, it seemed that such an idea was nothing more than an effort to excuse every horrible thing that might potentially happen to me or someone I love, leading me to wonder if I might be a more competent decision-maker than my own soul.

What I failed to understand, however, was the role time plays in each decision. To say that the soul "chooses" everything that happens to it is to assume that it is making personal decisions about everything that might occur. What it really means, however, is that the soul chooses to permit or, more correctly, accept, whatever happens within the context of any particular path we choose to follow. For example, just as there are benefits and consequences of every decision we make within our own lives, there are benefits and consequences to be realized within the larger decisions each soul makes. And, just as every decision we make puts into play an entire series of events, so too do the soul's choices put into effect a similar chain of events. As such, if some of the decisions that we put into motion result in some misfortune or catastrophe, that is a natural element of that path and so there is nothing "accidental" about it. The consequence was an inherent part of that choice, just as losing a leg to an exploding land mine is a natural consequence of walking across a mine field, regardless of whether the decision to do so is made consciously or unconsciously.

What this has to do with time, then, is that in recognizing that while we are moving forward through linear time unaware of what awaits us in the future, another aspect of ourselves—the soul—sees what's ahead but moves us toward it anyway, not because it is good for our spiritual development (it may very well not be) but because it has, in effect, already happened anyway. Whether we acquire any moral lesson or spiritual understanding as a result of it is beside the point; it is going to happen whether we learn from it or not.

Further, as a result of having free will within any incarnation, we have the option of changing what path we take, thus simultaneously suspending the consequences and benefits inherent to one path while opening ourselves to an entirely new set of consequences and benefits inherent to that new path. By way of an illustration, imagine that a man is walking through a forest and comes to a fork in the road. If he chooses to take the road to the right, the path will lead him deeper into the forest; if he chooses to go left, the road will lead him to a small fishing village on the coast. Each path will provide unique and distinct possibilities—as well as risks. One may lead to riches and fame, the other to destitution and hardship. Regardless, however, he must make one of three choices: either to take the left fork to the sea, the right fork into the woods, or choose to do neither (which is also a decision). There is no wrong path in this context, only different paths. Which one he chooses will immediately close off one future—with all its possibilities, adventures, realizations, and experiences—while simultaneously opening up another; which one he chooses to take will completely shape one reality while extinguishing all the other theoretical realities.

From the perspective of eternity, the new path, with all its adventures and experiences, is already written, but so are the results had the other path been taken. Both, and, potentially, countless more paths, effectively exist at the same time. In other words, we all have an infinite number of futures ahead of us depending upon which choices we make (or fail to make), and each of those potential futures are, in effect, already realized. They already exist, just as the final outcome of a movie already exists. The only difference is that this movie has millions of different endings, and each of them has already been shot and edited.

To bring this all together, when we step onto a doomed airliner, the possibility that the aircraft may crash is but one of thousands of possible scenarios. That it does crash is the result of physical forces outside of our control (weather, structural failure, pilot error, and so on) and not a result of our conscious or even "soul" choice. It simply is one of the potential consequences inherent with all decisions, just as our safe arrival after an uneventful flight is one of the potential results of our decision to board the aircraft. In effect, we do not "choose" to die in an airliner crash, but we do "choose" to experience whatever eventuality plays itself out as a result of our decision to board the plane. Either result, however, be it a safe flight or a crash, has already happened from the context of eternity, and our soul on some level already knows it. Yet it allows the incident to go on because it is all a part of the infinite number of choices eternity affords us.

Conclusion

I hope to have impressed upon the reader here that the universe is, if nothing else, a very complex place. I also hope I've made the point that it is a far more vast universe than we can begin to imagine, yet one in which not even the smallest detail goes unnoticed. Whether this leaves the reader with a sense of wonder or even fear is a personal choice; as for me, it leaves me with a sense of comfort knowing that despite the enormity of it all, everything works with absolute perfection. Nothing is wasted. There is no end to things (nor beginning, for that matter), and, most significant of all, everything is meticulously and marvelously interwoven into a single, vibrant plan. It is a far more wondrous and expansive place we live in, and one that is beyond the abilities of even the best imagination to fathom. The beauty of it is that we never need to fear for tomorrow, for there is nothing that exists within its vast expanse that we need be afraid of. If that doesn't make the troubles of today pale in comparison to the magnificence of the eternal and neverending journey we are on, I can't imagine what might do it.

chapter fifteen

BETWEEN INCARNATIONS AND CHOOSING THE NEXT LIFE

If one accepts reincarnation as a postmortem reality, it seems there can be no greater question than what happens to us between each incarnation. Do we exist in some kind of limbo state somewhere to await our next excursion into the physical world, or do we—as some suggest—experience a kind of "life review" or judgment in which our time on earth is carefully and exhaustively examined? And, finally, what of heaven? Is there room for such a place within the mechanism of reincarnation or is the idea of an "eternal reward" nothing more than a myth?

There are a number of ideas about what happens to our souls between incarnations, and each idea has its proponents and detractors. We will examine each in turn to determine their plausibility, but in the end it must be understood that all such musings must remain purely speculative. Unlike past-life memories, with their occasionally verifiable details to ponder, we have very little to go on when it comes to this particular question.

Since the intermediate state between incarnations is seldom examined in any great detail by regressionists,[1] the question of precisely what happens during this period remains largely unexplored (and, perhaps, unknowable). As such, much of what we discuss in this chapter, like much of the second half of this book, must remain purely conjectural—though not outside the realm of logic.

The Limbo State

The first and perhaps most frequent assumption to many is that nothing happens between incarnations—we simply die and immediately look for another fetus to inhabit. The Jainists of India adhere to this notion, as do some New Age purveyors. Research into conscious past-life memories in children done by noted reincarnationist investigator Dr. Ian Stevenson suggests this possibility as well, for he has found almost no memories of any intermediate state among his subjects; instead, most who recall their previous death usually attest to having almost immediately—sometimes within months or even mere weeks of their deaths—found another fetus to inhabit.[2]

Additionally, many of Dr. Wambach's subjects[3] were able to recall intricate details of numerous past lives but few reported memories of what occurred in the intermediate state. Most simply reported "drifting" between incarnations, while others were unable (or, perhaps, unwilling) to

---

1 One noteworthy exception is Dr. Michael Newton, a professional hypnotherapist from California who has written a number of books on the "in-between" state (see the bibliography). He describes a sophisticated and fairly complex between-state complete with guides, counselors, and carefully preplanned incarnations, some elements of which we will examine in detail in this chapter.

2 Of course, Dr. Stevenson never hypnotized any of his subjects to determine if they might have some intermediate-state memories locked away in their subconscious.

3 Dr. Wambach's demographic studies are recounted in more detail in chapter 3.

recall anything that occurred between lives, though there may have been a gap of many decades or even whole centuries between incarnations.

However, there are a few cases in which some information about the intermediate state emerges, though such memories are often unclear and confusing. They do give the impression, however, that the personality is conscious and aware during this time, though how active it is tends to be a matter of individual proclivity. Perhaps the best known of these is the celebrated (and subsequently pilloried) Bridey Murphy case, the alleged pre-incarnate personality of Mrs. Virginia Tighe and the subject of the 1956 bestseller *The Search for Bridey Murphy* (see chapter 1). She recounted being conscious after her death in 1864 and existing as something of a "wandering" spirit, capable of seeing others in the physical world but being unable to interact with them. She also recounted speaking with the spirits of others she had known in life, though even then there appeared to be no real substance to their conversations. In essence, "Bridey Murphy"—though apparently conscious and perceptive—seemed to simply drift along with no real point or purpose in the aftermath of her death until finally landing within the body of the woman known as Virginia Tighe in 1923, a full sixty years later.

So why are such intermediate-state memories so conspicuously absent or, at best, prosaic, during past-life regression sessions?

Beyond the possibility that nothing is recalled because nothing happens—the "limbo state" theory—is the very real possibility that what happens during that period is a very personal and private affair of the soul that is not always evident to the conscious personality. In other words, what occurs may be happening on a "higher level" than that upon which the personality resides. Much as important corporate decisions are often made behind closed doors, so too might the experiences and decisions of a past life be examined and considered on a higher level, and this does not filter down to make it into the conscious memories of either the previous or present personalities. As such, during a past-life regression the previous personality—now speaking through the present personality—really doesn't recall what occurred between the two lives because the lessons learned and the decisions made were done on a soul level and not a personality level. In essence, the personality doesn't remember what happened because it didn't happen to the personality; it happened to the soul. The events of a past life might be easily recalled because they are a part of the personality; the lessons that the events taught the soul, however, are not retained by the personality but are known only to the "higher self"—the soul—and cannot be as readily accessed.

If this is the case, the personality may not retain any between-life memories, so it may seem to be—at least from its limited perspective—merely "drifting" between incarnations. In fact, an entire process of life review and planning is going on elsewhere within the spiritual realm—a process that the personality is entirely unaware of. Bridey Murphy recalled a period immediately after her death during which she attempted to interact with the physical world and carried on only the most superficial contacts with a few others who had preceded her in death, but this period appears to have been short-lived. The next thing she recalls is being reborn in the body of an infant girl in 1923. But could something more have occurred during this interval as well, something even her own subconscious was unaware of?

HEAVENLY REST?

If we assume that the soul is conscious during these intermediate states— even if the experiences of this period may be inaccessible to us under hypnosis—the following question must be asked: "What possible environment might the conscious soul find itself in during this interval period? Is it a joyful one, a contemplative one, or even a mundane one? And, as I asked earlier, "What of heaven? Or hell, for that matter?"

One of the great hopes and comforts to most people is the idea that when they die their souls wing their way to heaven to be reunited with loved ones who passed before and live throughout eternity in a state of utter bliss. In fact, one of the most common complaints about reincarnation I've encountered is that it somehow "robs" people of their eternal reward by "making" them come back to earth; some even reject the entire idea of reincarnation on this basis alone.

The idea that heaven is somehow inconsistent with reincarnation is, however, incorrect. Reincarnation does allow for such a state of existence, though there are some significant differences in how the concept is interpreted between Western religionists and reincarnationists. The basic differences are twofold. First, reincarnationists do not believe that heaven is a reward one acquires for living a "good" life (or hell a punishment for an "evil" life) but that the soul returns to heaven—which is normally described in New Age literature as a place of light and joy—because that is all that exists within the spiritual realm. In other words, the soul goes to heaven simply because there is *no place else to go,* making heaven and the spiritual realm virtually synonymous terms.

The second significant difference between the heaven of Western religion and that of the reincarnationist is that for the former, heaven is eternal; once a person dies, his or her soul effectively remains in this blissful state forever, its brief sojourn on earth nothing more than a distant and rapidly fading memory. For the reincarnationist, however, heaven is only a temporary abode—a place of rest and reflection where the soul not only creates its own environment but recognizes that, like a wonderful vacation, it must end at some point so the soul may return to the "salt mines" of physicality.

How all of this actually works is unknown, of course, but the idea that the soul can be "at rest" while in the spiritual realm makes sense. This would seem especially true if the soul had just experienced an especially trying or traumatic incarnation and needed time to readjust and reflect upon what had just happened and acclimate itself to its "new" environment. Then, once it is refreshed, it may be ready for a return to physicality to continue the process.

The idea that this period is temporary is also misunderstood. From the soul's perspective, it may in fact appear to be transitory, but from the confines of the personality that the soul had previously manifested—a personality that now exists completely outside of the venue of linear time—it may well seem eternal. In reality, time itself is illusory, making any reference to *temporary* and *permanent* meaningless, though these illusions are necessary for both the soul and the personality to work through the process. As such, it remains entirely consistent to imagine that heaven is both a temporary abode of spiritual rest as well as an eternal state, depending upon one's perspective and whether the place is viewed from the context of a single personality or from the much larger context of a multi-incarnational soul.

Before leaving the subject of heaven entirely, however, it might be a good idea to mention something about hell. While hell as a place of eternal torment for "wicked" souls is clearly incompatible with a God of love and a spiritual realm of light and joy, the idea that a soul may experience anger, rage, and hatred during the intermediate state is also a distinct possibility, and might appear to the soul suffering such a fate to be a hellish experience. In essence, a soul that dies in "darkness" may hold on to its negative energy to such an extent that it finds it impossible to experience the endless bliss of the spiritual realm and remains locked in a kind of "dark limbo" state for a time until it can either work its way out of its predicament or be assisted by other souls out of its maze. Hauntings may be a good example of a soul that has refused to let go of its previous incarnation and remains trapped between the two worlds until it either tires of the torment it is putting itself through or is finally shown the way out. As such, while there is no hell in the absolute world of spirit, we are each capable of manufacturing our own hell and keeping ourselves imprisoned within it by our own obstinate refusal to let go of the past and turn to the light. Again, it is all a matter of personal choice, in the spiritual realm just as it is here in the physical.

THE LIFE REVIEW

While some reincarnationists doubt that a soul remains consciously active in the intermediate stage and others accept heaven as the soul's temporary abode, most manage to include somewhere within this period a time for reflection and review of the life just lived. To some, this may be a fairly simple process of careful self-evaluation, while others claim that a far more complex process awaits the recently deceased. The late Edgar Cayce (the Sleeping Prophet) maintained that a rather elaborate process of life review takes place between incarnations, during which the entire time just spent on earth is thoroughly reviewed and evaluated,[4] and suggestions are made by spiritual guides or counselors as to what the soul should attempt to achieve during its next incarnation. This idea is further reinforced by many of the intermediate-life studies carried out by Dr. Michael Newton and recorded in his popular book *Journey of Souls: Case Studies of Life between Lives.*[5]

This idea of an intermediate-life review is popular among New Agers and many who believe in reincarnation in general, and it possesses a certain logic that makes it hard to ignore. After all, it makes sense that one would want to review his or her past triumphs and mistakes if spiritual progress is the purpose of reincarnation, so it seems logical that there is an appraisal.

While it's possible that such appraisals are unnecessary simply because the events of a past life are no longer important to the growing soul—just as what happened to a person in second grade may no longer be relevant to him or her as a forty-year-old adult—it seems more likely that the personality would retain some sort of conscious memory of its time on earth,

---

4 Cayce maintained that this review was done at a central library-like facility known as the Hall of Akashic Records, where books containing the events of each life were kept and studied. This idea has worked its way into much New Age literature, though the concept did not originate with Cayce himself.

5 Dr. Michael Newton, *Journey of Souls* (St. Paul, MN: Llewellyn Publications, 1994).

and it is logical that it would still maintain the ability to judge and weigh its own actions while on earth in the light of its new spiritual environment.

But if a life-review does take place between lives, how might it work exactly? Certainly the idea of reliving one's more embarrassing or dishonest moments might be cause for some trepidation and, in some cases, even fear. This would especially be true if, as Newton and Cayce maintain, this review process is done under the auspices of spiritual guides or advisors. Of course, it needn't be a purely or even largely negative experience, for there is no reason to imagine that the more positive aspects of one's life might not also be examined along with the "negatives" and progress pointed out where evident. In fact, in many cases, the entire process might be an encouraging and even joyful experience, though, obviously, that would depend upon the quality of one's previous incarnation.

While all of this is purely speculative, I wonder if the pain or pleasure of such a process might not be entirely dependent upon the spiritual state of the soul being reviewed. In other words, a more advanced or mature soul might well perceive this process in a more objective and balanced manner—seeing its past-life "mistakes" as opportunities for growth and a part of the sometimes painful process of maturation—while a less mature soul might perceive a life review far differently. Most likely, a lesser-evolved soul is going to experience a more problematic incarnation, while its lack of spiritual maturity may result in it assessing that life from a more emotional perspective, making the process of review an excruciatingly painful experience.

What's important to recognize in all this, however, is that while this life-review process may appear on the surface to be similar to the concept of judgment day articulated in most religious literature, it is not designed to condemn or punish but instead to help us grow. It may seem unpleasant at points and even embarrassing to those souls who are still "ego heavy," but in the end each life lesson is a chance to learn and grow. As such, it's not difficult to imagine that even a "negative review" would be handled with compassion and gentleness, especially in the realm of the spirit. Aware of the trials and tribulations of each life, the environmental factors that shaped that life, and the general level of maturity of the soul involved, the reviewers undoubtedly understand better than anyone the reasons that an incarnation proved to be so difficult and would likely try to get the young soul to understand as well. There would be no effort to punish or humiliate the soul, but only to grade the progress it is making through each incarnation. There is no "pass" or "fail" in this test, only what happened and what might be learned from it.

Reincarnation is not interested in ridiculing, belittling, or otherwise humiliating us into changing, but in simply showing us where we are and how far we have yet to go. In its purest form, it is an optimistic and enlivening process, for it continually points us toward the direction our heart truly desires to go in any case—in the direction of joy and peace. It may seem a stern and even cruel master at times, but in the end we will emerge from the process thankful for the patience and gentleness it has shown. It is, after all, simply the process of God redefining himself and, in the course of doing so, moving all life toward new heights of self-achievement and fulfillment.

CHOOSING THE NEXT INCARNATION

As for how this process might shape the next incarnation, again it seems that this is a matter of how mature the soul is. To some, the next incarnation might be coolly and carefully planned to take advantage of the potential opportunities for growth the next life might promise, while for others it is chosen hastily or even reluctantly—like a schoolboy required to do his lessons when he'd rather be outside playing—yet neither procedure is right or wrong from the perspective of eternity. Each is simply a reflection of the maturity level of each soul.

To what degree the soul is capable of planning out the next incarnation is, not surprisingly, also a matter of debate. Some believe that every event of the next life is carefully scripted, with every significant detail being essentially preordained before the soul enters the fetus, while others see each life as a series of free-will decisions that may (and usually does) supersede any prebirth planning. Still others see an apparent randomness about each new life, as though it were a roll of the dice with the results being driven more by good fortune than good planning (a prospect we will discuss later as we examine teachings about karma). Yet if we are to use our own experiences in this present life as a guide, it seems that all three camps may have something to contribute to the debate.

What I'm suggesting is that just as we preplan events in this life, change our minds at the last minute, and sometimes seem to fall victim to forces beyond our control, the soul operates in much the same way. It may be able to choose a particular venue into which to incarnate, but it may not be able to plan out an entire incarnation in precise detail due to circumstances outside of its control and the impact of decisions it will make while in the flesh. As such, the process appears to be carefully planned, subject to change without notice, and apparently affected by factors completely outside of its control—*all at the same time.*

While this may appear on the surface to be contradictory, it perfectly mirrors life in general. Just as in life we make plans only to see them either come to perfect fruition or fall apart completely, so too within the spiritual realm we may well select a venue for our next incarnation—say, a specific gender, nationality, social class—and even a general timeframe into which we will be born. This especially makes sense if we work from the premise that the human soul possesses the same degree of free will in the spiritual realm as humans in the flesh do, in which case the argument can well be made that we should have a good deal to say about where we end up next. The soul, after all, is a creative "machine" that is, at its very core, utterly and completely free. Even when it is in the flesh, it manages to possess a considerable amount of free will, often even within the confines of a restrictive society. Are we to imagine that this capability ends at death?

Additionally, having access to all the cosmic knowledge of the universe may give us an especially ideal perspective from which to choose our next set of parents or even a specific family to be born into (assuming a developing fetus is available). We could gauge from our perch outside of time precisely what sort of circumstances we might find ourselves in, as well as the potential for growth that such a set of circumstances might afford. On the other hand, the soul may be content to simply let things happen and take advantage of whatever circumstances it finds itself born into, yet even that decision—the decision to *not* make any specific plans—is itself a free-will choice.

In either case, however, any planning the soul may do will take it only so far. Once it returns to physicality, it will again be able to choose the various paths it will take, each of which will open new doors while closing others. As such, over time the course it takes may—especially in younger souls—become increasingly at variance with any original plan to the point that any prior planning the soul may have done is moot. Other events, such as a war or a natural disaster, may also intervene in the process, impacting the course of events and completely superseding any previous soul planning that may have been done. A man may shoot an arrow into the sky and aim it precisely as he will, but once it leaves his bow it is at the mercy of wind and gravity and a host of other factors that will ultimately determine where it finally lands. In the same way, then, the soul may send the personality into the world with certain goals or intentions in mind, but where it ends up is anyone's guess.

But shouldn't the soul "see" the future from the spiritual realm and design its next incarnation around whatever external incidents are slated to occur within the venue the soul has chosen? In other words, wouldn't the soul know it was going to be born as a man who would one day be drafted into the military and die on a foreign battlefield before any significant "soul work" could be accomplished and simply change the venue?

While theoretically this makes sense, it fails to take into account that in order for the soul to realize the full range of human experience, it is imperative that it *not* know what is going to happen next. Just as a novel is not as easily enjoyed if the ending has been learned beforehand, so too would the experiences obtained in each incarnation be voided if the soul anticipated them beforehand. The not knowing what is going to happen next is as important as choosing the next venue. In essence, the soul and the personality it manifests may be equally surprised by what happens, but that is precisely the way it must be for the process to have its intended effect.

To better illustrate this point, imagine how bland life would be if we knew beforehand how every decision we make would turn out. For instance, if you *knew* the dollar token you put into a slot machine was going to pay off the million dollar jackpot—not *hoped* it would or *prayed* it would, but already *foresaw* that it would—how exciting would that be? Perhaps at first the newfound wealth would make it seem unimportant, but a moment's consideration would quickly demonstrate the grayness life would take on if we could predict the future. Further, imagine if you knew beforehand that a business venture you were planning was going to end in failure and bankruptcy, but since it was preordained, you had no choice but to go through with your doomed plans. How would you feel about life in general knowing that failure was assured and financial ruin was all you had to look forward to? Surprise, relief, excitement, and feelings of elation and exuberance would not be possible if the outcome were always assured; it's the uncertainties of life that make it worth living—no matter how excruciatingly frustrating those uncertainties may sometimes prove to be.

As such, we cannot blithely assume that the soul knows precisely what's going to happen to it in its next incarnation, and so even the most carefully planned venue could fall apart or be circumvented by any number of factors. This doesn't mean that the process has "failed," for growth of a kind, even if only short-term, may have still been possible; it's only that the soul did not realize the greatest "bang for its buck" in that particular incarnation.

However, it should be recognized that the success of an incarnation is not measured by the longevity or range of experiences the soul's personality realized. It is entirely conceivable that a soul may have a very limited agenda in mind for a particular incarnation, so it dies young or achieves very little (by worldly standards), yet still manages to meet each of its primary goals completely. It's impossible to know what a soul's agenda is from our side of eternity, and, as such, it's entirely possible that a child who dies in infancy and a man who has worked a long, hard life in a coal mine may have fulfilled their soul's agenda perfectly, even if we may not be able to see how.

Finally, even if we have the ability to plan the venue of our next incarnation, it's possible that such a gift is not taken advantage of by very immature souls intent only on continuing their adventure in the flesh. As such, those lesser-developed souls—those that we refer to as "young souls"—may put little thought into their next incarnation, simply choosing instead to inhabit the first available fetus they happen upon. Just as young adults who make important life decisions with little forethought frequently end up in difficult situations, so too may these young souls end up in extremely trying and difficult incarnations; in choosing their next fetus in haste, they may find themselves in the body of a crack-addicted infant or trapped within the prison of a child born into a near-vegetative state. This lack of prior planning may well explain why some souls end up in such horrific incarnations; careful planning and wisdom are needed as much in the spiritual realm as they are in the physical.

Yet there is nothing wrong with choosing a venue hastily. Just as there is nothing that requires a person to plan out his or her life in intricate detail, so too may some souls be content to go with the flow and land wherever the breeze blows them, completely unconcerned about pursuing any particular agenda at all. They have all eternity, after all, to mature, and so there may be no particular need to rush the process. Even the most immature children eventually grow up and become responsible adults; it seems likely that it is no different in the spiritual realm.

On the other hand, some very mature souls—realizing that all incarnations lead to some degree of growth—may also be content to travel down whatever road they find themselves on and purposely decide against making any specific plans. Like the old man who chooses to walk the breadth of America with nothing more than a walking stick and his dog along for company, so too may "old souls" occasionally enjoy living by their wits and taking on an entirely spontaneous incarnation. There is, after all, a certain freedom in not being tied to a single plan of action, but instead experiencing a day-to-day world completely free of deadlines or schedules.

For those of us somewhere in between, however, a preincarnate agenda might well be in order and some careful planning done—at least on a superficial level. Most of us are not comfortable enough to perform without a net; we want blueprints to follow, and we may well have those opportunities to craft them. How much choice we have in putting our plans together, however, may depend entirely on our needs and level of spiritual development; it may also be that along with greater spiritual maturity comes greater choice. Just as is true of maturity in general, once one becomes a more responsible decision-maker, the opportunities to make increasingly significant decisions increase as well.

Cultural Influences on a New Incarnation

The role that culture may play in this process is unclear, but it may figure prominently. Reincarnationist researcher Dr. Stevenson frequently noted that many of his subjects recalled having lived their previous lives in very close proximity to their current place of residence, and among the Tlingit Indians of Alaska (one of the Native American tribes that incorporate strong reincarnationist beliefs into their culture), he noted that sometimes the deceased soul returned to the same tribe or even family. Reincarnation in these cases also tended to take place much faster than the norm, with intervals of as little as eight to ten months between death and rebirth (as compared to a more common average of around thirty years). All of this suggests both a great deal of choice in the reincarnation process and a tendency for the soul to so closely identify with a particular culture that it insists on reincarnating within a very limited context, so, in essence, it willfully reduces its options. This would seem to be indicative of souls that are still either very young or so thoroughly identified with a specific place or culture as to be essentially "stuck" within a particular venue, though that doesn't mean spiritual evolution or maturation isn't still taking place on some level. Reincarnation is a patient process that is in no rush to achieve its ultimate goal, so a soul that insists on spending numerous lifetimes locked into a familiar and comfortable locale or social venue is not doing anything wrong; it is simply experiencing life at the level of its development. When it is ready it may finally move on to more fruitful pursuits and the process will continue.

More mature souls, however, may eventually develop an agenda and put more thought into the next incarnation. That's not to say that they automatically select "easier" incarnations—or, for that matter, "harder" ones (which are subjective terms in any case)—but that they will choose incarnations that will put them into situations where the chances for positive spiritual growth are optimal. A soul could still select poorly, of course, but the selection process itself may be far more deliberate than that shown by a younger, less mature soul. Yet even the wisest person still occasionally makes a mistake, so the process of rebirth has an element of randomness and, if one wishes, luck, involved among even the most "seasoned" veterans of multiple incarnations.

CONSIDERING AN ALIEN VENUE

It is generally assumed that a soul, if it chooses to reincarnate into the flesh, always reincarnates back on earth—an assumption that has found considerable support among past-life therapists. It is exceedingly rare to find a subject who recalls having lived on another planet in a past life (though occasionally people recall living a life on Atlantis),[6] which brings up an interesting point. It suggests that intelligent life—what we might refer to as "sentient" life—resides only on this single planet, with earth

---

6 See chapter 6.

being the single beacon of life alone among an ocean of stars. This seems rather unlikely, however, especially considering not only the vastness of our own galaxy, but the fact that there are literally billions of other galaxies much like our own throughout the expanse of the universe. Yet if life is ubiquitous, then why no memories of having lived as, say, an intelligent slug on the shores of the ammonia seas on Rigel's fourth planet? It seems that being continually reincarnated onto this single planet should be most limiting and even have the potential of restricting a soul's potential for growth. In other words, if it is the soul's goal to experience life on many levels, why are no extraterrestrial pasts thrown into the mix?

While several possibilities present themselves, the simplest answer is that the soul chooses to stay within the confines of what it knows best, restricting itself to a single venue through countless incarnations until it has learned all there is to learn there (and this may also be a part of the rationale behind same culture reincarnations as well). This would make sense, especially from a soul-growth perspective, for such would permit the soul to continue its growth unimpeded by the need to thoroughly readjust itself to a new physical reality each time it reincarnates.

Consider the likelihood that the universe is home to literally millions of species of sentient creatures, each of which exists within its own unique and distinct environment and culture. One creature may be completely aquatic and make its home at extreme ocean depths while another may do nicely floating in a pure methane atmosphere like a blimp. One may find temperatures of two-hundred degrees Fahrenheit most comfortable while another prefers a temperature only a few degrees above absolute zero. And culturally, they may possess an even more exotic and alien psyche, one so unlike our own as to make any similarities between us and them purely coincidental. As such, to move from one of these truly alien environments onto earth would not only be to take on a new body, but an entirely new physiology and mindset as well. If the traumas of a past life can come back to haunt us in our current incarnation, imagine how much more so a past life as an insectlike being that spent its days writing poetry and devouring smaller bugs might effect our current perceptions. In essence, it may be more than the soul can digest, making a return in a familiar form more desirable (and probably less traumatic).

Of course, there may be alien beings much like ourselves out there as well, but even if we shared a similar physiology with our extraterrestrial cousins, it's unlikely that we would share a similar culture, history, mentality, or morality, making an incarnation on earth still largely problematic. While we may one day leave the earth plane completely and move on to an entirely new venue (in fact, we may well be forced to once life becomes unsustainable on this planet), it seems logical to assume that when that happens, it will be more of a mass exodus than gradual emigration. Our reincarnating on this planet works for us because we've become acclimated to it; we stay here for the simple reason that we, in effect, understand the "rules" of earth, and find reincarnating here more useful.

Then again, it's entirely possible that some of us have lived on other planets before (I've known a few people whom I've suspected of this), but we simply don't retain the memory of having done so. Just as it seems that we are able to recall the last incarnation more completely than we can recall the one that preceded it, it is possible that if we go back far enough the memories of having lived in an alien world might well have evaporated. In the same way, perhaps one day our memories of having lived on this planet will similarly fade by the third or fourth incarnation on another world thousands of light years away, and all memories of having been an "earthling" will be lost.

It's also possible that due to the dramatic differences we experience when moving from one physical world into another, our soul simply expunges such memories from our subconscious, making them entirely unreachable to even the best past-life regression therapist. Perhaps there's a built-in "safety mechanism" designed specifically to prevent us from being too traumatized when a new incarnation is simply more than our psyche can handle, or maybe our past on another planet is so alien to our current personality—which is, after all, "filtering" past-life memories through its modern understanding—that it simply throws out those memories it can't relate to. As humans, we understand what it means to have been a human in a past life; we may have no context within which to understand a past life on an alien world, so we ignore those memories entirely, much like a child will ignore a complex algebraic equation written on a chalkboard because it's too complex for his or her undeveloped mind to fathom.

Finally, there is the possibility that as we mature spiritually and become more capable of grasping the nuances and complexities of an alien mindset, we may eventually develop a greater capacity to recall past lives lived on alien worlds. Additionally, some souls may be ready for the challenge another physical existence may provide and choose to leave the earth plane entirely and sample some "alien cuisine," with all the challenges and opportunities for growth that such a world might offer. The universe is, after all, a very big place, and we have all eternity to play in it.

CONCLUSION

It should be apparent that the process of rebirth is both complex and sophisticated, and undoubtedly takes into account many factors, some of which may lie far beyond our comprehension. It may appear in some ways to be beyond our understanding, but it is a process that works to perfection in helping us realize the divinity that resides within us. It may appear hopelessly complex, but it is this complexity that makes it such a superb tool for spiritual growth, for it takes everything into account. Even those elements that may appear at first glance to be random are figured into the mix, making it a perfect mechanism of spiritual evolution.

Therefore, the question of what happens to us between incarnations and, especially, the question of whether there is a judgment of some kind, should not fill us with trepidation and fear, but should be approached with confidence that the process not only knows what it's doing, but that it is compassionate and kind in carrying it out. It is not the process we need to fear, but our own doubts about God and his compassion and eternal love that we need to confront and vanquish if we are to realize the fullness and richness that each individual incarnation affords us on a daily basis.

chapter sixteen

THE MECHANICS OF COMING INTO THE FLESH

Having looked at the process of planning our next life in some detail, it might be interesting to look at the physical aspects of returning to the earth plane. The reason this is important is because of the impact it has upon those of us currently residing in the flesh in terms of the sanctity of life and questions having to do with birth control, abortion, euthanasia, miscarriages, and stillborns. While I can offer no firm and fast rules but only make a few observations and spout a great deal of speculation, I do so with the hope that some somber thought can be brought to the question of how all of this may impact the process of reincarnation itself. It is also my hope in visiting these issues that those who have experienced an abortion or the heartbreak of a miscarriage or stillborn birth may acquire a different perspective from which to consider their experiences, and perhaps find some reassurance and hope in the process.

THE START OF THE PROCESS

The question of precisely when a soul enters the fetus (in essence, the moment "life" begins) is not only an interesting philosophical one, but an emotional and moral one as well (and one replete with significant religious and even political overtones). After all, if life begins at conception, terminating a pregnancy at any point is effectively an act of murder; however, if life begins at the point that the fetus becomes viable—usually during the second trimester—it makes an early stage abortion a medical issue rather than a moral one. If one defines life as beginning upon the moment the first breath is drawn, then even late-term abortion is acceptable. The entire issue an important one to consider.

Perhaps the most common assumption made by both reincarnationists and traditionalists alike is that the soul enters the fetus upon conception, but this seems somewhat presumptuous. While some reincarnationists do teach this, most have maintained that the soul seeks out a fetus to "occupy" much the same way that a bird searches diligently for a tree within which to build its nest. The bird doesn't construct its nest within the thin branches of a sapling, but instead looks for a tree of sufficient maturity and size to support its own weight and provide shelter from the wind and rain. In the same way, then, the idea that a soul seeks out a fetus at a more mature stage of development makes sense, for this would allow the soul to determine the viability of the developing fetus and whether it had any inherent birth defects that might prove detrimental (or, for that matter, beneficial) to its spiritual agenda, as well as determine its parentage, nationality, gender, and so on. Then, once it has determined the fetus to be both viable and in alignment with its wishes, the soul enters the tiny body—either incrementally and progressively or, perhaps, all at once—to both wait out its traumatic birth and give it some time to readjust to the world of linear time and space once again.

When this might be is a guess of course, but since infants regularly survive premature birth and grow up with an apparently intact soul, it would seem reasonable to assume that the soul enters the fetus at some point immediately before a prematurely-born fetus might survive outside the womb (roughly speaking, late in the second trimester).[1] Of course, it's possible that some souls enter earlier and some much later (almost immediately before birth), but a late second-trimester timeframe seems reasonable from the standpoint of viability and logic.

This, however, brings up several interesting questions. For example, can a soul occupy and then abandon a fetus before birth, or, even more intriguing, is it possible for a person to be born without a resident soul at all? And, finally, is it possible for more than one soul to claim the same fetus? In effect, might souls actually contend for the right to occupy a particularly "choice" fetus? And what about identical twins? Are we looking at a single soul that has split or two contending souls? While none of these answers can be known with any certainty, we might hazard a few guesses that, while at first appearing to be a frivolous approach to an important subject, often prove to contain the answer within their core.

In terms of whether a fetus might conceivably be born without a resident soul, it is difficult to imagine how a personality could exist apart from a soul, especially if we assume that the personality is the product or reflection of the soul. Though it's possible that a soul might not enter until days or even mere hours before birth (some have even alluded to the possibility that souls could enter shortly *after* birth), if a fetus failed to acquire a soul prior to (or immediately after) birth, it is hard to imagine how the fetus might survive. Could this be what happens to those fully formed and apparently viable fetuses that are stillborn? It's an intriguing possibility.

As for whether a soul might abandon a developing fetus, this could be possible, but if it does occur, I'd imagine it to be exceedingly rare. As the fetus is developing in the womb, once the soul takes up "residence" it effectively grows and expands within the fetus, becoming larger and more fully realized as the fetus matures. To remove itself from the body

---

1 In some parlance, this is known as the point of "quickening."

at this point might not only be difficult, but even painful to the soul, making it more probable that it would choose to stay with its chosen "host" rather than abandon the project and look elsewhere for another fetus. It is, in effect, committed to the incarnation and can only be pulled away from it in the case of a miscarriage or abortion.

However, while probably rare, there is no particularly compelling reason why a soul couldn't change its mind even while in the spiritual realm, just as it frequently can and does in the physical realm, and decide to abandon a viable fetus of its own accord. Why a soul would choose to do such a thing remains enigmatic—perhaps it is an extremely immature soul that chose in great haste and decided that it was coming into an especially difficult incarnation it was not ready to deal with. This certainly has to remain a possibility.

On the other hand, abandoning a developing fetus may not necessarily be the decision of the soul, but determined, at least in part, by physiological factors. For example, a soul may take up residency in a fetus at an early stage only to discover that the fetus is developing a congenital defect that will result in it being born severely retarded or even in a vegetative state. If the soul decides that the defect may prove detrimental to its spiritual development,[2] it may choose to abandon the "project" entirely, resulting in a miscarriage. It's also possible that the decision to abandon the fetus may not be the soul's, but the fetus's. It's not unreasonable, for example, to imagine a fetus simply expelling its host soul once it became obvious it was not going to be viable, forcing the soul to seek out another host and effectively demonstrating how the physical and spiritual realms might work together in the quest for spiritual maturation.

---

2 Although it is also possible that such a "defective" fetus may be precisely what a more advanced soul would require for its development. Most likely, however, the average soul would probably opt to abandon the fetus and consider it a "false start."

THE ABORTION QUESTION

While the ethics and morality of aborting a viable fetus may be a hotly debated one, the question is rarely asked of what becomes of the resident soul once the decision to abort is made. Is the soul destroyed along with the fetus or does it continue its journey? Further, what responsibility does a soon-to-be mother have in this case? Is she acquiring "bad karma" for her decision to abort or does it not make any difference?

Part of the answer may have to do with what point in the pregnancy the procedure was performed; if very early, the fetus may be "unoccupied" by a soul so no real damage is done, making the procedure a purely medical issue rather than an ethical one (though it may still incur detrimental psychological/emotional effects for the mother later in life). If performed after the soul has taken up residency, however, an abortion would be the equivalent of destroying a bird's nest or obliterating a beehive: it would not destroy the soul, but it would force it to flee, possibly resulting in it taking up residency in another fetus that might prove to be less than ideal for it. As for whether this might result in "bad karma" for the mother, as we will look at in some detail later, the concept of karma—at least as generally understood in the West—is not a logical one. As such, the mother would not acquire *any* kind of karma for her decision, either good or bad; she would still have to live with the natural consequences of her decision and the possible guilt, remorse, and regret that might result, but it would have no impact on her next incarnation.[3] Additionally, as her decision to abort is a result of her own level of spiritual development, it would be illogical to punish her for simply acting within the context of her own level of spiritual maturity and understanding. The universe is nothing if not patient and forgiving.

Further, it may be possible for a soul to anticipate the emotional state of an expectant mother and how likely she is to abort, and delay joining

---

3 Except, perhaps, as a residual memory that manifests itself as a strong desire for a child in a future incarnation.

with the fetus until after the decision not to abort has been made. It is reasonable to imagine that such knowledge is available to the spiritual realm, especially if one accepts the idea that each soul has spiritual mentors to guide it into the next incarnation. What's not known, of course, is how extensive this information might be and if these "mentors" can actually see into the future or whether they simply make an educated guess based upon their knowledge of the level of maturity of the soul in residency within the mother. Perhaps it's a bit of both.

Fighting over Baby

The question of determining which soul gets which body is more problematic and, in my opinion, more intriguing. Certainly the idea of souls contending for some poor fetus like a pair of starving dogs fighting over an old bone is a ludicrous one, and I doubt the spiritual realm is quite as contentious as our physical world is, especially in regard to possessions. Perhaps there is some kind of seniority system in place in which more highly-evolved souls get to select first, with the youngest and most immature souls finally being allowed to pick over what's left. Perhaps some fetuses are specifically "tagged" for more advanced souls by spirit masters because of their potential value, while others are thought to hold such limited potential for significant growth that they are left for the younger souls. On the other hand, those fetuses being born into especially promising venues—spiritually speaking—might be set aside specifically for those younger souls who need maturing the most (with the assumption being that the older, more mature souls can do more with less). In either case, I imagine that the process is a lot less messy in the spiritual realm than it would be if played out in the physical realm. However, considering that there may be spiritually primitive souls involved in the process, one can never be certain that the process might not be any less pretty in the realm of spirit than it is in the flesh, despite what one might expect from the "other side."

The entire argument might be rendered moot, however, if we look at it from the perspective of eternity. No fetus may be considered better or worse or more promising or less promising than another; all may have—and probably do have—the same value in our maturing process. The developing fetus simply provides a particular venue from which to experience life in all its many facets; it is up to the resident soul to decide what to do with that life. As such, a child born into great poverty might, in the end, prove to grow far more spiritually in his or her short, deprived life than had he or she been born into great wealth. It is the difficulties of life and our abilities to overcome them that give birth to spiritual growth, not the time, place, and venue of our next incarnation. As such, fighting over a fetus may be pointless, especially from the perspective of eternity.

The Multiple Personality Disorder Phenomenon

However, the idea that souls might actually contend for the right to inhabit a developing fetus creates a host of other questions that need to be explored. For instance, is it possible for more than a single soul to occupy a particular fetus? We naturally assume we all have but a single soul and, as such, a single personality, but what if that is not always the case? Could multiple souls inhabiting a single body be one possible explanation for cases of multiple personality disorder (MPD)?

For those not familiar with this rare but fascinating condition, MPD is a psychological disorder in which a person exhibits more than one established, distinct personality (and may, in some rare cases, exhibit literally dozens of such personalities). What causes it is not entirely clear, but it seems to be a defense mechanism built into the human psyche that permits the personality to split or "shatter" during times of tremendous trauma, especially if the trauma is experienced during early childhood. In effect, the theory goes, in order to keep the psyche from complete disintegration, the personality breaks into smaller, compartmentalized parts (each of which apparently is safer from disintegration than a whole personality might be) resulting in numerous, often contradictory personalities emerging in later life. For example, one personality might be somber and restrained, while another is playful and vivacious; another might be sexually prudish while another exhibits itself as being promiscuous. Each is a part of the whole person, yet they are not integrated into a single seamless personality, putting the individual suffering from such a disorder in a difficult situation, especially because often many of the personalities are not aware of the existence of others, resulting in frequently embarrassing situations that leave the "primary" personality at a loss for how it got into a particular situation. It is only with considerable work and patience on the part of a good therapist (and a tremendous willingness on the part of the victim) that these pieces of the greater personality can be successfully fused back together, restoring order to the sufferer's life.

So what does this have to do with the idea of various souls contending for a developing fetus? In some cases of MPD, is it possible that some of these competing personalities are not fragmented pieces of a greater personality, but in often exhibiting evidence of being complete, whole personalities in their own right may, in fact, be "secondary" souls all inhabiting a single body?

Apparently many mental health professionals who deal with MPD patients note that some and indeed many of the personalities they encounter do not appear to be incomplete, as one would expect from a fractured element of a greater personality, but are fully intact personalities that exhibit a complete range of emotions, their own unique physiology, and even distinct brain wave patterns. For example, one personality may have a severe allergy to pollen while another does not, each may have different blood pressures and pulse rates, and one might even have better eyesight or hearing than another, even though they are all emanating from the same physical being. This leads one to conclude that either the brain has a remarkable and little-understood ability to dramatically affect a body's physiology, or there may be more than a single soul residing within a body.

Is it possible that in some unique cases the fetus may genuinely be inhabited by more than one soul—say either a series of primitive souls or a stronger primary soul and several "lesser" souls along for the ride—and that these "alter egos" don't appear until and unless there is some trauma that brings them to the surface? In essence, our body might be hosting more than a single soul but they remain hidden to us as long as our personality remains intact—in effect masking each of the more primitive souls within the shadow of a larger, more dominant primary soul.

While this may sound fantastic, it should be realized that most people exhibit wide-ranging mood swings. We have all had days when we just weren't feeling ourselves or seemed out of sorts for no apparent external reason. We may feel energized and optimistic one moment and depressed and tired an hour later; irritable and angry on one occasion and patient and forgiving on another; and even intellectually sharp one moment and frightfully dull another. Could these moods then be not simply a single soul manifesting particular energies from moment to moment, but in fact a series of personalities—some so subtle as to be almost indistinguishable—emerging under just the right conditions?

In this example a person is not exhibiting different personalities per se, but is merely experiencing a normal range of human emotions. Yet what if these different energies we put off at different times are the subtle efforts of very young and primitive personalities to exert themselves? Even if they're not powerful enough to dramatically impact the primary personality, could they be strong enough to still influence it to some degree?

It's an intriguing possibility that suggests that very immature souls may in effect "piggyback" onto more mature souls through an incarnation, much like an older, wiser sister might take the hand of her baby brother in a crowd. Is it possible that some souls are too immature to take on a solo incarnation and need to be shown "the ropes" by more seasoned souls, and that as long as the host does not suffer the sort of trauma that results in the personality shattering, it will reside deep within

the psyche of that person completely unnoticed throughout an entire lifetime? In essence, might not a very primitive soul be able to learn by simply staying in the background and watching the more mature soul live
out its incarnation and be more prepared the next time around to "fly
solo" in its own body?

This would have a number of benefits from the soul's perspective.
First, it would be a way of effectively shepherding a primitive soul
through the growth process instead of letting it take on an incarnation
before it's mature enough to handle it. Just as we don't let teenagers
operate an automobile until they've had some time behind the wheel,
perhaps the same might be true in the spiritual realm as well, with older,
more mature souls in effect taking the younger ones "along for a ride" so
they can get the feel of how an incarnation operates. This would also
have the effect of limiting the mischief underdeveloped souls could get
into, making the older souls, in effect, babysitters or surrogate parents to
the younger souls. As such, as long as the primitive souls are kept under
control, the human hosts need never be aware of their presence and
could live out their lives entirely unaware that they possessed a number
of younger souls within their psyche.

It would also be a means by which more mature souls might grow as
well, for in setting examples for the younger souls, they may be learning
a great deal themselves. Just as young men and women often mature
much more quickly once they become parents, so too might it be that
the maturing soul can make great leaps in its development if it serves in
the role of teacher for a time. If we work from the premise that all souls
are a manifestation of the divine and a part of a single, larger soul, it
makes sense that there would be considerable cooperation among the
various souls, both in terms of assisting others and being assisted by
others, all for their mutual benefit.

While a fantastic idea and probably an unnecessary appendage to
understanding reincarnation, it would account for some of the more
remarkable aspects of MPD and also have something to say about
"demon" possession (which may not be a "demon" at all, but simply a

primitive and angry soul that, out of fear, resists being cast out of its host). Additionally, it does answer some questions nicely, though admittedly it also creates a host of new questions in the process.

"Rogue" Souls

Finally, there is one of the lesser-known paradoxes to deal with, and that is the possibility that a particularly primitive soul might forcefully eject another soul from either a still-developing fetus or, conceivably, even from an already-born human. While admittedly this is one of the more intriguing possibilities regarding reincarnation, in looking at how souls may contend for a developing fetus or even piggyback onto another soul, isn't it possible that a "rogue" soul could decide to circumvent the rebirth process and simply seize an already occupied host body, effectively "claim jumping" or even expelling the previous, weaker occupant, committing a form of spiritual thievery? While probably unlikely, it is something to consider, and an important possibility to take a look at.

What brings the entire issue up are those rare cases Dr. Ian Stevenson encountered over the course of his studies of past-life memories in children when it appeared that the previous-life personality the child recounted had died shortly *after* the child's own birth. In effect, young Hamib could recall a past life as Muhammed that is both credible and verifiable only to later have it discovered that Muhammed did not die until nearly a year *after* Hamib was born. Of course, such should be utterly impossible if we are to imagine that incarnations are sequential, thus throwing the entire issue into doubt.

It might be imagined that this is something that only the most brazen and immature soul might try, and it's further difficult to imagine that there wouldn't be certain safeguards in place specifically to prevent such a thing from happening, but we cannot be certain of that. Also, there's the possibility that a more mature soul might willingly surrender its host to another soul if it felt the younger soul might benefit from taking on that particular incarnation. Precisely how this works can only be guessed at, but it is evidence that the mechanics of the rebirth process may be far more complex and free-will driven than we might imagine. It may even be that the process of returning into the flesh may lie well beyond our ability to understand at all, demanding instead that we simply learn to trust the process rather than try to comprehend it, which is probably the best advice of all.

THE QUESTION OF TWINS

Another interesting question within the realm of the mechanics of reincarnation is what to make of identical twins. That identical twins frequently share a significant number of personality traits is well documented, and while science explains this as the result of sharing the same genetic characteristics and similar environments, it fails to explain why such close parallels in personality are not as frequently found—or as pronounced—in fraternal twins as well, since they too are almost invariably raised under identical circumstances. Further, there is the question of those rare sets of identical twins who are separated at birth only to reunite years later to find that they share not only many physical characteristics and temperament, but also similar tastes in clothing, hobbies, professions, and even mates. Colin Wilson cites two examples in his extensive work *Beyond the Occult*,[4] where he writes of two cases of separated twins whose lives seemed to almost mirror each other's, right down to suffering similar mishaps at the same ages to marrying spouses with the same names and having the identical number of children!

This clearly seems to argue for at least a "soul mix" in identical twins, if not a single soul residing within two physical bodies. Yet it is hard to imagine how a single soul could manifest two near-identical personalities simultaneously and be able to work through both, especially when they are separated by great distances. But then, we so poorly understand this

---

4 Colin Wilson, *Beyond the Occult* (New York: Carroll & Graf Publishers, 1989).

process in any case that such may not only be possible, but even common. The fact that a single soul can occupy two physical forms at the same time should be no more remarkable than the idea that it can occupy a single human form; within the context of eternity, anything may be possible.

It is also possible there is such a thing as "complementary souls"—souls so close in temperament and personality as to be almost carbon copies of each other—that choose to travel together through multiple incarnations, always manifesting through sets of identical twins (or even triplets). Considering the almost unlimited combinations of soul and body experiences possible, it would not be far-fetched to imagine almost anything to be possible in the spiritual realm, right down to souls that travel like a pack of wolves—not in an effort to hunt down and destroy, but in an effort to facilitate and participate in each other's spiritual evolution.

The mechanism of reincarnation is often a mysterious one that produces as many questions as answers, and this could be one of these areas where we are fated to only guess. While it would be nice to understand this process more fully, it probably is not necessary that we do so. Perhaps one day, once we attain a higher level of spiritual understanding both individually and collectively, we may be ready to tackle these questions, but for now we shall have to settle for mere speculation.

CONCLUSION

The mechanics of returning to physicality are, most likely, complex and beyond our current understanding, and likely to remain that way for the foreseeable future. Fortunately, however, it is not necessary for us to understand the process to appreciate it for its inherent perfection and ultimate value. We all have questions as to why some people are born with heartbreaking deformities or genetic proclivities toward cancer or heart disease, yet we perceive the process from our very limited perspective and from this side of eternity. We can't always know or even understand what is going on within the spiritual realm when a person is born, or a miscarriage occurs, or even when a suicide takes place. Likely there are a great number of things happening simultaneously on many different fronts, each of them interrelated and joined to form the unique tapestry we call life. They are mysteries we can only ponder and accept as a part of the process of spiritual growth.

Fortunately, we don't need to understand all of the complexities of the process, but to retain the faith that the universe is a place of love and compassion, and to know that no matter what happens, everything will work out perfectly in the end. We may not always experience only joyous things—children and their mothers sometimes die in childbirth, and experiencing a miscarriage or a stillborn birth can be heartwrenching— but even so it is important to understand that the Divine is still in charge. Even the tragedies of life can be beneficial down the road (although when we can't see it at the time), so trust the process and learn what you can learn from each disappointment, for it is within the challenges and tribulations of life that the spirit of God glows most brightly. We must come to trust that life is not something to fear. It is a spectacular experience to immerse ourselves in; it is our playground of possibilities, the stage upon which we live out each act, and the venue within which God experiences himself. What happens to us, whether in life or between lives, is in God's hands, and we can rest assured that because of that we are safe, for God realizes that in dealing with each soul, he is dealing with the sacred.

chapter seventeen

A New Perspective on Karma

Perhaps no element of reincarnation has been more maligned or misunderstood than that aspect of it that is known as karma. It is the single most controversial teaching within reincarnation, and as such it requires the most careful thought.

Karma is a Sanskrit word that simply means "action," and is similar in many respects to the Western concept of cause and effect. It is the belief that the things we do or experience in a previous life impact our present life in ways both subtle and severe. For example, a brutal slave owner in a past life might find himself reincarnated as a slave, or, in a more extreme case, a despot who enjoys putting out the eyes of his enemies in a past incarnation may be born blind in a later incarnation to "atone" for his previous cruelty.

Since the human expectation that justice be served is universal, karma is not a difficult concept to accept even among those who have no belief in reincarnation per se. It does, after all, speak to the very basic human desire to see wrongs righted either through temporal mechanisms of justice (incarceration, execution, or restitution), or, if that fails, within the context of eternity (purgatory, hell, or rebirth into a negative incarnation). In fact, it is such a primordial instinct within the human species, it is difficult to imagine how any religion that does not address the issue of justice could be sustainable.

However, karma is not understood by everyone the same way. Like most belief systems, there are "schools of thought" on the concept, many of which are either vastly misunderstood or largely unknown in the West. For the sake of clarity, we will examine the three chief justifications behind karma, as generally taught, in an effort to understand the subtle but significant differences that exist between them, and we will take a brief look at one of the more persistent misunderstandings of the idea held by Westerners: "transmigration of the soul."

KARMA AS RETRIBUTION

The most prevalent view of karma is that it is primarily a punitive mechanism designed to punish a person for a past sin or wickedness. It works from the premise that there is a type of "accounting system" in place that demands that sin debts be repaid, if not in one lifetime, then in another. In some cases, this retribution can be fairly mild—a wealthy person may be born into a poor family or an abusive husband may be reincarnated as a woman—while in others it can be most severe (as in the above example of the evil despot reborn as a blind man). This assumption of retribution is why some cultures that embrace reincarnation believe that all birth defects are considered evidence of a wicked past life, and those born into great poverty and squalor are thought to be paying for an earlier life of selfish opulence and greed.

The problem with this idea—at least from a Western perspective—is that since the person being reincarnated has no previous knowledge of his or her wicked past, he or she suffers without understanding the reasons behind it, making it not only a poor tool for spiritual growth, but an unreasonable and cruel form of judgment. By way of example, let's say that "Black Bart"—the stereotypical criminal from the Old West—is captured and lynched in 1889, only to be reincarnated in the body of a boy named Fred in 1913. Now Fred, the unwitting reincarnation of the hated and feared outlaw, has a life that seems "snake-bit" from the beginning. Aside from suffering all his life from a badly deformed right leg—the same leg, incidentally, that old Bart once took a bullet in—throughout the course of his short, miserable life he also sees his parents murdered in a botched robbery, his fiancee raped and killed by a previous spurned suitor, and his own hard-earned savings stolen by an unscrupulous business partner. A broken man, he eventually dies from alcoholism at age thirty-five, his emaciated corpse discovered in an abandoned shack many weeks after his death.

From the perspective of punitive karma, Fred, being the reincarnation of Black Bart, got exactly what he deserved for his previous evil deeds. In fact, almost everything that happened to him perfectly corresponded to the actions that Bart had been guilty of in his life: the murder of his parents, the rape and murder of his fiancee, and theft were all the very crimes Black Bart had inflicted upon innocent people during his brief reign of terror. Experiencing the painful consequences of the actions carried out by his previous personality showed Black Bart—even in the guise of Fred—the enormity of his crimes, and, hopefully, gave the soul that was Black Bart the chance to atone for its sins.

Of course, the problem is that Fred is *not* Black Bart—at least in the practical sense—for he is an entirely separate personality who is uniquely distinct and completely removed from his past-life persona. Since he has no recollection of his past incarnation and has done nothing in his present life to warrant "God's wrath," from his limited perspective he is not experiencing the consequences of his previous crimes, but is simply suffering one calamity after another until it finally leaves him a broken man. He can't perceive the misfortunes that come upon him as a lesson, but instead sees them purely as a series of horrible and inexplicable miscarriages of justice. Further, there is no means by which he might understand the lessons karma is trying to teach him, nor can he appreciate the need that his past crimes be offset by his current suffering, for to him his past crimes are not his, but someone else's. It's akin to waking one morning in a wretched dungeon and being told that you are to remain there the rest of your life for a crime you have absolutely no recollection of committing. Even if you might agree intellectually that your punishment is just, with no memory of the crime itself the punishment will never have the effect of serving justice.

Yet from the perspective of retributive karma, none of that is important. It is the soul that is being punished for its crimes, not the personality it manifests; what incarnation it happens to find itself in at any particular time is beside the point—justice will be served regardless. From the soul's perspective, not only does all of this supposedly make perfect sense, but it also knows how important it is to be "cleansed of" its previous evil before it can go on. Therefore, it finds no injustice in Fred's horrific life and, in fact, would see it all as part of a perfect plan.

Unfortunately, we do not see through the eyes of the soul in this life, but through the eyes of the personality through which the soul has manifested. Even if we accept that the punishment may be justified (at least theoretically), the personality that is actually experiencing the consequences of that punishment is suffering for a crime it did not commit, but is guilty of only by association. Just as we would consider imprisoning a son for the crimes of his father to be profoundly unjust, so too should this scenario be rejected as patently unfair and, in fact, entirely in opposition to any concept of a loving God.

THE "NEED" FOR PUNISHMENT

The question that needs to be immediately addressed before moving on is why we assume evil needs to be "paid for" at all, and, further, if it is even *possible* for evil to be paid for, either through the mechanism of retributive karma or through the traditional Western mechanisms of purgatory or hell.

It seems an affront to some people to suggest that the wicked might not be punished in some way, as if retribution is the only thing that is capable of making things right. Unfortunately, it's a very human attitude that goes back to the dawn of time when we sought retribution against the other tribe for their perceived wickedness while interpreting our own brutality as righteous indignation or, at very least, prudent self-defense. It's also the reason that punitive karma attracts us: not only does it justify ourselves to ourselves, but it helps maintain the illusion that justice *can* be served.

But what is meant by justice being served? Clearly, no wrong has ever been righted through punishing the perpetrator. To do that, the very act of retribution itself would have to have the effect of undoing the consequences of the act that was committed, but, of course, we know it does not. If a person takes the life of another—either intentionally or accidentally— no amount of jail time (or even the death penalty itself) will undo that death. The victim's children, spouse, parents, friends, and family will still be without that individual, regardless of the severity (or, for that matter, lightness) of punishment the accused receives. Even if the criminal is executed, it makes no more difference to the ultimate outcome than if he or she were to get away with the crime scot-free.

While obviously a sense of justice does matter within the context of our present world and we should always strive to see that the human and civil rights of all people are secure, nothing we ultimately do in any single lifetime impacts eternity. The crimes we commit alongside the good deeds we do are reflections of our spiritual states; while they may have inadvertent repercussions within future lifetimes, in the context of the spirit realm they mean little. Therefore, punishment is not, in and of itself, a particularly useful tool for spiritual growth.

A person may learn from being punished for a crime, it is true, but that lesson has to come from within the human heart; it cannot be impressed upon a person from the outside. That's why two men may be imprisoned for the same crime and one will truly regret the path he has taken and strive to change his ways while the other will simply regret having been caught; the key to spiritual growth is not in suffering a punishment, but in recognizing what one is, and that can only come from within. Therefore, to punish a man for the crimes of his previous personality neither undoes anything he may have done nor teaches him anything new that might advance his spiritual development. As such, there is no such thing as retributive karma, for retribution can only be realized—if it can be realized at all—within the context of linear time and space.

This sounds as though I'm suggesting that we let people get away with their crimes, but I'm doing nothing of the sort. I'm simply recognizing the cold, hard fact that since everything we do is done within the context of linear time, there is no way to "pay for" anything that is done. We may apologize to our victims or even attempt to make restitution, but we cannot literally undo what has been done. It simply is not an option that linear time permits. Therefore, to punish someone in a future incarnation for crimes committed in a previous one is not only counterproductive, but an immense waste of time in that it has no capacity to achieve anything useful. What has happened has simply happened. Karma cannot change that. It is not designed to.

Of course, it could be argued that the purpose of retribution is not to undo the past, but to teach the soul not to repeat the same brutal acts through each incarnation, and while this has some merit, it fails to address the issue of just how the soul might change its nature by being punished. Punishment can modify behavior to some degree, but rarely does it change the underlying nature. If this were possible, we would see very low recidivism rates in our prison system. Unfortunately, of course, such is not the case, demonstrating clearly that punishment in and of itself has no inherent capacity to change human nature.

Further, punitive karma fails to take into account the negative circumstances surrounding a particular incarnation that are responsible for the direction the soul has taken through the course of a particular lifetime. Brutal and violent lives are often the result of growing up in abject poverty or in a particularly militant or vicious culture where aggressive tendencies are the norm. There are numerous external factors unique to any particular incarnation that often have less to do with the spiritual state of the soul than the circumstances of one's birth. Does it make sense, then, to punish the future personality for the difficult circumstances of a past one?

Transmigration of the Soul

Before moving on, it is first necessary to clear up one misconception many Westerners hold about reincarnation and bad karma, and that is the belief that reincarnation teaches that an especially wicked person may not return as a human in a lesser capacity, but may be punished by reincarnating in the form of an animal or some "lesser" creature. This belief, however—one that is persistently assumed by people unfamiliar with reincarnationist concepts to be a major component of the teaching—is actually an aberration of the idea, and one held to by few Western reincarnationists. Further, the idea is not technically even reincarnation at all, but an offshoot of it known as "transmigration of the soul."

Transmigration is thought to be the ultimate humiliation for the soul, for in binding it to a "lowly" creature, it is forced to endure a brutal and short life with little hope for redemption or opportunity to be reborn back into human form. It works from the premise that no matter how difficult a human life might be, even the most wretched of them is better than living out an incarnation as a "mere" animal, especially one of the lower creatures.[1] In some traditions, this concept is so completely entrenched that every effort is made to avoid killing animals, and in extreme cases believers will actually sweep the path in front of

---

1 Some beliefs even maintain that one might come back as a plant or, in an extreme case, a stone or some other inanimate object. While this sounds almost incredulous, it must be remembered that the Eastern mind accepts that all things—even inanimate objects—possess souls, and so it is no more difficult to imagine that one might inhabit a rock than it is to imagine that one might inhabit an ox.

them with a small broom in an effort to keep from inadvertently stepping upon an insect, lest they come back themselves as an insect as retribution for their negligence.

Transmigration has several serious problems inherent to it. First, it fails to explain how a soul might gain anything spiritually if it is born into a creature that does not possess sentience. A sense of self-awareness and a moral nature would seem to be the minimal prerequisite required in order to appreciate any spiritual growth, yet if the purpose of a lower incarnation is to induce the soul toward a higher level of consciousness, how is this to be realized within the tiny brain of a rat? As such, there seems to be no upward mechanism by which the soul might move toward spiritual maturity from within the context of transmigration, since animals are amoral creatures incapable of being either "good" or "bad."

Second, it assumes that life as an animal is a worse fate than life as a human, but this contention could be debated. Certainly it seems that some animals live a fairly carefree existence, and in the case of some birds or jungle predators (not to mention house pets) their lives might even be considered idyllic. Has one never fantasized about what it would be like to fly free like an eagle or be a powerful lion spending one's days hunting gazelle from the confines of a lush, cool jungle? If not, why do such phrases as "it's a dog's life" or "free as a bird" possess such positive connotations?

Third, most animals possess life spans that are far shorter than that of a human being, so an incarnation as an animal is more short-term, hence the period of punishment is greatly reduced. As such, it could be argued that a hard life as a man or woman might not only be more difficult than that of an animal, but as it would last longer it would make a human incarnation a much more severe punishment and a far better tool for rendering justice, if justice were the real issue here.

As such, it seems that transmigration of the soul is a far poorer mechanism for either extracting justice or teaching spiritual lessons than traditional reincarnation. If the purpose of the soul is spiritual maturity, then incarnating into the bodies of animals would appear to be a step in the wrong direction and utterly detrimental to what the rebirthing process is trying to accomplish. Except for those rare cases where a person might purposely enter into the body of an animal for some religious or symbolic reason,[2] it's difficult to see how transmigration would be useful.

Finally, the term "reincarnate" argues against the concept. To re-incarnate means to return once again as the same "kind" of thing one was before, not to return in an entirely different venue. As such, we must assume that humans come back as humans until their soul journey is complete, and it is with this assumption that we will move on to examine the other different "takes" on the role karma supposedly plays within human-to-human reincarnation.

Karma as Teacher

Another (and decidedly more popular) perspective on karma is that it is not primarily a means of exacting retribution but instead is better understood as a tool for teaching the underlying soul valuable lessons designed to enhance its spiritual development. While punitive karma is theoretically supposed to achieve the same thing, instructive karma really does attempt to shape the soul through finding useful circumstances it might use to experience a wider range of perspectives than would otherwise be possible within the course of a single lifetime. In other words, if the point of reincarnating is to apply the lessons from the previous incarnation to this present life in an effort to realize as rapid a spiritual growth as possible, then karma would seem to be the ideal mechanism to carry this out.

To see how this might be realized practically, imagine that the soul of a Nazi killed in the Second World War takes the time to assess its previous

---

2 Such teachings can be found within the traditions of many "earth religions," though even then such human-to-animal transitions are rare.

experience and determine its next best course of action. Realizing that having been born to anti-Semitic parents and growing up in a culture of mindless nationalism were what had largely shaped the hateful and arrogant personality it had become, it is determined that in order to offset those negative traits it will experience its next life from the perspective of a Jew. In this way, it is supposed, it will experience life from a viewpoint it had not encountered before and purge the poison of anti-Semitism from its blood, thus refining itself spiritually and growing toward ever higher levels of understanding and awareness. Further, this need not be an unpleasant experience either, for the lesson is realized whether the new incarnation's life is an easy or difficult one. It is the experience of living life as a Jew that is beneficial to spiritual growth, not the specific circumstances of that life.

Additionally, the theory goes on to suggest that a soul *may* decide to be born into decidedly unpleasant circumstances, not in an effort to punish itself for some previous evil, but to learn lessons only those born into poverty or suffering from deformity, weakness, oppression, or sickness can appreciate. In other words, the soul may choose an especially difficult incarnation because it feels that to do so will give it a fresh perspective that will prove vital in furthering its spiritual progress.

While this concept is far more positive than punitive karma, it unfortunately suffers from many of the same problems. Most significant among them is that just as in the case of punitive karma, teaching karma is equally lost upon the new personality. For example, just as Fred had no recollection of having been Black Bart in his past life, the Jew who was a Nazi in his previous incarnation retains no memory of his past, and without these memories there is nothing to be learned. One cannot appreciate what it is to be a Jew if he or she cannot also recall having been anti-Semitic, so the former Nazi can learn nothing from his new incarnation. As far as both personalities are concerned, the other does not exist, at least within their frame of reference. While the Jew may retain some characteristics of his "Aryan" past, unless he has the requisite memories to go with it there is nothing to compare the new experiences to. The entire process remains pointless, at least within the context of linear time, if there are no residual memories to give the experience meaning.

Of course, it is the soul that is supposedly learning these lessons, not the personality, but that only goes so far. Even if it is the soul that is benefiting from the change of venue, it is still the present personality that is living out the soul's choices and experiencing the consequences (or, for that matter, benefits) of those decisions, and that brings up the issue of fairness to deal with. If one chooses to reincarnate in some positive venue, that's fine, but what if one chooses to return as a muscular dystrophy patient? Even if the soul is learning all kinds of valuable lessons from the experience, the personality it has manifested itself as is still suffering, sometimes horribly. Suffering for the sake of the soul's spiritual enrichment may sound ennobling, but it is suffering nonetheless, and as such can have no place in the world of loving divinity. That some people are clearly born into unfortunate circumstances may be a fact of life and an element of linear time, but to decide that such incarnations are the result of some carefully thought-out plan is indifferent bordering on cruel. That a soul may incarnate within a deformed fetus is one thing, but to preplan such debilitating and painful circumstances can be nothing if not cold. To separate the soul from the personality is to concentrate on the "rights" of the one—the soul—at the expense of the personality, which renders the personality of no intrinsic value.

On the other hand, as we discussed earlier, it is not beyond possibility that a soul may choose a particularly difficult venue in order to affect some specific mission. A soul may choose to enter into a handicapped fetus if it believes that it can achieve some positive effects in the lives of others by doing so. Such a choice is not driven by karma, but by a very specific free-will decision of the soul. This is not karma as a tool for spiritual growth, but an attempt to affect the spiritual growth of others as a matter of personal choice.

That souls may enter into difficult incarnations, then, may be a reality, but it is only an assumption that such incarnations are a result of some rigid karmic law that cannot be broken. The effects may be similar, but it seems far more likely that such results are driven by free will rather than determined by karmic law, making karma as a tool for spiritual growth a result of faulty interpretation of external circumstances. In other words, while it may appear that the soul has entered into a difficult incarnation in an effort to learn a lesson it needs to learn, the reality might be something quite different. It is merely our limited understanding of how the process works that makes us interpret things the way we do.

Karma as a Balance of Negative and Positive Energies

A third idea about how karma works maintains that, unlike the other concepts that see each incarnation as either an inevitable consequence of a prior life or the result of a carefully crafted plan, this view of karma's role is that of an entirely indifferent and even amoral force that is not interested in either punishment or teaching, but merely in achieving spiritual balance. In other words, karma is simply a neutral mechanism of the soul by which negative energies are countered with positive energies in an effort to maintain a certain spiritual equilibrium. It is not "planning" things out, but simply righting a wobbling spirituality, the same way one might straighten a crooked picture on the wall.

The idea here is that the soul is inherently perfect, so when negativity, which is considered an imperfect element, enters into the picture, karma sees to it that everything is put right again. From this perspective, then, the soul is seen as a great "factory" that is constantly producing new personalities, and once negativity enters into one incarnation, the "factory" simply produces another, more positive personality to offset the negative effects of the earlier personality until complete spiritual harmony is restored. The effects are similar to the concept of learning from one's past mistakes by introducing a new personality to an incarnation that applies those errors, yet it is done blindly and naturally, without personal planning or judgment.

The problem with this concept, however, like the other concepts of karma, remains the same: it is still the unaware personality that essentially "pays" for the spiritual imbalance that the soul is attempting to correct. Even if one person's avarice and greed in one incarnation could be offset by a life of want in another in order to restore spiritual harmony to the larger soul, this still victimizes the personality born into desperate poverty, and as such remains an injustice that demands an explanation. It also doesn't explain *why* the soul requires itself to be spiritually balanced, or how a life of deprivation in one incarnation might actually "balance out" a life of selfish indulgence in another. If the soul's purpose is simply to appreciate what it is (pure, divine love) by experiencing being that which it is not (say, selfishness, greed, and indifference), then why does it require balancing at all? Isn't the experience itself sufficient to tell it all it needs to know?

And, finally, there is the problem of balancing out a positive energy with a negative one. If we work from the premise that the soul is seeking to keep its energy in perfect balance, shouldn't an especially positive incarnation be countered by an especially negative one, if we are to take this idea of spiritual balance to its logical conclusion? After all, it doesn't make sense that if you can push a picture a little too far to the right that you can't also push it a little too far to the left as well.

WHY KARMA AT ALL?

So, clearly, all three explanations that attempt to justify the rationale behind karma appear to be lacking on several fronts. They fail as an effective means of justice by punishing the innocent for the crimes of the guilty; they fail as a mechanism for enlightenment by teaching the required lessons to an unaware student; and they fail as a mechanism for balancing the soul's spiritual energy by both achieving that balance at the expense of the innocent and failing to justify the need for such balance in the first place.

As such, we are left with the question as to precisely what role karma, in fact, does play in reincarnation. In fact, to take it one step further, what if there is no such thing as karma at all? What if it simply doesn't exist, despite all the teachings to the contrary?

Few reincarnationists stop to ask themselves this question, preferring instead to simply accept whatever position personally appeals to them. Yet it is an important question to ask, for it is only in challenging the traditional teachings on any subject that we come to either understand it more completely or destroy it as a potential impediment to further learning. Such, I fear, is what must be done with the entire notion of karma.

It is perfectly reasonable to assume that since the point of reincarnation is spiritual growth, the experiences of each lifetime should shape us in ways both subtle and dramatic. Therefore, as we move through each incarnation, it seems inevitable that the vast number of experiences we've undergone will have much to say about what form our next incarnation may take. This concept, in fact, is a part of karma's counterpart teaching known as *dharma,* which is the notion that our underlying soul constantly improves as it moves through each incarnation, much like clay takes on a greater degree of refinement the longer it remains on the potter's wheel. And just as the imperfections and blemishes are constantly worked out of the clay through the natural process of the constantly turning wheel, dharma mimics this effect by serving as a type of spiritual bank account into which only positive characteristics are deposited while negative traits are discarded.

The problem lies in imagining this refinement process being realized only through a succession of preplanned incarnations rather than through purely natural and spontaneous processes. In other words, while karma maintains that a soul works out its refinement through a series of carefully orchestrated spiritual choices or, at the very least, through the effects of some impersonal tit-for-tat process of justice, the reality may be that such a process is entirely unnecessary for spiritual growth to take place. If both conscious past-life recall and regression therapy tell us anything, they demonstrate that the process of rebirth is apparently random, exhibiting

neither a balance between prior life and present life actions nor any meticulous and precise preplanning. A modern businessman, for example, may
recount, in turn, having been an eighteenth-century cobbler in England, a
rug maker in fifteenth-century Baghdad, an Indian girl in the ninth century, and a sailor in third-century Greece—none of which have any apparent connection between them. The English cobbler is not seen to be balancing out any negative actions of the Arab merchant, nor is the Indian
girl paying for the crimes committed as a third-century sailor. Instead,
each incarnation is a collection of very ordinary and unrelated lives that
together argue against most modern ideas about karma.

Only rarely does one find a potential link between a present incarnation and a past life, and these are frequently tentative at best. Occasionally
a person who suffers from chronic health problems and then recounts
under hypnosis having been a brutal and violence-prone husband in a past
life might be thought to be suffering a kind of "payback" for the harsh
treatment meted out to an abused wife in that prior incarnation. However, the "link" is purely an assumption based upon the notion that "what
goes around, comes around," whereas in reality the health problems may
be more a matter of bad genetics than bad karma. Usually, it's more commonly the case that there is no apparent link between this life and a past
one at all, and certainly nothing that might demonstrate a quid pro quo
between the actions of one incarnation and those of the next.

That doesn't mean that certain patterns won't emerge over the
course of several lifetimes, but such patterns do not suggest anything
approaching karma. They are more likely either the soul's effort to more
fully examine a specific venue by repeatedly incarnating into similar circumstances, or evidence of a soul that has gotten itself stuck within a
particular venue and is either unable to or unwilling to break the pat-
tern. In either case, there is no evidence that a soul is attempting to offset or pay off some incurred karmic debt by incarnating into similar, difficult lives; it's more likely that its repeated manifestations into trying
(or, at least, similar) circumstances are a result of the random process of
rebirth.

Additionally, there is no clear evidence that any single incarnation is necessarily planned out, but instead each is a spontaneous result of a process that operates quite independently of free will. That's not to say that the soul lacks any preferences for its next incarnation (as we discussed earlier); it merely suggests that the soul doesn't need to plan out each incarnation, or balance its spiritual energy, or pay for its past errors, in order to mature naturally. It will do so as a matter of course, quite apart from whether the next incarnation is carefully planned or utterly spontaneous. The process of spiritual maturation will go on regardless.

To appreciate this better, consider that over the course of a soul's "life span,"[3] it will incarnate scores or even hundreds of times before it reaches full maturity. As such, it is inevitable that it will experience almost everything imaginable to the human race (as both male and female and from the perspective of many races, cultures, social stations, and environments) *naturally*, without having to plan anything at all. A soul is going to incarnate into positive circumstances and negative ones repeatedly, know difficult lives and fairly easy lives, and experience life from both the perspective of a sinner as well as that of a saint many times before it is through, each of which will further shape its development.

If it's helpful, you can imagine reincarnation as a "crap shoot" in which the benefits are seen over the long term rather than immediately. For example, over a series of ten incarnations, a soul may find itself aborted, stillborn, or dying in infancy in three of them, existing in circumstances allowing little or no spiritual growth in three others, and experiencing growth of a kind in the remaining four incarnations. Overall, the soul has matured in four of the ten rebirths—the four "positives" offsetting the three "negatives" and the three false starts. And since the positives are retained into the next incarnation while the negatives are

---

3 Of course, a soul cannot die, so "life span" is an inadequate description. I simply mean here the time it takes for the young soul to grow to complete maturity before returning to its divine source.

purged, the soul still comes out ahead despite achieving a degree of spiritual growth only 40 percent of the time.

But what of the "negative incarnations"? Certainly it can be argued that reincarnating as a criminal—regardless of whether it is preplanned or accidental—should be detrimental to spiritual growth. With enough "negative incarnations," then, isn't one potentially capable of moving further away from spiritual maturity and sliding ever further into darkness?

That we may occasionally manifest under circumstances that are less than ideal for spiritual development may appear on the surface to suggest such a thing, yet even those incarnations that we might consider failures are, in fact, a part of the growth process. They show us where we are on our paths and help us appreciate the value in striving to move ahead. As such, there is no such thing as failure in the absolute sense of the word, for even failure is a necessary part of the greater matrix of illumination and understanding. We cannot ultimately fail, for failure is already figured into the mix.

Consider it this way: when an inventor is working on a new invention, he or she may initially encounter numerous setbacks, failed attempts, and dead ends. It is recorded that Thomas Edison tried literally hundreds of different materials as a filament for the light bulb before finally hitting upon magnesium. In the process, most of the materials he tried did nothing or immediately incinerated, while a few would burn brightly for a few seconds as electricity surged through them and then went out. Yet these were not failures in the strictest sense of the word, for Edison was working from a process of elimination. Each carefully-recorded failure brought him one step closer to finding a substance that would work until he finally developed a practical light bulb and revolutionized the industrialized world.

It is the same for the soul that is striving for spiritual growth. It may frequently turn out to be a two-steps-forward, one-step-backward process, but it is still progressing toward its own ultimate perfection. That this progress may be achieved through a process of randomness makes it no more or less efficient than if it were carefully planned, and, in fact, may make it an even more valuable process precisely *because* it is so random.

As such, we don't need karma to explain the mechanism of rebirth or even of spiritual evolution, for both are a byproduct of randomness. That's not to say that a soul may not have some choice in its next incarnation, at least in general terms, or that these incarnations are not instructive and useful toward maturing spiritually, but that they need not be pre-planned to be either. They simply are useful in the same way any new experience is an opportunity for growth and maturity—within reincarnation as well as within life in general. One need not carefully plan out every detail of a trip to Europe to find it an educational or enjoyable experience; in fact, sometimes too much planning can be an impediment to experiencing anything truly interesting. There is something to be said for spontaneity, after all. Could this be the case with reincarnation as well?

Suicide and Euthanasia

Before leaving the subject of the mechanics of rebirth entirely, it is important to visit one area that has been a frequent source of anguish and confusion within reincarnation, and that is the question of how, and whether, suicide and euthanasia impact our future incarnations. It has been commonly taught that such events incur "bad karma" because in cutting short an incarnation, they circumvent the growth process and retard the soul's spiritual development.

Certainly this is an issue that asks as many questions as it answers and remains among the most emotional aspects of reincarnation to deal with, but a few observations can be made that might bring some balance to the equation. First, much of the reason suicide (and, to a lesser degree, euthanasia) is singled out for karmic retribution has less to do with the supposed breaking of some universal taboo and more to do with society's anxiety and discomfort with the concept of self-destruction in general. As is common to most religious beliefs, we tend to perceive such difficulties through the limited lens of our own biases, and in so doing condemn those actions we personally consider wrong almost entirely on an emotional basis. As such, the belief that one acquires negative karma for taking his or her own life persists not because it is a greater crime than any other, but because we collectively find premeditated self-destruction to be the most frightening act a human being can engage in, and it is those things we fear the most that we want to punish the most. Yet is it a greater sin than others? Further, is it singled out within the spiritual realm for special punishment whereas "lesser" crimes might be simply dismissed as the ignorant errors of a young soul?

The reason suicide incurs such negative connotations is because it suggests we have tampered with the divine machinery of spiritual growth by ending an incarnation before it is time. However, since we have no way of knowing from the context of the physical realm when a life is "supposed" to end, a death at one's own hand is no more indicative of a circumvented incarnation than is one's accidental death in a plane crash; in effect, from the context of eternity there may be no "proper" time to die—when we do so is simply an element of our environment, our decision-making processes (is a two-pack-a-day smoker any less suicidal than a man who puts a gun to his head?), and the vagaries of fate.

Clearly the rights and wrongs of suicide are largely determined by a culture's own level of spiritual development and the impact its religious beliefs have on its moral values. We live in a society that fears death and considers dying an enemy that must be staved off at all costs. Yet from the standpoint of eternity, where the soul is indestructible and immortal, death is not only effectively harmless but even unimportant. How and when one dies is far less significant than what spiritual lessons the soul learned during that incarnation. Suicide may or may not be the sign of an immature soul, but, regardless, it has no impact on the soul's essential nature or ultimate fate.

That's not to say that a suicide may not have some negative effects, particularly on those left behind. Guilt, remorse, and anger are often a lasting legacy suicide leaves in its long wake, but even then such experiences are nothing if not a part of the process of spiritual evolution. We are on this planet to realize a wide range of emotions and experiences, both positive and negative, and the loss of loved ones, whether by natural causes, an accident, or even suicide, is a part of the mix. We can't expect to only experience the good and be surprised and shocked when we also experience the bad; they are both necessary to realize the fullest effects of the process.

As for the person who took his or her own life, the soul that inhabits that body is not acquiring bad karma but is simply moving through the process of spiritual growth from the perspective of its own level of spiritual development. The life review will examine the reasons it felt it necessary to end that particular incarnation and recognize what elements were active in bringing it to such a point of desperation. There may be some residual trauma that emerges in the next incarnation to deal with as a result, but in the end it will eventually be worked through.[4]

As far as assisted suicide or euthanasia goes, the same situation still applies. The soul is not harmed by choosing to end its own suffering (though it may not acquire the full benefits from choosing to experience suffering as part of the process of becoming more aware), nor has it done anything wrong. The notion that God is the only one who has the right to terminate a life is nonsense; if that were the case we should never be able to perform an abortion, fight a war, execute a criminal, or even take a life in self-defense. If we extend the argument further and assume that God has the ultimate say in whether we live or die, would we not be equally wrong to circumvent his will by prolonging and preserving life as well? To remain logically consistent, we should not attempt to cure a child of leukemia or perform open-heart surgery, lest we be taking events out of his hands. Trying to determine God's "will" is a fool's game at best, but one that humans seem to thoroughly enjoy playing.

---

4 Additionally, if reincarnation is a fact and we all experience living hundreds of lifetimes, I suspect we may all have to contend with a few suicides on our spiritual resumes, so one would be wise not to judge others too harshly for taking their own lives.

Reincarnation, in contrast, works from the premise that we are the captains of our souls and largely responsible for what happens to us. The decision to take our own lives must be one option always open to us, if only so we may truly remain utterly free to decide not to do it. Anything else restricts the growth process by limiting our choices, and renders the entire process moot. Whether we run aground through our own foolishness or run a good race, it must be primarily our decisions that get us there—which is precisely as it must be if we are ever to mature spiritually.

Conclusion

Karma as a tool for spiritual development appears to be, at least when examined from the context of pure reason, a nonstarter. It simply is an unnecessary appendage where spiritual growth is concerned, and, in some cases, may actually prove to be an impediment to appreciating the remarkable effectiveness and perfect function that lies at the heart of reincarnation.

While it seems undeniable that past lives may occasionally and sometimes substantially impact our present incarnation, for the most part the lessons they teach are far too subtle for the present psyche to appreciate. Reincarnation incurs spiritual maturity through a long, drawn-out process that is seen only in hindsight; its effectiveness in maturing the human soul is the result of a cumulative process seen over long periods of time and through countless incarnations.

Human beings are, by nature, an impatient lot who want to see the benefits of the process immediately. Reincarnation, however, is a timeless, ageless, and eternal process that feels no such urgency. If it takes a hundred incarnations to accomplish even a small bit of spiritual progress, it is as content as if it achieved the same results in just ten. The point is not to see who can finish first, but who can finish best; the prize in this case going not to the swiftest, but to the most determined, persistent, and, often, the most patient.

CONCLUSION

It is unlikely that any amount of evidence will ever convince the confirmed skeptic that the human soul might emerge in repeated incarnations over the span of many centuries, not because the possibility is so fantastic, but because it is so distracting. Thoughts of an afterlife and what might or might not happen to us when we die only serve to clutter our lives with unnecessary distractions, thereby preventing us, some think, from living our lives in the here and now.

Nothing, however, could be further from the truth. People who refuse to ponder their own mortality, I think, are living only one aspect of life. There can be no more important question of whether the human conscience survives the physical demise of the brain that houses it, for it is in pondering our own immortality that mortality is made bearable. The thought that we go on after this life—whether one chooses to accept reincarnation or not—is what gives life its meaning, without which everything we do, think, say, and believe are utterly pointless. It could almost be said that without an afterlife, there is no life at all, but merely a temporary existence. It is the eternal nature of the universe, of which we are a small but important part, that gives any of this meaning.

While I agree that we need to live in the present (which is, after all, the only thing that genuinely exists within our current frame of reference), considering reincarnation (or pondering any aspect of the survivability of the soul, for that matter), does not seem to take anything away from the fine art of living. In fact, I have found that it instead enhances it. Whether one looks into the possibility of life after death or not, there will always be bills to pay, aches and pains to endure, dirty dishes to wash, and traffic jams to contend with. A flexible and curious mind, however, will not only find a way to deal with the complexities of life in the present, but will include the past and the future into the equation, for it is only in fusing all three elements together that the present begins to make sense.

That is what makes reincarnation so important. It is more than merely an ancient Eastern hypothesis; if it is true, then it demonstrates that this life is not a single, temporary event but just one chapter in an eternal adventure. Once fraud, fantasy, and coincidence have all been eliminated as possible explanations, past-life memories demonstrate like nothing else can that the soul does survive death—not only does it survive, in fact, but it flourishes and grows.

It is more efficacious in demonstrating this fact than ghosts, which can always be dismissed as figments of one's overactive imagination, wish fulfillment, or fear playing tricks on the mind; it is more credible than NDEs (near-death experiences), which can always be explained away as oxygen-deprived hallucinations or the electro-chemical reactions of a dying brain; and it is certainly more substantial than the musings of psychics, mediums, and "channelers," whose supernatural communications can always be ignored as the ravings of a fantasy-prone personality. Even the pages of the holy books of our religions that clearly attest to the reality of post-mortem existence can be effortlessly pushed aside as the superstitious writings of long-dead and often self-proclaimed prophets, rigidly adhered to by those unable to accept their own fleeting existence.

Only reincarnation, however, stands up and defies the skeptic to explain how an otherwise normal and honest person can have detailed memories of a life lived long ago, in faraway places and even in the guise of another race or gender, and then have those memories verified by objective sources. This is either evidence of the inexplicable but unavoidable possibility that the human consciousness can make its way from a dying corpse to a quickening fetus with no more difficulty than we would have in changing clothes, or evidence that disembodied human personalities can somehow impress the memories of their former lives onto the still-living brain of a sensitive and willing human; either of which is possible, however, only if human consciousness survives the death of the very vessel of blood and tissue that houses it. This is what makes it not only an important question to explore and examine, but perhaps the single most important issue we can consider in this lifetime. What we decide about it will determine how we choose to live out this life. It's that important.

Reincarnation allows us to see our existence not in the context of a single brief earthly visit, but in the context of a hundred such visits. It allows us the luxury of recognizing that our deaths won't be the end of our lives, but the beginning of another, and permits us to live out our lives without self-recrimination, knowing that everything we've done— no matter how selfish or evil—is a part of the sometimes painful process of spiritual maturation. It also permits us the dignity of securing our own salvation not through some carte blanche absolution resulting from membership in a particular religion or by professing a specific creed, but by taking responsibility for our own lives and actions and learning to grow beyond our very human frailties and weaknesses.

Reincarnation also gives us the gift of accepting that we don't need to realize every hope and dream in the context of this single brief lifetime, for the opportunities we wish we'd had in this life may be realized in the next lifetime, or in the one after that, or the one after that. Consider how many people might find comfort in this life knowing that those things they've always wanted to do but lacked either the time, resources, energy, or courage to try may be realized in a future incarnation; that the unrealized dream of being a great musician or an acclaimed actor, a gifted leader or a daring explorer, or even of simply bearing the children a barren womb has robbed one of are not out of reach, but merely on hold. Or how much joy might the knowledge that those things we once loved doing but can no longer do now because of age, sickness, or distance can be realized once again, albeit in another time and place. The music may stop playing, but the band is only taking a break; the music will eventually play again, and the joy of dancing will be ours once more. Reincarnation is the mechanism through which we may live the very life we've always wanted—or relive the one we've always loved—upon a stage from which we may act out a million possibilities, dream a billion dreams, and live an effortless eternity. If that fails to appeal to the deepest longings of the human heart, then I can't imagine what might do it.

"Yes, but isn't that the problem?" the materialist might ask. Couldn't our desire for immortality—for wanting to find a way to realize those dreams or relive a golden past—cause us to "invent" reincarnation? In effect, could our desire to live forever be the very thing that allows us to deceive ourselves into imagining we live on through multiple incarnations? For that matter, aren't all of our musings about an afterlife in general really nothing more than a feeble effort to give our admittedly otherwise pointless existence some meaning? Aren't we, in effect, simply victims of our own delusions?

Of course, such is a possibility, but the question of whether we live on forever is one we must ask ourselves irrespective of whether or not we choose to believe in reincarnation. Whether life is significant or whether it's all one cruel lie is something we must decide for ourselves. However, it is a fallacy to accept the oft-quoted adage that we invent those things we require to make us happy or give our lives significance. Things that make us happy exist, but they exist whether we take advantage of them or not. If an afterlife is merely a self-delusion designed to bring meaning to our life, then why can't we just as easily imagine for ourselves a whole slew of things that will make us equally as content? Yet even when we try to convince ourselves we are content in a dull job or happy in a loveless marriage, a part of us still realizes we are miserable and lonely, despite how badly we want it to be otherwise. Further, a belief in an afterlife doesn't necessarily make us happy or give our lives more meaning; it *can* do those things, but there is abundant evidence to suggest that it usually does not. Therefore, the premise that we have invented the idea of an afterlife—of which reincarnation is merely one possibility—just to make ourselves happy is untenable. The afterlife either is or it isn't; it's not there merely because we want it to be.

The belief that reincarnation is true must remain an element of faith, but if we deny that it is at least a possibility, are we not then left with more mysteries to solve? It would mean discounting thousands of case studies from reliable, stable individuals who, often against their own wishes, recounted lives lived long ago in foreign lands and within different bodies. I for one find the skeptics' job the more difficult one, and wish them luck in their efforts to stem the growing tide of those who believe in reincarnation. I personally believe that their efforts will ultimately prove to be a lost cause.

As for myself, I can only say that the idea that this life is all there is and that our consciousness does not survive death is like imagining that love does not exist, but is only a silly notion we have invented to keep ourselves from feeling lonely and unappreciated. Yet we know that love is real because we have all felt it. It is as real as the affection we feel for our spouses and the tears we shed the first time we hold a newborn child, so I choose to believe that love and life, like the universe we live in, are eternal as well.

And while reincarnation is the way I see eternity being played out on the human stage, we would be wise to remember that it is only one small part of the equation, and not even the most important part. Yet it was in embracing the concept of reincarnation that I realized the enormity of the universe and the untapped potential of the human spirit. It was in demonstrating to myself that we live through multiple incarnations that I found a rhyme and reason to the cosmos I never knew existed before, and for that I am eternally grateful.

That is the gift reincarnation gives us. It is the gift of God.

APPENDICES

appendix a

RECONSIDERING THE BRIDEY MURPHY CASE

The famous Bridey Murphy case, briefly recounted in chapter 1, not only remains one of the most famous past-life memory cases on record but is also notable for being one of the few that has been both successfully debunked and subsequently "un-debunked."

Though savaged by its critics within months of the story's release in 1956, it has managed something of a rebound among reincarnationists over the years, who have been able to punch holes in the skeptics' best explanations for the mysterious Bridey Murphy's apparent recall of a full life lived in nineteenth-century Ireland. Even the venerable Dr. Stevenson, considered by many the most practical and objective of the reincarnationist investigators, accepts the Bridey Murphy case as credible, despite the decades of debate that have raged around it.[1] As such, I thought it might be interesting to briefly reexamine the case here, for it

---

1 Dr. Ian Stevenson, *Twenty Cases Suggestive of Reincarnation* (American Society for Psychical Research, 1966), 340.

is a perfect example of how any paranormal account can be demolished with a few well-placed shots, and then just as easily resurrected with a few return salvos. This is not a story of reincarnation per se, but a quick look at how the skeptical community operates and how it is just as willing to grasp at straws in its determination *not* to believe in the possibility of life after death—usually in any capacity—as the proponents of postmortem existence are to embrace evidence in support of their beliefs. In other words, this should demonstrate how both sides basically think alike, though from very different perspectives, in their quest to prove their position. It's all part of human nature, I suppose, and human nature can be as fascinating a subject for study as even the most inexplicable mysteries often prove to be.

The Basics of the Bridey Murphy Story

Bridey Murphy was the name of the alleged past-life personality recalled by a hypnotized twenty-nine-year-old Pueblo, Colorado housewife by the name of Virginia Tighe. Put into a deep trance in November of 1952 by a self-taught hypnotist named Morey Bernstein, Tighe, speaking in a mild Irish brogue, claimed to have been born in the town of Cork, Ireland in the year 1798 and went on, over the course of the session (as well as through four subsequent sessions) to describe in considerable detail a life lived in nineteenth-century Ireland. Among the details she recounted were of having been born to a barrister father named Duncan and his wife Kathleen, of marrying a Catholic man from Belfast named Brian McCarthy, and her death after a fall down a staircase in 1864 at the age of sixty-six.[2] Further, she named a number of places (including the names of locations that had long since been renamed but were in use in nineteenth-century Ireland) as well as acquaintances from her previous life in intricate detail, and, even more impressively, used archaic terms that only

---

2 Actually, she did not die from the fall directly, but supposedly broke her hip and subsequently died of her injuries some weeks later.

someone who studied the local dialects of Ireland would have recognized. She also correctly named several household items by their proper nineteenth-century terms and identified the currency of the era (which included a little-known monetary denomination known to exist only during the early nineteenth century). In all, Tighe made more than two dozen specific statements that provided precise details of a verifiable nature, many of which were later demonstrated to be correct. She did all of this, we are assured, with no prior knowledge about or interest in Ireland or Irish folklore, history, or customs (and, we are told, possessing no prior interest in reincarnation either). Even the most casual observer, it seemed, was impressed with both the quantity and the quality of the information she provided, and the subsequent book about the event that Bernstein went on to write proved to be a bestseller upon its release in January of 1956.

Enter the Debunkers

Within weeks of Bernstein's book hitting the shelves, objections to the story emerged. The criticism came primarily from three camps: from the religious detractors who considered reincarnation incompatible with their Christian beliefs; from the medical/scientific community who questioned both the validity of hypnosis itself as a tool for accessing subconscious memories as well as the idea of life after death in general; and from the press, who challenged the supposed evidence designed to bolster the credibility of the story. While the religious opponents attacked from the standpoint of Biblical inerrancy and the medical and scientific communities worked from the premise that it all lacked empirical evidence, it was the press that proved to be most damaging to Tighe's claims. Doing their own digging, they were the ones who, writing through a series of damning exposés, torpedoed Bernstein's book and reduced the Bridey Murphy story from that of a metaphysical mystery to a textbook case of cryptomnesia.

It wasn't the fact that there were no written records of a Bridey Murphy, her parents, or her husband (all of which Bernstein acknowledged in his book) that was most damning. Record keeping in nineteenth-century Ireland was notoriously bad, and considering the commonality of the names Murphy and McCarthy, such a lack of physical evidence was understandable. What the critics had the most success with was in delving into Tighe's past, where they made the following "discoveries":

- As a girl growing up in Chicago in the 1920s, Virginia Tighe[3] had a neighbor by the name of Bridie Corkell, whose maiden name was Murphy. Obviously, this was the subconscious origin of the name Bridey (though spelled differently) Murphy.

- For a time Tighe lived with an aunt of Irish descent who apparently "regaled" the impressionable young girl with tales of Ireland. These stories were subsequently forgotten by the young girl but remained as "hidden" memories that were later to serve as the basis for much of the later Bridey Murphy mythology.

- A Chicago clergyman by the name of Reverend Wally White, whose church Tighe had supposedly attended as a child, admitted that the girl had proven especially precocious and had a notable interest in all things Irish. He was a major source of information to the reporters of the *Chicago American* in writing their series of exposés debunking her story.

- Tighe supposedly learned how to speak in an Irish brogue and perform Irish jigs from a teacher named Saulnier in Chicago when she was twelve years old. Apparently, she had a considerable gift for

---

3 Tighe is, of course, her married name. I never found any mention of her maiden name, and so I will refer to her as Mrs. Tighe even during those periods when she was single. In the book, Morey Bernstein used the pseudonym Ruth Simmons to protect her anonymity and privacy. Tighe died in Denver in 1995 at the age of seventy-two. Mr. Bernstein passed away four years later.

acting and dancing, elements of which would later play an important role in her Bridey Murphy persona.

- Bridey Murphy remembered having a brother who died in infancy. According the first exposé, Tighe also had a brother who was stillborn, which undoubtedly served as the source for Bridey's memories of losing her brother.

- There was no evidence of a Father John Gorman or a St. Theresa's Catholic Church in Belfast, where Bridey and her husband were supposedly married, existing at the time Bridey lived. Even if record keeping was poor, it is unlikely something as substantial as a church would not be found somewhere in the public record.

- Bridey described herself as growing up in a wooden house at a time when wood was scarce in Ireland and rarely used as a building material. Bridey also recalled scratching paint off of the bedposts of her iron bed as a child, years before iron beds had been introduced to Ireland.

- There were a number of other objections and inconsistencies as well, most having to do with some of the phraseology she used, as well as other historical inconsistencies.

The conclusion, then, was that Tighe was the unwitting victim of cryptomnesia (lost or hidden memories accessible only through hypnosis) along with a fertile imagination, all enhanced and encouraged by a self-taught hypnotist and author who was to realize a tidy profit from the story. Within months, the debunkers had successfully destroyed Bernstein's credibility and the subject quickly faded from public interest, along with serious interest in the subject of reincarnation in general.

The Counterattack

Just as much of the public had been quick to accept Bridey Murphy's story at face value, they were equally as quick to accept the verdict of the "professionals" that it was much ado about nothing. Unbeknownst to most people, however, Bernstein did not take having either his reputation or the competency of his work sullied without a fight. Aided by a reporter for the *Denver Post* by the name of William Barker (the man who had first run the Bridey Murphy story in 1953) and assisted by a number of allies, Bernstein fought to set the record straight.

Several months of investigation, including a careful study of Tighe's background, revealed that the debunkers themselves had been less than honest in their "facts." Not only did they make numerous erroneous statements concerning the woman's upbringing, but they were frequently caught portraying the *opinions* of "experts" as though they were irrefutable facts. Writing a supplement to later reprints of Bernstein's book, Barker successfully debunked every point the skeptics had made, using careful investigation and corroborative facts to make his case that the Murphy story, while not irrefutable proof of reincarnation, was not mere nonsense either. Following are some of the more interesting discoveries he made:

- While Virginia Tighe did in fact have a neighbor in Chicago by the name of Bridie Corkell, who had indeed grown up in Ireland, it was never clearly established that her maiden name was actually Murphy,[4] nor was it obvious how Tighe would have learned her maiden name. She was not a close associate (Tighe barely remembered her, according to her own account), plus children rarely were privy to what

---

4 Later requests to interview Bridie Corkell were repeatedly denied, making it difficult to determine the validity of her claims. Further, her son John was the editor of the *Chicago American,* the very paper that first "debunked" the Murphy story! Who says there's no such thing as coincidence?

would have been considered personal information such as the first and maiden names of nonrelated adults. Additionally, if Corkell was the source for Bridey Murphy, why would Tighe have used her maiden name rather than her married name? If indeed Bridie Corkell was the source for Virginia Tighe's past-life persona, wouldn't it have been more consistent for her to have referred to herself as Bridie Corkell rather than Murphy?

Finally, Corkell was not from Cork as Bridey Murphy claimed to have been, nor had she ever been to Belfast; she grew up in Mayo in western Ireland, a region of Ireland Bridey Murphy made no mention of during her detailed regression sessions.[5] Again, if Bridie Corkell was the source of Bridey Murphy, why the abrupt and inexplicable change in locales?

- Tighe's "Irish aunt" Marie, who had lived with her family briefly when Tighe was eighteen years old, was not from Ireland, but was born in New York City and lived most of her life in Chicago. Contrary to what the skeptics have maintained, she did not regale Tighe with stories of Ireland, simply because she had never been to the place nor had any particular interest in it. In any case, eighteen years of age is a bit old for one to acquire "hidden" memories. Had Tighe actually heard her aunt speak of Ireland, this should have been easily recalled in later years—if not the specifics, at least the fact that she had spoken of the place—implying either that there were no stories for Tighe to remember, or that she was being less than honest when later asked about them.

---

5 Skeptics have never actually claimed that Corkell was the *source* for Tighe's memories of Ireland in any case; only that she had appropriated her name for the story. Furthermore, even if Tighe did inadvertently appropriate the name Bridey Murphy from Corkell, could that not be just as easily explained by the human propensity to want to "fill in the gaps" in incomplete memories by borrowing or fantasizing the missing pieces in an effort to make it complete? In effect then, could Bridey Murphy be a fictional name for a genuine person whose real name Tighe could not recall?

Additionally, even if we accept the possibility that Tighe's Irish aunt had told her stories of Ireland, where would the aunt have gotten such a considerable amount of richly detailed information, especially considering she had never been to Ireland herself? Further, even if she had read about Ireland somewhere and inadvertently passed that information on to an apparently easily impressionable eighteen-year-old girl, how did she accrue such a wealth of little-known historical facts and the unique details "Bridey Murphy" was later to reveal? Obviously, someone had to have done his or her research with no one being the wiser for it, and then that same someone had to have lied about the fact—a contention that has never been validated.

- It turns out Tighe had never heard of the Reverend Wally White until he showed up on her doorstep some months after the release of the book, offering to "pray" for her. Not surprisingly, he went on to be a major contributor to the *Chicago American* article exposing Tighe's supposed past, despite having never known the woman as a child at all. Clearly, if this was the case, then Reverend White was apparently a self-imposed "plant" designed to discredit the story because reincarnation was incompatible with his religious beliefs and was considered a threat that needed to be eradicated. There is no evidence that the *American* knew the good Reverend was mounting his own one-man disinformation program,[6] but likely simply accepted his word that he had known the woman based upon the presumption that being a "man of the cloth" made it unlikely for him to lie. (Note: history has repeatedly demonstrated that even deeply religious people—and, in some cases, *especially* deeply religious people—will lie, distort, and withhold information if they believe it is for the greater good. Did the Reverend fit into this category?)

---

6 Though one investigator from the *Denver Post* quoted the Reverend as admitting that his rationale in helping was to "debunk reincarnation because of its assault upon established religious doctrines."

- Tighe did take "elocution" (acting) lessons from a Mrs. Saulnier in Chicago when she was twelve years old, but, according to later investigators who managed to locate and interview the woman, Tighe apparently demonstrated no particular gift for acting and never learned Irish jigs from her.

- Though Bridey Murphy claimed to have had a brother who died in infancy, thus paralleling Tighe's childhood memory of having a stillborn brother, this proved to be completely erroneous: Tighe had no such ill-fated sibling, and never claimed to have. Where this information came from is anyone's guess.

- While admittedly there was no evidence of either a Father John Gorman or a St. Theresa's Catholic Church in Belfast, it had to be remembered that there were literally hundreds of small parishes peppered throughout Belfast in the early nineteenth century. While larger churches would likely be found in the public record, it would not be difficult to imagine smaller parishes flourishing for a time before dying out, moving, or being renamed without leaving a trace in the public record that they ever existed. (The fact that Bridey recalled having Father Gorman over to her house on numerous occasions would seem to imply that he was able to spend considerable time away from his congregation, which would only be possible if his "flock" was a reasonably small one.)

- While much has been made of Bridey's supposed wooden house (a scarce building material at the time), it has to be remembered that her home was apparently in a meadowed, forested area outside of Cork itself, which might have made a wooden house (or at least a partially wooden one) plausible. There is also some confusion as to whether she said on the tape that she lived in a "wood" house or a "good" house. Her Irish brogue was, at times, difficult to make out and the tapes, being produced on an early recording machine, were not of the highest quality. The fact that Bridey also recalled scratching paint off of the bedposts of her iron bed as a child, years before iron beds had been introduced to Ireland, is also a nonstarter. Later research demonstrated that while iron beds were not common in Ireland at the beginning of the nineteenth century, they were not unheard of either. Since Cork was a major Irish seaport that served as a conduit for a large number of imports, it's not inconceivable that her father may have been able to procure an iron bed, even at such an early date.

Other objections and inconsistencies later proved to be largely red herrings as well, leaving much of the skeptics' case in tatters. Additionally, Barker noted that two of the Belfast merchants Bridey named, a Mr. Carrington and a Mr. Farr, *were* found listed on a registrar of Belfast merchants from that era, straining the chances of coincidence to its limits. Even a local coin Bridey named (a tuppence) that was originally dismissed as nonexistent turned out to have been in common use during the time that Bridey lived. In all, while there were a few small discrepancies and some elements of the Bridey Murphy saga that proved to be unverifiable, for the most part Tighe's story proved to hold up better under scrutiny than did those of her skeptics, a point that has since been largely lost on most people.

CONCLUSION

While the Bridey Murphy story is not the strongest case of reincarnation on record, it is not the weakest either. What's most curious about it is that even though the debunkers were themselves debunked—which they have never addressed, it might be added—skeptics of reincarnation continue to use these objections today, over fifty years later, without a second thought. I assume most are simply unaware of these points, or refuse to accept them because they do not conform to their preconceived biases.[7] While the pro-reincarnation lobby is occasionally just as

---

7 In my research, I found a remarkable amount of erroneous material from critics regarding Bridey Murphy, Morey Bernstein, and Virginia Tighe. It is almost

guilty of this themselves, it seems that men and women who pride themselves on accuracy should know better. No one is demanding that people accept the Bridey Murphy story as true, but it strikes me as dishonest and unprofessional for skeptics to continue to use long-ago discredited material to make their tired and oft-repeated case for cryptomnesia. It simply isn't there, and saying so—even fifty years later—does not make it so.

---

as if not one of the skeptics had bothered to read Bernstein's book before attacking it, but rather copied what others had written without bothering to check the accuracy of the information. This propensity for sloppy research does not fill one with great confidence in the validity of the skeptics' arguments.

THE SAGA OF THE USS SHARK

Rick Brown's remarkable account of a man who claimed to have died onboard an American submarine during World War II as recounted in chapter 9 is an extraordinary claim that demands careful scrutiny, not just from the standpoint of logic, but from the perspective of history as well. Since Bruce Kelly's story of having lived and died while a crewman onboard the USS *Shark* contains a wealth of historical data—information that was too voluminous and tangential to be properly included in the body of that chapter—I thought it might be helpful to examine those claims for their historical plausibility in an effort to better gauge how well his story holds up in the light of objective criticism. Of course, since there were no survivors from the *Shark* and therefore no one to confirm Kelly's story, his account would seem to possess only limited value in validating his contention that he is recalling a past life. However, it does contain enough very specific information that, while not proving what happened to the *Shark* and her crew, does at least allow us to examine the story for its military and historical accuracy, which, in itself, could prove useful. After all, if the story has little or no bearing on the known historical facts or is inconsistent with military tactics of the time, the validity of the entire event can be brought into question. On the other hand, while historical accuracy wouldn't necessarily prove that Kelly had a genuine past-life memory, it would at least make it more credible, especially coming from a nonveteran with no prior interest in naval history, submarine warfare, or ship operations in general which he might draw upon to manufacture a plausible scenario. Nonveterans, as a rule, have little understanding of how the military operates in general (and are even less likely to appreciate what serving onboard a World War II–era submarine might have been like), and so are unlikely to be able to weave together a believable tale, either consciously or unconsciously. While movies on the subject might give a person some sense of what World War II submarine warfare was like, their recollections—if dependent upon Hollywood movies for their source material—would be as flawed and limited in scope as these movies inevitably prove to be. In other words, a fantasy created from a couple of old submarine movies would probably be limited to looking through periscopes and firing torpedoes. With very few exceptions,[1] movies are unlikely to provide enough useful information about submarine operations from which to manufacture a credible story. It would undoubtedly sound like a confabulation from the beginning, and likely reveal itself as such fairly quickly.

Being a naval veteran myself and something of a World War II history buff, however, I thought I might be in a better position than most to gauge the plausibility of Kelly's story. While I never served onboard a submarine, I have been onboard several and know enough about basic submarine construction and tactics to make a reasonable, though not flawless, assessment of his story from something of an "insider's" point of view. If nothing else, it might at least prove interesting to provide a fuller account of the USS *Shark's* brief and tragic war record in an effort to

---

1 The German film *Das Boot* is probably the most accurate portrayal of life onboard a submarine to date, but even it is still extremely limited in its breadth of detail.

appreciate just how dangerous submarine duty was and recognize the valiant efforts of the nearly four thousand American "submariners" who lost their lives in the "silent service" during the dark days of World War II.

A Brief Overview of the USS Shark (SS-174)

Before examining Kelly's story in detail, it is first useful to know a few things about the main player in his drama, the USS *Shark* itself. Since such a vessel did indeed exist, it may prove helpful in judging the plausibility of Kelly's story if we at least have a few hard facts about the ship from which to start our inquiry.

The *Shark* was one of ten "porpoise" class submarines built between 1933 and 1937 by the Electric Boat Company of Groton, Connecticut. One of only a few dozen submarines in the small but growing prewar US Navy, it boasted state-of-the-art technology for the 1930s and was a prototype for the later classes of submarines that were to enjoy so much success in World War II. Measuring just under three hundred feet in length and displacing around 1,400 tons, she was somewhat underarmed by modern standards (she carried just six torpedoes—four forward and two aft), but her four powerful diesel engines could drive her at a top speed of twenty knots (ten knots submerged on batteries) and gave her a range of some eleven thousand miles, making her a powerful and dangerous weapon by the standards of the day. Typical of submarines of that era, despite being cramped, noisy, and dirty, she was still considered home to her standard crew of six officers and fifty enlisted men.

Her prewar history is brief and typical of submarines of the era: after her initial shakedown cruise and commissioning in 1937, *Shark* transited the Panama Canal and was assigned to the submarine base at San Diego, California, arriving there on March 4, 1937. She operated her entire life in the waters of the Pacific Ocean, first off of San Diego and later out of Pearl Harbor, Hawaii. In December of 1940, *Shark* was assigned to the Cavite Navy Base near Manila Bay, Philippines, which is where she found herself when war broke out in December of 1941.

Unfortunately, *Shark's* war record is short and tragic. She spent the first few weeks of the war patrolling the Philippine coastline, where she saw only limited action. On December 19, she was ordered to evacuate Admiral Hart and his staff from Manila to the new allied command base at Surabaya, Indonesia (then the Dutch East Indies), which she successfully completed on January 2, 1942. Upon completing that task, she was immediately ordered back to sea to search for and attack Japanese targets of opportunity in and around the important Dutch naval base at Ambon. Departing Surabaya on her second and final war patrol on January 5, 1942, over the course of the next five weeks the *Shark* was attacked on one occasion (and possibly others) by Japanese destroyers while she attempted, apparently without success, to torpedo Japanese shipping in the Molucca Sea.[2]

The allied naval base at Surabaya received its final transmission from the *Shark* on February 7, 1942, when the ship reported an empty Japanese cargo ship in her operating area. The following day she was ordered to the Makassar Straits (the large passage between the islands of Borneo and Celebes), which was being used by the Japanese as a prime invasion route in its conquest of the islands of Borneo and Java. Apparently *Shark* did not reply to this message, but this was not unusual during combat operations (when transmissions can be intercepted by enemy listeners and a vessel's position compromised), and it was assumed that the *Shark* received the order and was proceeding to her new duty assignment. However, no further word was received from the vessel, and on March 7, 1942, the Navy officially declared her and her fifty-eight-man crew missing in action and presumed lost. She was the first American submarine lost at sea during World War II, and the first lost with all hands.[3]

---

2 It's not known whether *Shark's* lack of success was due to crew inexperience, a lack of good targets, or because of problems with the Navy's torpedoes, all of which proved to be serious problems in the early months of the war.

3 The USS *Sealion* was the first American submarine lost to enemy action during World War II, but she was sunk at pier-side at Cavite on December 10, 1941, during a Japanese air raid. The *Shark* was the first submarine lost *at sea* with all hands, however.

These are the known facts about the *Shark*. How, where, or even exactly when the vessel was lost is unknown. Many historians, assuming she had received and obeyed her orders to proceed to the Makassar Straits, naturally imagine that she must have gone down there. A more careful study of the operational records of the Japanese Navy after the war, however, suggests that she most likely was destroyed by naval gunfire from the Japanese destroyer *Yamakaze*[4] on February 11, 1942, about 120 miles east of Menado (a city on the north end of the island of Celebes). Though never officially confirmed (the Japanese Navy reported two other engagements in the region during the month of February, 1942, that could have also been the *Shark*),[5] this is considered by most authorities to be the most likely time and place of her loss.

BASIC ELEMENTS OF THE REGRESSION SESSION

With this basic information out of the way, it is now necessary to examine the individual claims made by Kelly while under hypnosis to see how they stack up to the known historical record, what is known of early submarine operations and tactics, and logic. The first thing that is apparent from Brown's transcripts of the many sessions he recorded is that Kelly possessed a significant knowledge of what life onboard a submarine was like during the early months of World War II, knowledge that would be difficult to obtain without having spent some time onboard these vessels or

---

4 Rick Brown, in a side-note to his article on the case, claimed that the *Shark* was sunk by the Japanese destroyer *Amatsukaze* rather than the *Yamakaze*, but this is wrong. He may have confused the *Shark* with another submarine that was sunk a few weeks later, the USS *Perch*, which probably was, among other vessels, the victim of the *Amatsukaze*. Officially, it is the *Yamakaze* that is credited with the *Shark's* demise.

5 Japanese combat reports were notoriously incomplete, especially in the early months of the war. The *Yamakaze's* claim, however, is thought to be the most credible of the bunch. Additionally, if the *Yamakaze's* victim wasn't the *Shark*, who was it? She appears to have been the only submarine lost in the area at the time.

having, at a minimum, spent countless hours studying submarines from outside sources. As such, he includes details that are not only uncannily accurate, considering the overall scenario, but are probably beyond the realm of pure imagination. That being said, however, he also makes a number of claims in recounting his past life as seaman Johnston and the events that led to his death that are not only curious, but a few are significant enough to raise warning flags. While I'm not prepared to do a line-by-line assessment of each statement Kelly/Johnston made during his hypnotic sessions, there are a few points that are most unusual and deserving of careful consideration.

Bruce Kelly's Claim: Kelly claimed that the *Shark* was attacked around 11:30 a.m. on the morning of February 11 while the vessel was underway and submerged. He also believed that the ship was attacked by a "couple" of Japanese destroyers, and further maintained that the ship was hit with two depth charges and fatally holed before he (Johnston) could get to his battle station. The ship, being doomed within seconds of the first battle alarms being sounded, sank within minutes, taking all hands, including Johnston, down with her. While there is no one alive who can either confirm or deny this scenario, there are a number of problems with it, which we will examine in detail.

Problem #1: First, though the date of February 11 is the one most consistently accepted by military historians, official reports from the *Yamakaze* stated that the attack occurred at night, shortly after 1:30 a.m., and not late in the morning as Kelly recounts.[6] While the precise time of attack is not a hard and fast fact, it's unlikely that the Japanese would have gotten this wrong. As one who used to be in charge of keeping the ship's deck logs while serving onboard the cruiser USS *Albany*, I can assure you that no one would knowingly invent an attack and record it in the official log. Deck logs are as sacrosanct as the Bible (if not more so) and only observed

---

6 Harry Holmes, *The Last Patrol* (United States Naval Institute Press, 2001), 18.

events are to be entered into it. Supposition, interpolations, guesses, and conclusions as to what might or might not be happening are strictly *verboten*. Therefore, if the *Yamakaze's* official log said that they fired upon an unknown American submarine at 1:37 a.m., one can be fairly certain that that's correct, which brings us immediately into conflict with Kelly/Johnston's timeline.

Problem #2: Kelly's assertion that he "thought" there was more than one attacking ship is problematic. There was no way of knowing from within the confines of the crew's berthing section whether they were under attack by a battleship or a sampan, and there would have been neither the time nor opportunity to find out. As such, there is simply no way Johnston should have known how many destroyers were attacking, leaving us to either assume he was merely guessing or making things up.

Problem #3: More curious is Kelly's contention that Johnston "believed" the *Shark* was submerged at the time of the attack and, further, that it was holed by depth charges. While possible, this seems unlikely. World War II–era submarines were basically diesel-powered vessels that normally ran on the surface so the engines had both sufficient air to operate and adequate ventilation. (This is also what gave them their tremendous range.) While they also had batteries to operate under water, these were only good for a few hours at most and reduced the ship's speed and range, and would normally have been used only when the ship was making or evading a surface attack. As such, submarines generally remained on the surface whenever possible in an effort to extend their range and to better observe enemy ships and planes. While it's possible that the *Shark* was indeed submerged when she was attacked, it seems more likely that she was surfaced and dead in the water, which would have been standard procedure for a submarine trying to conserve limited fuel supplies.

Problem #4: What is important about whether the *Shark* was submerged or surfaced at the time of attack has to do with Kelly/Johnston's assertion that the ship was sunk by depth charges. A depth charge (essentially a fifty-five-gallon drum packed with explosives and designed to explode at preset depths) uses water pressure to crack the hull of a submarine rather than penetrating the hull through explosive force as with a conventional bomb or shell. Therefore, since they need to explode at the same depth as the submerged submarine in order for the concussion to stave in the vessel's hull, they are only used to attack a submarine when it is submerged. If the *Shark* were on the surface at the time of the attack rather than submerged, however, it would not have been attacked with depth charges (at least not immediately) but would most likely be engaged with surface guns first in an effort to hole the ship before it could dive to the comparative safety of the ocean depths. (This is, in fact, precisely what the *Yamakaze's* logs clearly indicated had occurred. It claims to have attacked an enemy submarine with surface guns. There is no mention made of a depth charge attack as well; a point that surely would have been carefully recorded in the logbook.) As such, the question of whether the vessel was on the surface or submerged becomes vitally important in determining the mode of attack that the Japanese used, as well as in determining the credibility and historical accuracy of Kelly's past life memory.

Possible Explanations

While at first glance these problems with Kelly's account seem fatal to the veracity of his story, there are a couple of points that need to be taken into account. First, it is important to recognize that this past-life memory is being told from the perspective of a twenty-one-year-old sailor confined within the interior of a terror-stricken, foundering ship as recounted through the filter of Kelly's own brain. It is not unreasonable to imagine, therefore, information being juxtaposed or confused, or just plain guessed at. In fact, a seamless memory would be cause for suspicion. People's memories—especially if told through, in essence, a "third party" (Bruce Kelly)—could not help but be fuzzy. As such, with just a little effort it is not difficult to find reasonable explanations for all of the discrepancies in Kelly's story.

Problem #1 Solution: The timing of the attack seems to be a point of some concern here, especially since the disparity between Kelly's account and that of the official record (of the *Yamakaze*) differ by almost eleven hours. However, it was never confirmed that it was the *Yamakaze* that in fact sank the *Shark* at all; it is merely considered the most likely vessel to have done so, considering all the known facts.[7] As such, if it wasn't the *Yamakaze*, the discrepancy in time immediately disappears.

However, it is probably more likely that Johnston, confined to his bunk due to an injury received in an earlier attack (as claimed in one of the regression sessions), simply got the time wrong. Other than bridge crews, the average crewman onboard a submarine, especially in wartime and deep within enemy waters, was unlikely to venture above deck. Not remarkably then, in such an environment time can often be distorted, especially with no external stimulus to set one's internal chronometer to. Is it conceivable that in not seeing the sun for several days, Johnston simply lost track of time and genuinely had no idea what time it actually was? Was his guess of the time then, which he seems vague about in any case, nothing more than a shot in the dark? Still, there are clocks onboard ships (it's not known whether Johnston had a wristwatch or ready access to a wall clock), so it remains something of a mystery in any case.

Problem #2 Solution: Likely, James Johnston—speaking through the filter of Bruce Kelly—simply confused one attack with another. It is a recorded fact that the *Shark* reported to Surabaja that it had been depth-charged by Japanese warships on February 2, while Kelly, under hypnosis, recounted a second depth-charge attack taking place on the 8th. Is it possible that Johnston simply confused one attack, and, by extension, the timing of the attack, with one of the earlier attacks? This would not

---

7 The *Yamakaze* never actually claimed it attacked the *Shark* specifically, only that it fired upon an American submarine. It did, however, report spotting an oil slick and floating debris immediately afterward.

be remarkable or unusual, especially in a panic-driven and confusing crisis situation.

Problem #3 Solution: Kelly's claim that the *Shark* was submerged at the time of the attack is, as was his estimation of the time of attack, based entirely on the perspective of an off-duty seaman lying in his bunk in the crew's berthing compartment, where he would have been unlikely to know whether the ship was submerged or not.[8] A surfaced submarine running on diesels is extremely loud, but when it is dead in the water or running submerged on batteries, it can be remarkably quiet. That the vessel's loud diesel engines were not running as they normally would be when surfaced may have been misinterpreted by Johnston as meaning the vessel was running submerged on batteries. Johnston may have simply *assumed* they were submerged because of the silence (which is why he *assumed* the vessel was attacked by depth charges). In fact, the ship may have actually been simply sitting on the surface dead in the water waiting for a target of opportunity to appear. This would have been an especially common tactic at night, as well as a way to conserve limited fuel supplies. Of course, all of this is merely supposition, though not unreasonable supposition considering the nature of the vessel and the traditional tactics of the day.

Problem #4 Solution: While the fact that Kelly believed that the *Shark* had been attacked with depth charges when the *Yamakaze's* logs indicate that it was engaged with surface guns appears to be, on the surface at least, a serious contradiction, but it need not be fatal to the validity of Kelly's past-life memory when a few points are taken into consideration. First, it must be realized that Kelly was recounting what Johnston *thought* was happening, not necessarily what was *actually* happening. A past-life memory is no more likely to be 100 percent accurate than a current-life

---

8 Further, firemen generally worked in the engineering sections of the ship and rarely ventured onto deck. As such, it would be understandable if he couldn't tell whether they were running on the surface or not.

memory, and is subject to the same misconceptions, exaggerations, guesses, and inaccuracies common to any recalled event (especially if it's traumatic and stress-induced). Further, it's not certain whether a young sailor with little combat experience like Johnston would be able to differentiate between the impact of a hit from a surface gun and that of a depth charge. A frightened novice may not be able to tell the difference, especially if he's never been subjected to both types of fire, and might imagine that *all* explosions are "depth charges."

More important, Kelly's account of the attack on the *Shark* is more consistent with what would be seen in a surface gun attack, especially in terms of how quickly the ship was hit and mortally damaged. Kelly claimed, for example, that Johnston was in the crew's compartment when the attack began but was unable to get to his duty station before the first hit. Since the distance from the crew's berthing room to his combat station at the escape hatch in the forward torpedo room was only about 120 feet, this would imply that the vessel was hit within mere seconds of the first alarm being sounded. This is far too soon for a depth-charge attack but perfectly consistent with what might be expected in a surprise surface gun engagement. The speed of such an attack would also contribute to the *Shark's* rapid sinking, as most watertight hatches would not have had time to be properly secured, making it especially vulnerable to a sudden hull breach.

A depth-charge attack, in contrast, is a much slower affair in which the attacking vessel has to close thousands of yards to where the enemy submarine is observed to have submerged and then roll depth charges off the fantail directly over where it imagines the fleeing vessel to be hiding. Had the *Shark* been subjected to such an attack, the crew would have had several minutes of warning as the destroyer closed the range (the sounds of which could be monitored on hydrophones), easily enough time for Johnston to have made it to his duty station in the forward torpedo room. Additionally, Kelly/Johnston claims the ship took better than a minute to sink, which is more consistent with what one would expect had the hull been breached by a round from a surface gun as the ship attempted an emergency dive. Depth charges, in contrast, use the pressure of the water around the submerged submarine's hull to essentially split the skin of the ship through the force of concussion; a submarine struck by a depth charge would fill with water almost immediately. Had the *Shark* actually taken a depth-charge detonation close enough to breach the hull (especially near his position, as Johnston claims), the young man would probably have never known it: the blast and resultant wall of water would have killed him instantly. The fact that Kelly claims the ship took a second, even more powerful hit a few seconds later is also consistent with a surface engagement; once a gunner onboard the *Yamakaze* found the range, the other batteries on the attacking vessel would zero in on those coordinates and have a much better chance of scoring a second hit. This appears to be precisely what happened as the *Yamakaze's* gunners bore down on the doomed submarine.

Confirming the Evidence

While at first glance the fact that Kelly's recollections appear to be in serious error in regards to the *Shark's* sinking would seem to invalidate his story, they may in fact have precisely the opposite effect. Kelly's account of the sinking of the *Shark*, while disagreeing with the historical record, in fact contains all the ingredients necessary to confirm the memory as genuine and authentic.

Though believing the ship to have been the victim of a depth-charge attack, Kelly's actual description of the battle instead better confirms the historical record that maintains that the vessel was most likely the victim of surface gunfire. Had the story been hoaxed, it seems unlikely that Kelly would have missed such a vital point. The only other option is that he simply "guessed lucky" and fabricated a story, either consciously or unconsciously, that accidentally turned out to be historically accurate, which, while not out of the realm of possibility, seems highly unlikely.

THE LOCATION DISCREPANCY

Finally, there is one last point to consider, and while perhaps appearing insignificant at first glance, it may do much in further confirming the authenticity of Kelly's story. The problem has to do with the question of precisely where the *Shark* was when it sank and what it was doing there in the first place.

As noted earlier, many sources erroneously report the *Shark* to have been lost in the Makassar Straits, but if she was lost 120 miles *east* of Menado—as seems most likely—that would have placed her in the area of the Molucca Sea, hundreds of miles from the Makassar Straits. What's significant about this is that if the *Shark* had been ordered to the Makassar Straits by high command in Surabaja on February 8, as recorded, the fact that she was still in the area of Menado three days later would seem to indicate that she never received those orders. While this could have been due to radio malfunction, poor atmospherics, or even possible Japanese jamming of the airwaves, Kelly may have almost innocently given us a clue as to what really happened, and in so doing introduced a detail that further enhances the authenticity of his story.

During his regression session, Kelly claimed that the *Shark* had experienced a series of depth-charge attacks over the course of several days. The first of these was on February 2 (which was reported to Surabaja at the time and confirmed by the historical record). He also reported a second attack, however, six days later (on February 8), when one of the *Shark's* bulkheads was supposedly cracked and during which a metal pulley broke loose and struck Johnston in the side (allegedly resulting in several broken ribs and forcing Johnston to be confined to his bunk). Additionally, the attack also, at least according to Kelly, *damaged the ship's radio.*[9] Now, if this attack occurred the very day the *Shark* was

---

9 Rick Brown, "The Reincarnation of James the Submarine Man," the *Journal of Regression Therapy*, vol. 5, no. 1 (Dec. 1991), 195.

ordered to the Makassar Straits by naval authorities in Surabaja—a message that, apparently, was never acknowledged (no transmissions of any kind were received from the *Shark* after February 7)—could this have been the reason why?

While it's possible that the *Shark* did receive the orders from Surabaja to move west and simply decided not to acknowledge them (due to operational requirements vessels sometimes did not acknowledge receipt of incoming messages), what is unusual is that if the *Shark did* receive such orders, she apparently made no effort to obey them. If she was, as is thought, attacked on February 11 and 120 miles east of Menado, she was *hundreds* of miles from where she was supposed to be. Even at a leisurely ten knots, the *Shark* would have made 240 miles per day, and so should have easily completed the six hundred miles from the Molucca Sea to the Makassar Straits in those three days between when she received her orders to proceed west and when she was attacked by the *Yamakaze.*

So why was she so far from her assigned station? Doesn't this suggest that she never received the order from Surabaja to change stations—an order that was never acknowledged and simply assumed to have been received and obeyed? And why wouldn't she have received the order or acknowledged receipt of it when she had demonstrated the ability to send and receive just the day before? Could Kelly have been correct when he maintained that the ship's radio was damaged by a depth-charge attack on February 8?

Clearly, it all fits together neatly and goes far in explaining why the *Shark* was not where she should have been and why nothing more was heard from her after February 7. Did a past-life memory inadvertently provide a missing piece of the puzzle to help us solve the mystery of what happened to the *Shark*, and in doing so lend an air of credibility to Kelly's account in a way nothing else could?

ONE POSSIBLE SCENARIO

Considering all the facts—the historical record, Kelly's testimony, the capabilities of World War II–era submarines, wartime operations and tactics, and other logical points—I propose here what I believe to be the most likely scenario of what happened to the USS *Shark* one terrible day over sixty years ago. It might be wrong, but it is a scenario that at least takes into account all the facts as they are known and makes some reasonable assumptions about what is not known.

I propose that in the predawn hours of February 11, 1942, the *Shark*—no longer able to communicate with Surabaja due to her damaged radio and continuing to carry out her last known orders to hunt for targets of opportunity in the Molucca Sea—was on patrol some 120 miles east of Menado, intent on engaging the enemy. Her engines idled (to conserve dwindling fuel supplies), she sat quietly on the dark surface waiting for Japanese ships to pass by, not aware that she had unfortunately been spotted by the patrolling Japanese destroyer *Yamakaze*.[10] Possessing a main armament of five batteries of 5-inch guns, each with a range of five to seven miles, upon spotting the American submarine, the *Yamakaze's* captain quickly decided to engage the submarine with its surface guns before it had the chance to dive, and, making the most of its lucky break and demonstrating some uncanny gunnery skills in the process, the ship's gunners managed to hole the submarine with one of their first salvoes before the *Shark* had time to completely submerge.

Onboard the *Shark*, the sudden appearance of an enemy destroyer undoubtedly surprised the lookouts manning the conning tower (who perhaps didn't notice it until the first shells began landing around them), and the *Shark* began her desperate emergency descent—which usually takes about a minute to complete—a few seconds too late. (Kelly did

---

10 Since the bridge on a destroyer is substantially higher out of the water—thus providing greater line-of-sight visibility—than that of a submarine, the destroyer likely had the decisive advantage of spotting the *Shark* first.

note that the ship was in a "nose down" attitude as it sank, suggesting that the vessel was making an emergency dive at the time.) As the ship began its dive, one of the Japanese shells scored a direct hit and punched a relatively small but strategically located hole through her thin iron skin. Exploding within the ship's cramped interior with tremendous force, this had the additional effect of temporarily knocking out power throughout the vessel (as Kelly recounted) and disorienting the panicked crew. A second and perhaps closer hit than the first (explaining why Johnston thought of it as a "bigger" explosion) may have wreaked further carnage inside the ship and tore a second hole into the vessel just as it was sliding beneath the waves.

The presence of not one but two gaping holes in the ship's hull exposing the interior of the ship to the sea meant that several compartments within the *Shark* would have filled with water very quickly—though not instantly—and doomed her. Even if some of the watertight hatches had been secured in time, the additional weight of thousands of gallons of seawater would have made the *Shark* too heavy to "blow tubes" and resurface, putting her into a fast dive from which there was no hope of recovery. Depending upon the depth of the water, she either hit the seafloor hard enough to split her hull, or passed her test depth and imploded (unless she was completely filled with water by then). All of this could conceivably take place within minutes of the first shots being fired (and the alarm being sounded), and would have been entirely consistent with Kelly's account of the vessel's sinking.

CONCLUSION

While Kelly's account that the *Shark* was sunk by depth charges appears to be the most damaging inconsistency in his story, being that the details he goes on to provide are more consistent with the historical record of a surface engagement, he inadvertently strengthens his contention that he is the reincarnation of James Johnston. In an ironic twist, far from bringing the entire story into disrepute, Kelly/Johnston's "misses" actually strengthen the case that Kelly had a genuine past-life memory.

Considering that the entire perspective of the incident is that of a young and frightened sailor with little combat experience and is told from within the cramped confines of a darkened and flooding submarine (and is further being "filtered" through the modern sensibilities of a civilian with no military experience), Kelly's account of dying within the confines of a World War II submarine appears quite credible. Further, I contend that it is the very erroneous assumptions that Kelly makes that give the story a ring of truth and makes it less likely to have been either a hoax or a fantasy (or, for that matter, a forgotten memory), all of which would be expected to more closely conform to the known historical record. While the story does not prove reincarnation, it does strengthen the case for it in that it is the only plausible explanation that neatly takes into account all the variables of this case. While the skeptic can dismiss it as a series of coincidences or a neatly-managed fraud, if Rick Brown's story of Bruce Kelly is accurate and honest, it remains one of the better cases on record and one worthy of serious consideration.

appendix c

REINCARNATION IN THE BIBLE

As I began studying reincarnationist literature, I soon became aware of how both sides are often dishonest in their use of the Bible in defense of their position. It was increasingly evident early on that reincarnationists commonly read more into a particular passage of scripture than was intended and build arguments from silence while opponents of reincarnation are often equally as guilty of misapplying or misinterpreting certain verses as well as "lifting" passages out of context to bolster their position. In effect, both sides have been guilty of "making" the Bible say or imply what they wish it to rather than letting the texts speak for themselves.

Such is to be expected, of course, for all of us are occasionally guilty of using propaganda to defend deeply-held positions or, at a minimum, parroting what we have been told by those whose opinions we have come to trust and respect. However, if our study of reincarnation is to be either fair or complete, we must be willing to look at books like the Bible from an objective perspective, which can only be done by examining it from outside the venue of faith. Such is not easy to do, of course, but it is the only way to bring some balance to the debate and keep it from disintegrating into the shouting match it frequently turns into when a religion's holy books become involved.

And remaining objective is not the only hurdle one must jump when looking for pro-reincarnationist and anti-reincarnationist passages in the Bible: one must also overcome the limitations imposed by the scriptures themselves. Translating from the original Greek or Hebrew into modern tongues is a less-than-precise process that can frequently result in considerable confusion. Often the meaning of certain passages can hinge on the use of a single word that can be absent or rendered differently from one translation to another. Such is a natural limitation one encounters when attempting to translate from one language to another, and must be accounted for.

Of course, such difficulties were a problem that hampered the translators themselves, as attested to by the many footnotes denoting alternate definitions found in the margins of most modern Bibles. Plus there is the issue of how complete the scriptures are in terms of their teachings. There's a whole body of writings that did not make it into the modern Bible (some of which we will briefly look at in appendix D), so one is immediately hampered by having only the sanitized orthodox or "official" version of the Bible to consider.

As such, for our purposes we will consider only those verses that appear in the pages of the authorized Protestant Bible when examining whether the scriptures have anything to say on the subject of reincarnation. Of course, I will endeavor to be as fair as possible, for I am fully cognizant of the exalted status the scriptures play in the hearts and minds of many professing Christians, and do not wish to diminish the status of these inspirational writings in any way. I hope the readers will find that I have succeeded in this endeavor, even if I fail to convince them of any particular position.

DESTINED TO DIE ONCE, AND THEN THE JUDGMENT: HEBREWS 9:27

The most commonly quoted passage of scripture used to disprove reincarnation is contained in one of the lesser-known books of the New Testament: the Epistle to the Hebrews. Originally believed to have been penned by the apostle Paul, scholars today are nearly unanimous in their opinion that it was written some years after Paul's death in AD 64 by an unknown author. Nonetheless written by a man who obviously knew a great deal about Judaism and how it related to the emerging Jewish sect called Christianity, while most of Hebrews is a fairly long treatise on how Christ fulfills the law of ancient Judaism, in the ninth chapter we find the following quotation: "Just as man is destined to die once, and after that to face judgment, so Christ was sacrificed once to take away the sins of many people . . ." (Hebrews 9:27–28).

On the surface this seems pretty straightforward, and as such anti-reincarnationists use it with damning effect on the unwary reincarnationist. Unfortunately, this is one of the best examples I can find of how a passage can be lifted out of context and made to address an issue its author never intended.

The subject of Hebrews chapter nine has nothing to do with reincarnation or life after death in general. Instead, it is an eloquent defense of how Christ's single sacrifice was eternally sufficient to cleanse mankind of all unrighteousness. The writer is making the case that Jesus supersedes the old Mosaic laws and explains how his sacrifice displaced their previous traditions of achieving salvation through animal sacrifice (or, more precisely, the shedding of blood).

The problem is with the word translators frequently use for "man" in this passage. The word is *anthropos*, which is normally translated either as men (plural) or, more figuratively, mankind. Many translations, however, improperly translate this word in the singular as "man" rather than the more all-encompassing "men" or "mankind" demanded by the word *anthropos.* (The more proper word for a man in the singular, personal sense would be *aner*, which is used frequently in this sense throughout the New Testament.) The difference is small but important, for if we interpret the passage properly, it should read something to this effect: "Just as *mankind* died and so came under judgment (the fall), so Christ's onetime sacrifice 'fixed' the problem."

The point is, then, that just as mankind fell (in the Garden of Eden) once, Christ's sacrificial death needed to be performed only once to successfully atone for all the sins of mankind; the one-time death alluded to here being not physical, but spiritual in nature. Mankind sinned once (with Adam) and came under judgment; Jesus died once (on the cross), undoing the consequences of that earlier disobedience. As such, the author of Hebrews is simply using metaphorical prose to note that Christ's death offset the consequences of the fall. There is nothing about reincarnation in the passage at all—either in support of or in opposition to the idea. To see it in there is simply a subjective choice based upon a preconceived bias against the idea and nothing more.

As a sidebar, however, I have encountered another take on this verse from a reincarnationist perspective I found interesting. Some reincarnationists do read the verse in the traditional manner—interpreting it to mean personal judgment following physical death—but interpret it to mean that once each incarnation ends, the person is judged and reaps the rewards or suffers the consequences of that life in the next incarnation. In effect, the person is judged "once" for each incarnation and then sent back into the flesh to do it all over again—which is the essence of the Hindu concept of karma. Of course, this interpretation is simple conjecture, again based upon one's personal preference and bias. Just as the traditional position is guilty of lifting this verse out of context to make it an anti-reincarnationist–proof text, so too is the reincarnationist guilty of reading more into the verse than is there. Such, however, is human nature.

In conclusion, Hebrews 9:27 is not the ironclad case against reincarnation it is assumed to be. While it does not support the reincarnationist position in any way, neither does it demolish it. It simply has nothing to say on the subject and should not be read as though it does.

THE CASE OF THE MAN BORN BLIND

The Christian reincarnationist has his or her own "proof text" that is often pointed to as being indicative or at least suggestive of reincarnation. In the ninth chapter of the well-known Gospel of John, Jesus and his disciples happen upon a man who had been born blind. Immediately, one of his disciples asks Jesus: "Rabbi, who sinned, this man or his parents, that he was born blind?"

"Neither this man nor his parents sinned," Jesus is recorded as replying, ". . . but this happened so that the work of God might be displayed in his life" (John 9:2–3), at which point Jesus then promptly restores the man's sight.

Reincarnationists rightfully point out that the disciples seem to suggest some form of preexistence here, for when else could the man have sinned to deserve being born blind except during some preexistent spiritual state or in a prior incarnation (which, incidentally, would be consistent with many traditional beliefs about the role that karma teaches). They also point out that had Jesus not believed in reincarnation (or, at least, the preexistence of souls) he overlooked a golden opportunity to set his disciples straight on the subject. How do we explain Jesus's silence? Did he also believe in preexistence, or did he simply ignore his followers' misconceptions and move on? It's hard to say.

However, there is more to the story than is immediately obvious. Note that the disciple's question is a two-parter. Not only does it suggest that a man might sin before he is born, implying some sort of preexistence, but the disciple also wonders if his condition could have been the result of his parents' sins, a common theme that runs throughout Old Testament literature. (Remarkably, this Jewish belief that assumed any deformity in a child to be God's punishment for a sinful act on the part of the child's parents—the "punishing the son for the crimes of the father" theory—is close to some teachings on karma.) However, notice that Jesus doesn't address that idea either, but instead ignores both choices the disciple offers. Since Jesus doesn't address that element of the equation either, however, couldn't the case be made that Jesus also believed in hereditary punishment (or karma) based purely upon his silence in not addressing it?

This is the "argument from silence" technique that reincarnationists are famous for. Since Jesus didn't correct his disciple's error (in believing in preexistence), it is reasoned, that means that he must have believed it himself, or at least was content to let his disciples believe it. If that's the case, however, it can be argued that he also believed in hereditary retribution—a close cousin to karma—for he failed to correct that assumption as well. See the problem with arguments from silence?

Still, this verse does demonstrate one thing. It strongly suggests that there was an undercurrent of belief in preexistence or even reincarnation itself evident among the Jews of Jesus's day, which, considering Israel's proximity to the major trading routes of Asia, would not be difficult to imagine. Additionally, there was a substantial Hellenized Jewish community in existence throughout the Roman Empire,[1] making it a virtual certainty that other philosophies and ideas would have been encountered by the people of the region, and even occasionally integrated into their own belief systems. It's curious, though, that Jesus seems unconcerned about it. Perhaps he considered such beliefs too trivial to deal with or maybe he believed that once the Holy Spirit came

---

1 A Hellenized Jew is a Jew who has been heavily influenced by the Greek philosophies of the day, resulting in him or her having more in common with the Romans than with his or her own people. Undoubtedly, some of these Jews had contact and influence with the more traditional Jewish community in Israel, making it likely that reincarnationist ideas might well have worked their way into the consciousness of various segments of Jewish society (much as reincarnation has worked its way into the consciousness of our society today). This would also explain why the Kabbalists and Hasidic Jews maintain a tradition of reincarnation today. Obviously, the idea had been an element of Jewish thought from antiquity.

upon his followers to lead them "into all truth" they would eventually figure it out for themselves. Or could he have even embraced some of these ideas himself and didn't bother to correct his followers because he considered them self-evident truths? In any case, if Jesus seems so nonchalant about the issue, why do we fret so?

Elijah and John the Baptist

Perhaps the most powerful reincarnationist passages in scripture are those linking the Old Testament prophet Elijah with the New Testament prophet John the Baptist. In Malachi 4:5 the ancient prophet writes: "Behold I will send you Elijah the prophet, before the coming of the great and dreadful day of the Lord." Later, in several gospel passages, we see John the Baptist alluded to as being that very Elijah. In fact, Jesus himself makes it clear that John was the one prophesied in Malachi when he says: "For all the prophets and the law have prophesied until John. And if you are willing to receive it, he (John) is Elijah who was to come" (Matt. 11:13–14). Jesus further reiterates this idea in Matthew 17:10–13 and again in Mark 9:13.

On the surface, it sounds as if Jesus is indeed implying that the Old Testament prophet had reincarnated as John the Baptist (this, despite John's own denial of the fact in John 1:21). Traditional Christianity refutes this idea, however, by insisting that John was a *type* of Elijah and worked under the power and spirit of Elijah—not that he was *literally* the Old Testament prophet come back to life (Luke 1:17). In response, reincarnationists are quick to point out that nowhere does the text in either the Old or New Testament make this clear. In this case, they interpret both Malachi and Matthew quite literally, accusing the traditionalist of being the one who is guilty of "spiritualizing" the text rather than accepting it at face value.

There are two problems with these passages that reincarnationist literature rarely deals with, at least as far as I've read. First, there is the problem that, according to the Old Testament book of 2 Kings (chapter 2, verse 11), Elijah never died. He was instead "swept up" by a flaming chariot and spirited away, presumably to heaven. Even a reincarnationist can't explain how someone can be reincarnated if he or she hasn't first died. Of course, the reference to the "flaming chariot" could be a euphemism for death, or perhaps he was simply "translated" into spiritual form directly without experiencing the trauma of death itself. This might even explain how Elijah could appear alongside the long-dead Moses in the story of the Transfiguration (Matthew 17:1-13 and Mark 9:2–8), implying that both figures were in the same spiritual state (though their means of acquiring their final spirit form may have been different). What's important to note is that Elijah did not appear as John the Baptist, but apparently as his old mortal self. If he had reincarnated as John the Baptist, in this instance at least, he was appearing in his earlier earthly incarnation also—a clear case of regressive incarnation if ever there was one.

Obviously, something is wrong here. Presumably Elijah can't be both John the Baptist and himself at the same time. For that matter, if Elijah didn't die, he couldn't be anyone else, either.[2] This is the best evidence yet that John was a "type" of Elijah in that his ministry mirrored the earlier prophet's insistence that the people prepare for the return of God.[3]

On the other hand, it is possible the Elijah/Moses appearance (if indeed it literally took place) was purely a vision and not an actual appearance of the two long-dead prophets. In other words, could the transfiguration experience have been less a genuine spiritual visitation than a type of "waking dream" or shared vision in which John, Peter, James, and Jesus not only saw the Old Testament patriarchs but were

---

2 Unless one accepts the idea that a soul, which exists outside of the constraints of linear time, may maintain multiple incarnations simultaneously, even though the various manifestations may live thousands of years (and miles) apart—an idea we explored earlier.

3 Yet it is significant that Jesus tells his listeners that John *is* Elijah, and not some archetype of the ancient prophet, a wording that, if taken literally, strongly implies reincarnation. Would Jesus—arguably the world's finest judge of human nature—have been so careless with his wording?

able to speak with them? This would not be remarkable in the Bible, which has several accounts of extremely realistic visions occurring to the Old Testament prophets in which figures both spoke to and seemed to interact with them. Could this have been the case here also? If so, however, that would render the case against reincarnation entirely moot, for if Elijah is simply a vision, there is no problem with the notion of John the Baptist being a later reincarnation of the man.

Another possibility is that since the spiritual realm exists outside of linear time, spiritual beings could appear at any time regardless of what incarnation their soul was currently experiencing in the world of physicality. As such, Elijah—being outside of linear time—could feasibly appear to the disciples as himself while also existing as John the Baptist *at the same time* without any conflict. It only would appear contradictory from the perspective of linear time; from the realm of the spirit, no such problems would exist. If so, the reincarnationist has a better argument in maintaining the John the Baptist/Elijah connection—especially in light of Jesus's later repeated affirmation of that link (Matthew 17:11–12 and Mark 9:11–12). Unfortunately, the text can be read to support either interpretation, so it seems to be another dead end.

Another point about this incident that Christian opponents of reincarnation often point out is that John the Baptist himself *denied* being Elijah when asked directly (John 1:21)—a point they feel destroys the entire notion of an Elijah/John soul link. This is not as ironclad as it appears, however, for John may simply not have *known* he was the reincarnation of Elijah (though Jesus did), just as most people have no idea who they may have been in a previous incarnation. A point frequently overlooked by traditionalists is that John also denied being a prophet (John 1:21), whereas Jesus clearly refers to him as such in the Gospel of Luke (7:26–28). So who should know better: Jesus or John?

Finally, there is one last possibility. If John was not merely a "type" of Elijah or the actual reincarnation of the ancient prophet, the only other possibility that remains is that Elijah *himself* returned to earth still in his previous body just as predicted in scripture. Obviously, since there was no one alive at the time who would have known what the prophet actually looked like, he could have simply taken the name John the Baptist and continued his interrupted ministry. Why he would do such a thing remains a mystery, of course, and it does play havoc with accounts of John's birth as recorded in Luke, but it is a possibility, albeit an unlikely one.

OTHER PASSAGES

The reincarnationist's and traditionalist's other passages are less impressive than those we've already covered so I won't go into great detail on them. However, a brief review might be helpful.

The reincarnationist points to John 3:3 as stating that Jesus was implying reincarnation when he said: ". . . no one can enter the kingdom of God unless he is born of water and the (Holy) Spirit. Flesh gives birth to flesh, but the (Holy) Spirit gives birth to (human) spirit." These verses are clearly dealing with salvation, however, and not reincarnation. Being born "of water" is usually understood to mean baptism or, more symbolically, repentance, while being born of the "spirit" means to be infused with eternal life by God's Holy Spirit, both things the "flesh" cannot give us. In essence, Jesus was saying that unless people allow themselves to be washed (symbolically) of their sins so that the Spirit of God may infuse their life, they cannot see the kingdom of God. To read reincarnation into that is unnecessary and unwarranted, although, admittedly, it does appear to brush upon some of the symbolism of rebirth.

Another verse reincarnationists use is Revelations 3:12: "Him who overcomes I will make a pillar in the temple of my God. Never again will he leave it." The use of the word "again" in this passage implies that one may have left the temple of God before (through being reincarnated?) but in the end will return to the temple and remain there forevermore.

This is, however, a very weak reference to reincarnation at best, especially when one compares this translation (taken from the New International Version, which, though a good, readable translation, is not always true to the original Greek) with the more familiar King James Version, which renders Revelations 3:12 as: "Him that overcometh will I make a pillar in the temple of my God, and he shall go no more out . . ." The original Greek manuscripts do not contain the word "again" in this verse at all, and without that, the verse may simply be interpreted to mean that once one is made a pillar in the temple, he or she will stay there forever. Finally, even if one does accept the idea of leaving the temple numerous times before returning to it in the end, this does not say *what happens* once one leaves or imply that he or she is reincarnating; it simply says that once a person returns and overcomes, he or she will never leave. On the other hand, since reincarnationist beliefs often contain the idea of returning to the Creator as the ultimate goal of spiritual evolution, this passage could be read as a reincarnationist text as well. However, I personally find it a very weak reference to reincarnation.

Reincarnationists also interpret such verses as Mark 10:29–30, Matthew 26:52, and Exodus 21:24–25 as promises to be realized in the next earthly life; not in a future noncorporeal existence. As such, when Jesus says that one who lives by the sword shall die by the sword or assures us that no one who gives up family or land for his sake will fail to be rewarded many times over "in this present age and in the age to come," the reincarnationist sees this as being possible only in multiple lifetimes. Metaphor, apparently, is not the reincarnationist's strong suit—at least in this case.

The traditionalists are not much better off, however. Besides the disingenuous use of Hebrews 9:27 (discussed above) to refute reincarnation, they usually point to the various references concerning resurrection versus reincarnation and the idea that upon death one goes immediately into God's presence and into judgment. The Christian reincarnationists, however, do not have a problem with the resurrection or judgment. To them the term "resurrection" could be construed as simply denoting the final state of human spiritual development, with the various birth and rebirth cycles being intermediate steps that ultimately bring one to that point. And as for being judged, reincarnationists are often open to the idea of punishment occurring between incarnations, believing that the truly wicked work off some of their "bad karma." In other words, they don't necessarily see anything permanent about punishment for wicked deeds, nor do they necessarily see judgment and punishment as being realized only through an earthly manifestation into the next incarnation.

Finally, the use of Paul's admonishment in 2 Corinthians 5:6–9 that to be absent from the body is to be present with the Lord likewise fails to impress the reincarnationists. They have no trouble with the idea that in our disembodied spiritual state we may, in fact, see Jesus. Some suggest that he may even help prepare us for our next incarnation or point out areas we need to work on. I'm sure this is not what Paul had in mind when he penned his thoughts, of course, but this demonstrates how reincarnationist concepts can be easily read into the very verses the orthodox use to deny the idea. Exegesis can be a cruel sport not to be played by the weak-hearted.

Conclusion

It is apparent from a careful study of scripture that the Bible has next to nothing to say on the subject of reincarnation. Beyond the suggestion that some Jews of Jesus's day seemed to hold to reincarnationist or pre-existent beliefs of some kind and some word play around Elijah being John the Baptist, it is clear that scripture simply doesn't deal with the subject. What also seems abundantly evident is that Jesus did not openly, clearly, and unequivocally teach the concept. It simply isn't there. Jesus seems far more concerned with redemption and resurrection than with reincarnation, and that is how he teaches. As such, efforts by reincarnationists to use the Bible in support of their beliefs are tenuous at best and positively dishonest at worst.

However, it's equally true that Jesus never clearly taught *against* the idea, which to me remains inexplicable (especially if it is as incompatible and, indeed, even harmful, to his teachings as many people insist). This is unfortunate because as reincarnation is becoming such a major belief element of humanity, it certainly should have been mentioned in Holy Writ, yet it is not.

Of course, simply because a subject is not specifically addressed doesn't demonstrate that it is invalid. The concept of the Trinity, for example, is not clearly articulated in the Bible (the word itself is never used), yet it remains a cornerstone doctrine of orthodox Christianity. Issues such as abortion, euthanasia, birth control, cloning, gene splicing, and a whole host of modern ethical issues also are not directly addressed in scripture, yet that doesn't mean that they don't exist as well.

The reincarnationist often maintains that the scriptures are silent on the issue for two reasons: first, the apostles clearly were anticipating Christ's imminent return and with it the end of the age, thereby possibly ending all future incarnations and rendering any teaching on the subject superfluous, and, secondly, it was well known that teachings on the subject fell into disfavor with the early church fathers, in which case any writings in support of the position may have been intentionally suppressed for the sake of orthodoxy.

While the first point has some potential, it is the second point that is probably closer to the truth. Clearly, history has aptly demonstrated that the early church did make a concerted and apparently successful effort to suppress reincarnationist teachings and omit any writings that did touch upon the subject from the final canon. In fact, the church even went so far as to declare reincarnationist teachings a heresy punishable by death, thus stilling reincarnationist voices for the last 1,500 years and demonstrating how thorough and successful the efforts of Christendom were to expunge any thought of multiple rebirths from its long shadow. Why such a response was deemed necessary remains a point of debate; certainly, many really believed that in reincarnation being so closely associated with the mystical teachings of the Gnostics, it really was anti-Christian, and sincerely convinced themselves that they were doing "God's work" by crushing it. However, I suspect that it had considerably more to do with the more immediate concerns of the church fathers, for a person who believes that he or she has a "second chance" is a person who is not as easily controlled, and control was an important element of the early church. Clearly, reincarnation was a threat to the natural order of things, just as it remains for many people today, which is why it is unlikely to be even tentatively embraced by the modern church. The concept is simply too radical for any but the most liberal branches of Christianity to embrace, just as it always has been and will likely remain.

appendix d

REINCARNATIONIST BELIEFS WITHIN GNOSTIC CHRISTIANITY

What if, in the church's zeal to stamp out any teaching it disagreed with, it inadvertently purged itself of a deeper truth? If reincarnation was a part of Jesus's teachings that was subsequently suppressed by the early church, might not Christianity have lost a big part of itself—perhaps even the very mechanism by which it might better understand the process of salvation among the heathen? In that case, might reincarnation itself be a bit of orthodoxy lost to history now in the process of being rediscovered?

The idea that the Bible might not be complete and perfect does not sit well with most Christians, who prefer their faith clearly laid out and devoid of uncertainties. As such, any ancient texts that challenge the conventional thinking about Jesus are generally perceived as an attack on "orthodoxy" and, as such, something to be ruthlessly suppressed. Like most religions, Christianity is not a flexible faith that grows and changes over the years. Instead, it is a belief structure that has been shaped by almost two thousand years of church tradition into a largely defensive mechanism designed to identify and eradicate doctrinal error wherever it finds it. As such, new ideas (or even rehashes of old ideas) do not generally fare well. Could reincarnation be one such idea doomed from the start by the intransigence of the entrenched church and two thousand years of orthodoxy? Fortunately, there are nonbiblical (or unauthorized) writings that survived the church's attempts to destroy them that suggest that very possibility.

"Secret" Teachings of Jesus

As alluded to earlier, there is a body of literature that does touch upon the subject of reincarnation, though it is by no means the central theme. These writings are known as the Gnostic (or "lost") Gospels, and contain the writings and teachings of a small but important branch of early Christians who believed that salvation came from the direct knowledge (gnosis) of God. In other words, the Gnostics were essentially Christian intellectuals and mystics, heavily influenced by Greek philosophy, who saw in Jesus's message much more than just forgiveness and redemption from sin, but an effort to restore the "knowledge" of God that mankind had lost in the beginning. This work isn't of sufficient scope to outline all the basic tenets of the Gnostic belief system, but among them was the idea that the soul evolves chiefly through gnosis (knowledge) via reincarnation until it achieves sufficient "gnosis" to break the cycle of endless rebirth. Knowledge to the Gnostic Christian was true salvation; reincarnation, though an element of their belief system, was the result of failing to learn those lessons and having to repeat the birth cycle.

The Gnostics were considered dangerous heretics by the early church and were later successfully repressed and the bulk of their writings destroyed, but what has survived is fascinating and has major implications for orthodox Christianity in many ways. From the reincarnationist standpoint, these writings do record Jesus teaching the concept of reincarnation as part of his "secret" teachings (alluded to in Mark 4:11). Whether one accepts these writings as accurately recording the sayings of Jesus is a matter of subjective opinion of course, but the point still stands that orthodox Christianity cannot maintain with any degree of integrity that reincarnation was never taught by some branches of the faith or that there are not ancient manuscripts that unequivocally quote Jesus as teaching the idea.

The Nag Hammadi Texts

In 1945 an Egyptian fellah with the unlikely name of Muhammad Ali discovered an earthen jar near the small village of Nag Hammadi. Far from containing gold as Mr. Ali had hoped, the jar instead contained something of far greater value—if not to Mr. Ali, at least to modern historians. Inside the single container were a number of ancient parchments and scrolls that were later examined by archeologists and determined to be surviving remnants of a number of Gnostic writings, probably buried by local monks during the height of Gnostic persecution in the mid-fourth century. Largely unknown prior to their amazing discovery, the thirteen codices contained within this simple earthen jar brought to light a body of teaching that had been lost for centuries.

Highly metaphorical and mystical in nature and often difficult to interpret, a few of these manuscripts, most of which purport to be secret teachings Jesus revealed to his disciples shortly after his resurrection, do contain reincarnationist concepts. The clearest teaching of this kind is recorded in the *Secret Book of John,* a text that allegedly preserves a number of Jesus's most mystical teachings about the afterlife. In the fourteenth chapter, the disciple John is recorded as asking Jesus about the fate of souls in various states of enlightenment. Jesus responded that the enlightened ". . . will be saved, and will become perfect, worthy of greatness, and free of all evil and interest in wickedness . . ." (SBJ 14:3) but that the "contemptible soul" (that which is not enlightened by its own choice) will be "hurled down into forgetfulness." He then adds: "After the soul leaves the body, she is handed over to the authorities. . . . They (will) bind her with chains, throw her into prison, and abuse her, until finally she emerges from forgetfulness and acquires knowledge. This is how she attains perfection and is saved" (SBJ 14:15–17). How this abuse helps the soul obtain salvation is implied in verse 20 when Jesus is recorded as saying: "This soul needs to follow another soul in whom the Spirit of Life dwells, because she is saved through the Spirit. Then she will never be thrust into flesh again" (SBJ 14:20, 81–82)—an unmistakably clear reference to rebirth.

Since to the Gnostic, matter and, as such, life in a human body was considered the lowest form of existence (when compared to pure spirit), it's easy to see how the idea of being "thrust into flesh again" would be considered a type of punishment, with the body serving as the "prison." It also explains why we don't seem to recall our previous lives, as we are "hurled down to forgetfulness" as an element of this purging process.

Further, this idea is again implied in another well-known Gnostic Gospel, the Book of Thomas. Here, in chapter 4, verse 17, Jesus is recorded as teaching: "Then the fire that those people see will make them suffer, because of their love for the faith they once had. They will be brought back to the visible realm."

What does being brought back to the "visible realm" mean from a spiritual perspective if not reincarnation? This idea is further reinforced later in the book when Jesus says: "Watch and pray that you may not be born in the flesh, but that you may leave the bitter bondage of this life" (BT 9:5, 50). Again, the implication is that one would want to avoid being "born in the flesh," which, from a Gnostic standpoint, would be the equivalent of flunking school and having to repeat all the grades over again.

What's interesting about the Book of Thomas is that so much of it parallels the teachings of Jesus as recorded in the four "accepted" Gospels of the modern Bible, almost to the point that one suspects the Gnostics either stole ideas from the canonical scriptures, or the recognized Gospels borrowed heavily from the Gospel of Thomas. No fewer than twenty-two sayings, teachings, or parables of Jesus in this book (over half) are almost word-for-word parallels to those contained in the recognized (or canonical) Gospels. While it's not certain which came first, most likely the synoptic Gospels (the Gospel of John and the Gospel of Thomas) were all outgrowths from an even earlier body of work known cumulatively as the Q source, a collection of Jesus's sayings and actions probably accrued shortly after his death that likely predate the earliest Gospels by decades.

Why the Gospel of Thomas didn't make it into the canon, however, isn't difficult to understand when one looks at the entire book, which goes off on esoteric tangents that seem at variance with traditional church orthodoxy and teaches—among other things—the concept of rebirth or reincarnation. As such, it is easy to see why parts of it were not included in the canon and, indeed, why they *could not* be.

Again, this does not prove that Jesus taught reincarnation, but it does demonstrate that writings exist—writings every bit as ancient as many of the books currently included in the modern New Testament—that clearly record Jesus speaking on the subject as if the idea is self-evident. The rationale for accepting half of the Gospel of Thomas (through osmosis in other canonical writings) while rejecting parts of it is not clear, beyond the obvious point that church politics seem to have been involved.

Intellectual honesty demands that we be willing to explore everything that was written during that remarkable time, even when it lies outside of the realm of recognized scripture. Only in this way can we judge if reincarnation is heresy or a lost idea that needs to be reintroduced. The Gnostic writings were largely unknown to Christianity for almost seventeen hundred years. Since then, we have had the opportunity to examine for ourselves how others who considered themselves Christians thought about and understood Christ. Such is an opportunity that has not presented itself in a very long time, and one we would be wise to take advantage of.

BIBLIOGRAPHY

Bannerjee, H. N. *Americans Who Have Been Reincarnated.* New York: Macmillan, 1980.

Bernstein, Morey. *The Search for Bridey Murphy.* New York: Doubleday, 1956.

Brown, Rick. "The Reincarnation of James the Submarine Man." *Journal of Regression Therapy* 5, no. 1 (December 1991).

Cranston, Sylvia, and Carey Williams. *Reincarnation: A New Horizon in Science, Religion, and Society.* New York: Julian Press, 1984.

Fiore, Edith. *You Have Been Here Before.* New York: Ballantine Books, 1978.

Goldberg, Bruce. *Past Lives, Future Lives.* New York: Ballantine Books, 1982.

Lenz, Frederick. *Lifetimes: True Accounts of Reincarnation.* New York: Ballantine Books, 1979.

MacGregor, Geddes. *Reincarnation as a Christian Hope*. Hampshire, UK: McMillan, 1982.

———. *Reincarnation in Christianity: A New Vision of the Role of Rebirth in Christian Thought*. Wheaton, IL: Quest Books, 1978.

Moody, Raymond. *Coming Back: A Psychiatrist Explores Past-Life Journeys*. New York: Bantam Books, 1991.

Newton, Michael. *Journey of Souls: Case Studies of Life Between Lives*. St. Paul, MN: Llewellyn Publications, 1994.

Pagels, Elaine. *The Gnostic Gospels*. New York: Random House, 1979.

Snow, Robert L. *Looking for Carroll Beckwith: The True Story of a Detective's Search for his Past Life*. Emmaus, PA: Daybreak Books, 1999.

Stevenson, Ian. *Twenty Cases Suggestive of Reincarnation*. New York: American Society for Psychical Research, 1966.

Wambach, Helen. *Reliving Past Lives: The Evidence Under Hypnosis*. New York: Bantam Books, 1978.

Weiss, Brian. *Many Lives, Many Masters*. New York: Simon & Schuster, 1988.

Whitton, Joel L. *Life Between Life*. New York: Warner Books, 1986.

Wilson, Colin. *Beyond the Occult*. New York: Carroll & Graf, 1989.

Woolger, Roger. *Other Lives, Other Selves*. New York: Bantam Books, 1988.

Index

 # LLEWELLYN ORDERING INFORMATION

 ## Order Online:
Visit our website at www.llewellyn.com, select your books, and order them on our secure server.

 ## Order by Phone:
- Call toll-free within the U.S. at 1-877-NEW-WRLD (1-877-639-9753). Call toll-free within Canada at 1-866-NEW-WRLD (1-866-639-9753)
- We accept VISA, MasterCard, and American Express

 ## Order by Mail:
Send the full price of your order (MN residents add 7% sales tax) in U.S. funds, plus postage & handling to:

Llewellyn Worldwide
P.O. Box 64383, Dept. 0-7387-0704-X
St. Paul, MN 55164-0383, U.S.A.

Postage & Handling:
Standard (U.S., Mexico, & Canada). If your order is:
$49.99 and under, add $3.00
$50.00 and over, FREE STANDARD SHIPPING

AK, HI, PR: $15.00 for one book plus $1.00 for each additional book.

International Orders (airmail only):
$16.00 for one book plus $3.00 for each additional book

Orders are processed within 2 business days.
Please allow for normal shipping time. Postage and handling rates subject to change.

Destiny of Souls

New Case Studies of Life Between Lives

MICHAEL NEWTON, PH.D.

A pioneer in uncovering the secrets of life, internationally recognized spiritual hypnotherapist Dr. Michael Newton takes you once again into the heart of the spirit world. His groundbreaking research was first published in the best-selling *Journey of Souls*, the definitive study on the afterlife. Now, in *Destiny of Souls*, the saga continues with seventy case histories of real people who were regressed into their lives between lives. Dr. Newton answers the requests of the thousands of readers of the first book who wanted more details about various aspects of life on the other side. Destiny of Souls is also designed for the enjoyment of first-time readers who haven't read *Journey of Souls*.

1-56718-499-5

384 pp., 6 x 9, illus. $14.95

Spanish edition:

Destino de las almas

1-56718-498-7 $14.95

Practical Guide to Past-Life Memories
Twelve Proven Methods

RICHARD WEBSTER

Past life memories can provide valuable clues as to why we behave the way we do. They can shed light on our purpose in life, and they can help us heal our current wounds. Now you can recall your past lives on your own, without the aid of a hypnotist.

This book includes only the most successful and beneficial methods used in the author's classes. Since one method does not work for everyone, you can experiment with twelve different straightforward techniques to find the best one for you.

This book also answers many questions, such as "Do I have a soul mate?", "Does everyone have a past life?", "Is it dangerous?", and "What about déjà vu?"

0-7387-0077-0
264 pp., 5⅜₆ x 8   **$9.95**

Spanish edition:
Regrese a sus vidas pasadas
0-7387-0196-3   **$12.95**

Death: Beginning Or End?

Methods for Immortality

DR. JONN MUMFORD
(SWAMI ANANDAKAPILA SARASWATI)

This book is an exhilarating celebration of life—and death. It is a thought-provoking and interactive tool that will alter your perceptions about death and prepare you for reincarnation. Explore the history of death rituals and attitudes from other ages and cultures. Uncover surprising facts about this inevitable life event. Moreover, discover the ultimate truth about death, knowledge that is guaranteed to have a profound impact on how you live the rest of your life!

Learn how your experience of life after birth will impact your experience of life after death. Personally engage in five "alchemical laboratories"—five of the most crucial "stocktaking" exercises you will ever do. Learn a traditional Hindu meditation that will provide a psychic and mental refuge as well as deep physical relaxation. Practice a mantra that can liberate you from the endless wheel of blind incarnation. Use the tools provided in the book and avoid the death's biggest tragedy: to not ever discover who you are in life.

1-56718-476-6

224 pp., 5³⁄₁₆ x 6 $9.95

BY THE AUTHOR OF BEST-SELLING
JOURNEY OF SOULS & DESTINY OF SOULS

LIFE
BETWEEN
LIVES
HYPNOTHERAPY
FOR SPIRITUAL REGRESSION

MICHAEL NEWTON
Ph.D.

Life Between Lives

Hypnotherapy for Spiritual Regression

MICHAEL NEWTON, PH.D.

A famed hypnotherapist's groundbreaking methods of accessing the spiritual realms.

Dr. Michael Newton is world-famous for his spiritual regression techniques that take subjects back to their time in the spirit world. His two best-selling books of client case studies have left thousands of readers eager to discover their own afterlife adventures, their soul companions, their guides, and their purpose in this lifetime.

Now, for the first time in print, Dr. Newton reveals his step-by-step methods. His experiential approach to the spiritual realms sheds light on the age-old questions of who we are, where we came from, and why we are here.

0-7387-0465-2
240 pp., 6 x 9, illus. $14.95

To order, call 1-877-NEW-WRLD

Prices subject to change without notice

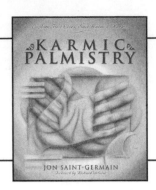

Karmic Palmistry

Explore Past Lives, Soul Mates, & Karma

JON SAINT-GERMAIN

Follow your personal roadmap to your next stage of spiritual development...

At birth, both of your palms are very similar, representing your genetic and karmic potentials. As you mature, your dominant hand changes to reflect the direction your life actually takes, while the passive hand shows what you were meant to be.

Look at your own hands. Is the right hand significantly different from the left? If so, you will find this book especially useful. You will learn how to determine your individual karmic cycle, discover ways to maximize the quality of your life, explore past lives, choose a satisfying career, find soul mates, and assure a happier future.

0-7387-0317-6
264 pp., 7½ x 9⅛, illus. $14.95

To order, call 1-877-NEW-WRLD
Prices subject to change without notice